Essex County, Virginia

Deed Book

1728–1733

Ruth and Sam Sparacio

HERITAGE BOOKS

2018

HERITAGE BOOKS
AN IMPRINT OF HERITAGE BOOKS, INC.

Books, CDs, and more—Worldwide

For our listing of thousands of titles see our website
at
www.HeritageBooks.com

Published 2018 by
HERITAGE BOOKS, INC.
Publishing Division
5810 Ruatan Street
Berwyn Heights, Md. 20740

International Standard Book Number
Paperbound: 978-16-8034-924-5

pp.
1-
3

THIS INDENTURE made the Seventeenth day of February in the year of our Lord one thousand seven hundred & twenty eight Between WILLIAM JONES of the Parish of St. Ann's in the County of Essex Planter of one part & ROBERT BROOKE of the Parish & County aforesd Gent. Witnesseth that the said WILLIAM for the sum of ten pounds Currt. mony hath sold unto said ROBERT BROOKE his heirs and as- signes forever one peice of land & Marsh containing twenty acres in the Parish & County aforesaid and bounded Beginning at a white Oake Swamp the beginning Corner of TOBIAS INGRAM on a point of high land Between the Creeks CHEESETUXSEN & WAS- SANOUSEN and running thence along the said INGRAMs line South West to CHEESETUX- SEN CREEK side thence down the same till a Course South West will strike the beginning thence to the same the said peice of land & Marsh being part of a PATTENT for sixty two acres & a quarter granted to the said WILLIAM JONES on the twentieth day of November in the year of our Lord one thousand Six hundred & eighty Nine with all its rights whatsoever thereunto belonging To Have and To Hold the said Land & Marshes & all the premises unto the said ROBERT BROOKE his heirs and assignes forever. In Witness whereof the parties above named have set their hands & Seals
in presence of SALVATOR MUSCOE.   WILLIAM /M\ JONES
            ROBERT JONES, JAMES NOELL

At a Court held for Essex County on the 18th day of March 1728 WILLIAM JONES acknowledged this his Deed indented to ROBERT BROOKE Gent. which on his motion is admitted to record
                                Test   W. BEVERLEY C E Cur

Memorand. that full possession and Seisin was given and deliver'd by WILLIAM JONES unto ROBERT BROOKE To hold to him and his heirs forever by Turf & Twigg the Seven- teenth day of February one thousand and seven hundred and twenty eight
in presence of ROBT. JONES,
            JOHN WOOD, TOBIAS INGRAM,
            JAMES NOELL

This livery and Seizen of the land & premises was acknowledged in Essex County Court on the 18th day of March 1728 by WILLIAM JONES to ROBERT BROOKE gent and admitted to record
            On margin: The Release herein mentd. is recorded in ye Book No. X. folio 307
& altered accordingly   Test   W. Beverley C E Cur

            The Within Release was altered and amended this fourteenth day of June 1728 in the presence & by the Consent of the within mentioned ABRAHAM MAYFIELD who like- wise desires the record may be made to agree herewith in Witness herof I have here- unto set my hand
in presence of NATHL. FOGG,   ABRAHAM MAYFIELD
            WILLIAM WD DICKERY, THOMAS HOWARD

At a Court held for Essex County on the 18th day of March 1728 This writing together with the Alteration mentioned was proved by the Oaths of all the Wittnesses thereto on the Motion of ROBERT BROOKE It is order'd that the record be made agreeable with the said Release & that the said writing be recorded

pp.   THIS INDENTURE made this Seventeenth day of March in the year of our Lord
3-   one thousand seven hundred and twenty eight Between SUSANNA COOK on the
5   one part and WILLIAM COOK on the other part Wittnesseth that said SUSANNA
        for the natural love & affection which she bears to the said WILLIAM her Son
also for the sum of Fifty pounds Sterling she hath given unto said WILLIAM & to his
heirs and assignes all that two hundred and twenty acres of land being the land and
plantation whereon the said WILLIAM now dwells lying and being in the Parish of St.
Ann in the County of Essex being granted by PATTENT to FOGG and WEST and afterwards
purchased by TIMOTHY PELL Father of the said SUSANNA which land by Virtue of the
last Will and Testament of the said TIMOTHY PELL fell to lott of said SUSANNA and
binding on the lands of BENJA. CLARK and SAML. HENSHAW and the Reversion & right
whatsoever of her the said SUSANNA & her heirs all which premises now are in the
actual possession of the said WILLIAM by Virtue of one Indenture of Bargain and Sale to
him made for one year and the Statute for Transferring uses into possession and all the
profits To Have and To Hold the said Seat or Tract of Land unto the said WILLIAM COOK &
to his heirs & assigns forever. In Witness whereof the said parties have put their
hands and Seals
in presence of JOHN COOK,   SUSANNA 𝒰 COOK
        ANN ✝ BRADBURY, WIL LICORISH
   At a Court held for Essex County the 18th day of March 1728
SUSANNA COOK acknowledged this her Endented Release of land to WILLIAM COOK wch
on his motion is admitted to record

p.   KNOW ALL MEN by these presents that I BENJA. CHALKLY of the County of
5   HENRICO Taylor for diverse good causes do ordain my Trusty friend Mr. RICHARD
        TYLER JR. of the County of Essex to be my Lawfull Atto. for me and in my name to
acknowledge Deeds of Lease and Release unto Mr. WILLIAM BROOKE of the County of
Essex a certain tract of land containing one hundred acres of land wch I bought of Mr.
HENRY ADCOCK by Deeds as will appear Ratifieing what my said Atto. shall lawfully do as
Witness my hand & Seal this 7. of December 1728
in presence of NICHO. SMITH,   BENJA. CHALKLY
        DANL. DOBYNS, SAML. CLAYTON
   At a Court held for Essex County on the 18th day of March 1728
This Power of Atto. was proved by the oaths of NICHO. SMITH & SAML. CLAYTON two of
the Witnesses thereto and admitted to record

pp.   THIS INDENTURE made the twelfth and thirteenth day of January in the year of
6-   our Lord one Thousand seven hundred twenty and eight Between BENJAMIN
8   CHALKLEY of the Parish of (blank) in the County of HENRICO Tayler of one part
        and WILLIAM BROOKE of Southfarnham Parish in the County of Essex Gent. of
the other part Witnesseth that Whereas said BENJAMIN CHALKLEY by Indenture
bearing date with the day before the date hereof did bargain and sell unto ye said WIL-
LIAM BROOKE his heirs and assignes a certain parcell of land containing one hundred
acres which said land formerly did belong to SAMUEL JONES Brother to the Wife of the
said WILLIAM BROOKE concluded in a PATTENT of Mr. JOHN SCOT and also all Tenements
and buildings thereon standing and advantages whatsoever To Have and To Hold the
said Lands and buildings unto the said WILLIAM BROOKE during the term of Six month
to the end that by Virtue thereof & of the Statute for transferrring uses into possession
the said WILLIAM BROOKE might be in actual possession of the premises Now This
Indenture Witnesseth that the said BENJAMIN CHALKLEY in consideration of the sum of
Seven pounds Currant money by WILLIAM BROOKE to him paid the said BENJAMIN

CHALKLEY doth grant unto the said WILLIAM BROOKE his heirs and assigns forever all that parcel of land houses and appurtenances thereunto belonging To Have and To Hold the said parcell of land with the premises to WILLIAM BROOKE his heirs and assigns forever. In Witness whereof the said parties have set their hands and Seals in presence of THOMAS BROOCKE.   BENJA. CHALKLY
   HUGH WILLIAMS, SAMLL. BROOCKE
 At a Court held for Essex County on the 18th day of March 1728
BENJAMIN CHALKLY by RICHARD TYLER JUNR. Gent. his Attorney acknowledged this his Indented Release of land to WILLIAM BROOKE which on his Motion is admitted to record

pp. THIS INDENTURE made the forteenth day of February in the year of our Lord one
9- thousand seven hundred & twenty eight and in the Second year of the Reign of
11 our Sovereign Lord KING GEORGE the Second Between THOMAS OSBORN of RICH-
   MOND COUNTY and Parish of Sitenburn of one part and GEORGE WRIGHT of the
County of Essex and Parish of Southfarnham of the other part Witnesseth that said THOS.
OSBORN for the sum of Sixteen pounds Currt. money of Virga. do sell unto the said
GEORGE WRIGHT in his actuall possession now being by virtue of a bargain and Sale
made for one year and by virtue of the Statute for transferring uses into possession all
that tract of land in the Parish and County aforesd containing Seventy nine acres and
bounded Beginning at a red Oak by a Ridg PATH near WILLIAM COXes which leads from
JOHN PICKETs old plantation running thence North West to a white Oak and South East to
a white Oak near WILLIAM COXes plantation thence West to a red Oak by the aforesaid
PATH thence along the said PATH to the beginning together with all priviledges whatsoever belonging also all the Estate right of the said THOMAS OSBORN unto the said
GEORGE WRIGHT his heirs and assigns forever. In Witness whereof the parties have set
their hands & Seals
in presence of THOS. HEALY,   T. OSBORN
   JAMES BROWN
 At a Court held for Essex County on the 18th day of March 1728
THOS. OSBORN acknowledged this his Release of land indented to GEORGE WRIGHT which on his motion is admitted to record

p. THIS INDENTURE made the twentieth and sixth day of Aprill in the year of our
11 Lord one thousand seven hundred and twenty & One Betwixt BENJAMIN EVANS
  of the County of ALBEMAR and Province of NORTH CAROLINA of one part and
THOMAS EVANS of the County of Essex in Virginia of the other party Wittnesseth that
said BENJAMIN EVANS doth Lease and lett unto said THOMAS EVANS all that land and
plantation to him belonging in Essex County in Virga. which land adjoyning to land of
said THOMAS EVANS for the full term of Ninety and Nine years to him his heirs and assigns To Have and peaceably enjoy without the Molestation of me my heires or assignes
whatsoever dureing the term and time heer above exprest in consideration the said
THOMAS EVANS is obliged to pay unto BENJAMIN EVANS his heirs and assignes the rent
of three yeers of Corn a year and also to pay yearly the quitrents of the said land
during the term of time mentioned and to the true performance of every Article here-
above expressed said BENJAMIN EVANS binds himself his heirs in the penal sum of
Forty pounds Sterling. In Wittness whereof said BENJA. DAVIS hath hereunto set his
hand & Seal
in presence of us JOHN JORDAN,   BENJAMIN EVANS
   JOHN ʔ EVANS   JANE X EVANS

At a Court held for Essex County on the 18th day of March 1728
On the motion of THOS. EVANS this indented Lease from BENJA. EVANS & JANE EVANS to him is admitted to record

p.
12
KNOW ALL MEN by these presents that I HUGH ROBERTS late of Virginia but now of LONDON Carpenter have and by these presents in my stead put my trusty friend Mr. JOHN VAWTER of the County of Essex in Virga. Planter to be my lawfull Attorney to my use to ask and Receive of all such pesons whom it may concern all Tobaccos and Sums of Money due unto me and whatsoever or howsoever giveing and granting unto my said Attorney all my Lawfull power as fully as I myself would do for the receiving thereof and Releases or any discharges for me to make confirming all whatsoever my said Attorney shall lawfully do about the premises. In Wittness whereof I said HUGH ROBERTS have sett my hand & Seal the twenty fifth day of October 1728, And in the Second year of the Reign of our Sovereign Lord KING GEORGE the Second in presence of us JOHN HOWELL, HUGH ROBERTS
JOHN WORTHY, W. LOURY

At a Court held for Essex County on the 18th day of March 1728
This Power of Attorney was proved by the Oath of JOHN HOWELL & JOHN WORTHY & admitted to record

p.
12
KNOW ALL MEN by these presents that we Wee JOHN EDMONDSON and JAMES EDMONDSON are held and firmly bound unto our Sovereign Lord GEORGE in the full sum of Ten thousand pounds of Tobacco this 18th day of March 1728

THE CONDITION of this Obligation is such that Whereas JOHN EDMONDSON hath obtained a Lycence to keep an ORDINARY at his Dwelling House if therefore the said JOHN doth constantly find and provide in his ORDINARY good wholesom and cleanly Lodging and Dyet for travellers and Stableage fodder and provender or Pasturage & provender as the Season shall require for their Horses for the term of one whole year from the day of the Date hereof, and shall not suffer any unlawfull gameing in his House nor on the Sabbath Day suffer any to tipple more then is necessary, that then the above Obligacon to be void else to remain in force

JOHN EDMONDSON
JAMES EDMONDSON

This Bond was acknowledged by JOHN EDMONDSON & JAMES EDMONDSON in Essex County Court on the 18. of March 1728 to be their act and deed which is Ordered to be recorded

p.
13
KNOW ALL MEN by these presents that we JOHN VAWTER and WILLIAM GRAY are held and firmly bound unto our Sovereign Lord GEORGE in the full sum of ten thousand pounds of tobacco this 18th day of March 1728

THE CONDITION of this Obligation is such that Whereas JOHN VAWTER hath obtained a Lycence to keep an ORDINARY at his now Dwelling House if therefore said JOHN VAWTER doth constantly find and provide good wholesom and cleanly lodging and dyet for travellers and Stableage fodder and provender or pasturage & provender as the Season shall require for their Horses for the term of one whole year from the date hereof, and not suffer any unlawfull gameing in his House nor on the Sabbath day suffer any to Tipple more then is necessary, that then the above obligacon to be void else to remain in force

in presence of WIL. LICORISH JOHN VAWTER
WILLIAM GRAY

This Bond was acknowledged in Essex County Court the 18th day of March 1728 by JOHN VAWTER and WILLIAM GRAY to be their acts and deed wch was order'd to be record'd

pp.   THIS INDENTURE made the Twenteth day of May in the year of our Lord one
13-   thousand seven hundred & Twenty nine Between WILLIAM KETON & ELIZABETH
14   his Wife of the County of KING & QUEEN and Parish of Drysdale of ye one part
and JOHN PICKET of the aforesaid Parish of Drysdale & County of KING & QUEEN
of the other part Witnesseth that said WILLIAM KETON & ELIZABETH his Wife for the
sum of Fifty pounds Sterl. money of England paid by said JOHN PICKET wee the said WIL-
LIAM KETON and ELIZABETH his Wife hath granted unto the said JOHN PICKET his heirs
and assigns a Certain Tract of land in the Parish of Southfarnham & County of Essex
containing Eighty acres Beginning at the Mouth of the MIREY BRANCH & running up
the Western Branch of MAJER ELLETs line & up the said line to COXes line & along the
said line to the begining To Have and to Hold the said Tract of land & premises unto the
said JOHN PICKET his heirs or assigns from the day before the date hereof unto the full
term of one year paying the rent of one Ear of Indian Corn at ye feast of St. Michael ye
Arch Angel if lawfully demanded that by virtue of these presents & of the statute for
the transferring of uses into possession the said JOHN PICKET may be in the actual possession of the premises and be enabled to accept of a grant of the reversion. In Witness
whereof the parties have set their hands and Seals

in presence of WM. C COX,   WM: M KEATON
        FRANCIS COX   ELISABETH KEATON

  At a Court held for Essex County on the 20th day of May 1729
WILLIAM KEATON & ELIZABETH his Wife acknowledged this Indenture to JOHN PICKET
(the said ELIZABETH being first privately examined by THOS. STHRESHLEY JR. gent on
his motion is admitted to record

p.   BE IT KNOWN to all men that we WM. KEATON & ELIZABETH his Wife of the County
14   of KING & QUEEN & Parish of Drysdale am holden and bound to JOHN PICKET in
    the sum of fifty pounds Sterl. money of England by these presents
THE CONDITION of this Obligation is such that if WILLIAM KEATON & ELIZABETH his
Wife at all times hereafter upon request & charges of WM. KEATON & ELIZA. his Wife
their heirs or assignes by such Lawfull Act in the Law whatsoever as by said JOHN
PICKET his heirs or assigns shall reasonably require and sufficiently grant unto the
said JOHN PICKET a certain tract of land in the County of Essex and Southfarnham
Parish containing Eighty acres & otherwise keep harmless from all manner of former
sales whatsoever that then this obligation to be void otherwise to remain in force
Test   BENJA. RENNOLDS   WM. M KEATON
                                      ELISA. KEATTON

  At a Court held for Essex County on the 20th day of May 1729
WILLIAM KEATON & ELIZABETH his Wife acknowledged this their bond unto JOHN
PICKET wch on his motion is admitted to record

pp.   THIS INDENTURE made this Seventeenth and Eighteenth day of December in the
15-   year of our Lord one thousand seven hundred & twenty eight Between JOHN
17   BUSH and SARAH BUSH his Wife of the Parish of South farnham in the County of
    Essex of one part & JOHN BROOKES of the same Parish & County Planter of the
other part Witnesseth that for the sum of thirty pounds Sterl. to the sd JOHN BUSH &
SARAH BUSH in hand paid they do grant unto the said JOHN BROOKES in his actual possession now being by Virtue of a bargain & Sale made for one year & by force of the
Statute for the transferring of uses into possession & to his heires & assignes all that
tract of land containing fifty acres or thereabouts in the Parish of Southfarnham in
the County of Essex and bounded Beginning at a black Oak near and on the North side of
PICKETS ROAD thence its course to a Hickory the Norwest side of a Branch thence fifty

poles to a Holley in the Eastward Branch falling to the old MILL BRANCH thence along the said Branch Westward to a black Oake on the side of the aforesd ROAD thence along the said ROADE to the place it began To Have and To Hold all & singular the premises to the use of the said JOHN BROOKES & his heirs & assignes. In Witness we have set our hands and seals

in presence of R. CURTIS JUNR.,   JOHN ✝H BUSH
    ROGER MAGWIRE, WM. STREETON   SARAH 𝄞 BUSH

At a Court held for Essex County on the 20th day of May 1729 JOHN BUSH and SARAH BUSH acknowledged their Release of Land indented to JOHN BROOKES which on his motion is admitted to record

Also ye same day the said SARAH BUSH freely relinquished her right of Dower of in & to the Land & premises conveyed by this Release to JOHN BROOKES wch on his motion is admitted to record

KNOW ALL MEN by these presents that I JOHN BUSH am held and firmly bound unto JOHN BROOKS of the County of Essex in the sum of Sixty pounds Sterl. money of great Brittain the 18th day of December in the year 1728

THE CONDITION of the above obligation is such that if JOHN BUSH shall faithfully keep all the agreements mentioned in Indenture which on the part of the said JOHN BUSH are to be kept that then this obligation to be void Otherwise to remain in full power

in presence of us R. CURTIS JUNR.,   JNO. ✝ BUSH
    ROGER MAGWIRE, WM. STEETON

p. 17   KNOW ALL MEN by these presents that wee PETER DUDLEY, JOSEPH LEEMON & JOHN PICKET are held and firmly bound unto our Sovereign Lord GEORGE in the full sum of Tenn thousand pounds of Tobacco this 20th day of May 1729

THE CONDITION of this obligation is such that Whereas the above bound PETER DUDLEY hath obtained a Lycence to keep an ORDINARY at his House Now if therefore the sd PETER DUDLEY doth constantly provide in his ORDINARY good wholesome & cleanly lodging & dyet for Travellers & Stableage fodder & provender or Pasturage and Provender as the Season shall require for their Horses dureing the term of one whole year from the day of the date hereof & shall not suffer any unlawfull gaming in his house nor on the Sabbath day suffer any to Tipple or drink more then is necessary that the above obligation to be void Else to remain in full power

PETER DUDLEY
JOSEPH ∫ LEEMON JOHN PICKET

This Bond was acknowledged in Essex County Court the 20th day of May 1729 by PETER DUDLEY & JOHN PICKET to be their act and deed which was ordered to be recorded

p. 18   KNOW ALL MEN by these presents that we SUSANNA ROBINSON Wido. and JOHN ARMISTEAD Gentl. are held and firmly bound unto SALVATOR MUSCOE, ROBERT BROOKE, NICHOLAS SMITH & THOS. STHRESHLEY JUNR. Gentl. Justices of the County of Essex in the sum of one thousand pounds Sterl. this 20th day of May 1729

THE CONDITION of the above obligation is such that if the above bound SUSANNA ROBINSON Guardian of ANN ROBINSON Spinster her heirs & Admrs. do truly pay unto the sd Orphan all Estates that now are or hereafter shall come to the hands of the sd SUSANNA ROBINSON as soon as said Orphan shall attain to lawfull age or when required by the Justices for the County of Essex as also keep harmless the said Justices from all trouble that may arise about the said Estate, that then this obligation to be void else to remain in full power

SUSAN ROBINSON
JNO. ARMISTEAD

At a Court held for Essex County on the 20th day of May 1729
SUSANNA ROBINSON and JOHN ARMISTEAD Gent acknowledg'd this bond to be their act
and deed which is order'd to be record'd

pp.   KNOW ALL MEN by these presents that we JUDITH DIKE, JOHN EDMONDSON and
18-   RICHARD JONES Planter are held and firmly bound unto ROBERT BROOKE,
19   NICHOLAS SMITH, RICHARD TYLER JUNR. and THOS. STHRESHLY JUNR. Gent Jus-
       tices of the County of Essex in the sum of two hundred pounds Sterling this 20th
day of May 1729
THE CONDITION of this obligation is such that if the above bound JUDITH DIKE Admrx.
of all the goods chattels and credits of JOHN DIKE deced do make or cause to be made a
true and perfect inventory of all the goods chattels and credits of the said Deced which
have come to the hands of the said JUDITH or any other pson the same so made do exhibit or cause to be exhibited in the County Court of Essex at such time as she shall be
thereunto required by the Court and further do make a true and just and true account
of her actings and doings therein when required & deliver and pay unto such persons
as said Justices by their Order shall direct & if it shall hereafter appear that any last
Will and Testament was made by the said Deced and the Executr. named exhibit the same
into the said Court and said JUDITH being required do deliver up her Letter of Admon.
approbation of such Testament being first had & made in the sd Court that then this
obligation to be void & Otherwise to remain in force
                                        JUDITH ∫ DIKE
                            JOHN EDMONDSON   RICHD. JONES pl.
   At a Court held for Essex County on the 20th day of May 1729
JUDITH DIKE, JOHN EDMONDSON & RICHARD JONES Planter acknowledgled this their
bond to be their act and deed wch is ordered to be recorded

pp.   THIS INDENTURE made the thirteenth day of May in the year of our Lord one
19-   thousand seven hundred twenty & nine Between ROBERT STOKES of the Parish of
21   St. Ann in the County of Essex Plantr. of one part & SALVATOR MUSCOE of the
       aforesd Parish and County of other part Wittnesseth that said ROBERT STOKES for
sum of Twenty pounds Currant money of Virginia doth sell unto the said SALVATOR
MUSCOE his heires & assignes forever all his right in one plantation & wood land
ground containing fifty acres in the Parish & County aforesaid joining to the land formerly purchased by the said SALVATOR from my Brother WILLIAM STOKES & is bounded
as followeth (Vizt) Beginning at a marked Popler by a Branch side by the plantacon
whereon JOHN KIRGAN now lives Corner tree of sd SALVATORs, from thence along his
line North East to a corner red Oak of sd SALVATORs by the MAIN ROAD thence North
East to a pesimon tree in the Old field under the hills thence North West to a small
pesimon tree in the old field thence South West to a live Oak standing by WM. JONES's
BRIDGE in MOSE's SWAMP corner tree to AARON PERRY & the said SALVATOR MUSCOE
thence along AARON PERRY's lines to SAMUEL DAVIS's land from thence along DAVIS's
line to the land purchased by ARTHUR McDANIEL from WILLIAM STOKES thence along
the lines of the said ARTHUR McDANIEL to the Popler where it first began including all
the land between the land of AARON PERRY & the land of the said ARTHUR McDANIEL
which said Plantation wood land with the appurtenances thereunto belonging he the
said ROBERT STOKES hath should or ought to have after the Deced of MARY LAREMORE
Mother to the said ROBERT which said Plantation ground and Premises RICHD. STOKES of
the Parish & County aforesd Deced late Father of the said ROBERT STOKES party to these
presents by his last Will and Testamt. dated the Seventeenth day of Janry. one thousand
seven hundred & Eight devised, bequeathed unto the sd MARY then Wife of the said

RICHARD STOKES deced revertion thereof to the said ROBERT STOKES in fee To Have and
To Hold all the Estate right of the said ROBERT STOKES to the said premises immediately
from & after the decease of the said MARY Mother of the said ROBERT STOKES unto the sd
SALVATOR MUSCOE his heirs & assignes forever & the sd MARY LAREMORE Mother to
the sd ROBERT STOKES do for the consideration before mentioned & paid to her Son
ROBERT STOKES give Release & quit claim unto the sd SALVATOR MUSCOE & his heirs all
her Estate right whatsoever to the aforesaid Plantation. In Wittness whereof the said
ROBERT STOKES, MARY LAREMORE & SALVATOR MUSCOE have set their hands and Seals
in presence of THOS. TUNSTALL,   ROBT. STOKES
       THOS. STHRESHLEY, WM. GRAY   MARY **W** LAREMORE
  At a Court contd. & held for Essex County on the 21st day of May 1729
ROBERT STOKES and MARY LAREMOORE acknowledged their Deed indented to SALVATOR
MUSCOE Gentl. which on his motion is admitted to record
  Memorandum that full possession was delivered by ROBERT STOKES & MARY LAREMORE
to SALVATOR MUSCOE by Turff & Twig this thirteenth day of May in the year one thou-
sand seven hundred Twenty nine in presence of SAML. EDMONDSON, WM. GRAY
  At a Court continued & held for Essex County on the 21st day of May 1729
ROBERT STOKES and MARY LAREMORE acknowledged their livery & seisin of the lands
and premises within mentioned to SALVATOR MUSCOE Gentl. wch on his motion is admitted to record

pp.   THIS INDENTURE made the 19th day of May in the year of our Lord one Thousand
22-   seven hundred Twenty Nine Between ROBERT BROOKE of Saint Ann's Parish in
23   the County of Essex Gentl. of one part and JOHN COOKE of the Parish & County
         aforesd Planter of other part Wittnesseth that for the sum of Two thousand five
hundred pounds of Merchantable Tobo unto the said ROBERT BROOKE in hand paid by
said JOHN COOKE hath granted and doth fully grant unto the said JOHN COOKE his heirs &
assigns forever all the HALF part or Moiety of a GRIST MILL comonly called & known by
the name of TANDYS MILL with the Land & Appurtenances to the said Moiety To Have
and To Hold the half part of the said GRIST MILL with the land & appurtenances thereunto belonging to the sd JOHN COOKE his heirs & assignes forever. In Wittness whereof
the parties named have set their hands & Seals
in presence of THOS: JONES,   RO. BROOKE
        DAVIDSCOTT
  At a Court held for Essex County on the 20th day of May 1729
ROBERT BROOKE Gent. acknowledged this his Deed indented to JOHN COOK which on his
motion is admitted to record
  Be it Remembered that full possession of the Moiety of said MILL and Premises was de-
livered by ROBERT BROOKE unto the said JOHN COOKE according to the meaning of the
Indenture on the 19th day of May in the year 1729
in presence of JOHN **R** PRICE,   RO. BROOKE
        THOS. **X** DOWNS, SARAH **H** DOWNS
  At a Court held for Essex County on the 20th day of May 1729
ROBERT BROOKE Gent acknowledged this his Livery & Seisin of the MILL & premises to
JOHN COOKE wch on his motion is admitted to record

pp.   BY THIS PUBLICK INSTRUMT. of Procuration or Letters of Attorney Be it Known
23-   unto all Those who shall see these presents or hear the same read That on the
24   Eighteenth day of Novembr. 1728 and in the Second year of the Reign of our
         Sovereign Lord GEORGE the Second & before me RICHARD WISE Notary & Tabel-
lion Publick resideing in LONDON by Royal Authority duly admitted & Sworn Wittnesses

personally appeared Mr: JONATHAN FORWARD of LONDON Mercht. who declared to have appointed & by these presents doth make Mr. THOS. WAREING of Virginia Merchant (at present in LONDON) his true & lawfull Attorney giving unto his said Attorney full power in his name & to his use to Ask Sue for receive from all persons whom it may concern Inhabiting either in Virginia or MARYLAND all sums of money, goods, wares, Effects whatsoever due to him the said Constituant by bond, note, bill accts, or by any other ways and upon recoverie & receipt to give Acquittances or other sufficient discharges in due form of Law but in case of refusal to compel by all Lawfull waies & means to appear before any Lords Judges in any Court thereto concerning the premises & generally to perform whatsoever shall be necessary as effectually as he the said Constituant might do hereby promising to rattifie whatsoever his said Attorney shall lawfully do about the premises Thus done & passed in LONDON afforesaid in prence of

                                                             JONA. FORWARD

being first duly Stamp'd in presence of
    GEORGE TILLY, JOHN FRIE   RICHD: WISE Not Publ 1728

  At a Court held for Essex County on the 20th day of May 1729
This Power of Attorney from JONATHAN FORWARD to THOMAS WAREING Gent was proved by the Oath of GEORGE TILLY & admitted to record
  At a Court held for Essex County on the 21st day of May 1729
This Power of Atto. was also proved by the Oath of JOHN FRIE the other Witness and admitted to record

p.   THIS INDENTURE made the 20th day of May in the year of our Lord one thousand
25   seven hundred & twenty nine between WILLIAM DAINGERFIELD, ALEXANDER
       PARKER, NICHOLAS SMITH and THOMAS STHRESHLEY JUNR. gentl. Justices of the County of Essex of the one part and JAMES WALL of the Parish of Saint Ann's in the County of Essex Planter of the other part Witnesseth that said WILLIAM DAINGERFIELD, ALEXANDER PARKER, NICHOLAS SMITH and THOMAS STHRESHLEY JUNR. have & do by these presents bind an Orphan Boy named WILLIAM ROBERTS about the age of ten years unto the said JAMES WALL and MARY WALL his Wife to serve him the said JAMES WALL and MARY WALL his Wife for & during the term & untill he shall attain the age of one & twenty years during all which term he shall faithfully serve their lawfull commands gladly every where obey, he shall do no damage unto his said Master or Mistriss nor see it to be done by others without giving notice thereof unto his said Master or Mistriss he shall not comit fornication nor contract matrimony dureing the said term at unlawfull games he shall (not) play whereby his Master or Mistress shall be damaged he shall not absent himself day or night from Service without their special leave but in & by all things behave himself as a good and faithfull Servant ought to do during the said term And the said JAMES WALL & MARY WALL his Wife shall sufficiently provide for the said Servant meat drink Apparrell washing and Lodging fitting for a Servant during the term & shall learn the said Servant or cause him to be learned to read and write and to the true performance of the Covenants above mentioned of the parties bind themselves by these presents. In Wittness whereof the parties their hands & Seals have set this day & year

in presence of us LEWIS LATANE,   JAMES P WALL
    W. BEVERLEY ClCur
  At a Court held for Essex County on the 20th day of May 1729
On the motion of JAMES WALL this Indenture is admitted to record

p.   KNOW ALL MEN by these presents that I SARAH THORP of the Parish of Saint
25   Anns in the County of Essex do hereby appoint MR. THOMAS HAWKINS as my
        lawfull Attorney for and in my name to relinquish the right of dower which I
have in One parcell of land which my said Husband WILLIAM THORP sold to JEREMIAH
BISWELL. Wittness my hand and Seal this 17th day of May 1729
in presence of JNO. VAWTER,   SARAH ✚ THORP
        JNO. HODSON
  At a Court held for Essex County on the 20th day of May 1729
This Power of Attorney from SARAH THORP to THOS. HAWKINS was proved by the Oaths
of both the witnesses thereto & then the sd THOS. HAWKINS by Virtue hereof relinquish'd the said SARAHs dower in lands conveyed by her husband WILLM. THORP to
JEREMIAH BISWELL which on his motion is recorded

pp.   THIS INDENTURE made the 17th day of May in the year of our Lord one thousand
26-   seven hundred & twenty Nine Between THOS. EDMONDSON and CONSTANT his Wife
27   of the Parish of Southfarnham in the County of Essex of one part and DANIEL
        TAYLOR of the aforesaid Parish & County of other part Wittnesseth that said THO-
MAS EDMONDSON & CONSTANT his Wife for sum of Seventeen pounds of good & lawfull
money doth sell unto the said DANIEL TAYLOR his heirs & assigns forever all that par-
sel of land in the abovesaid Parish & County and part of the Dividend of land whereon
the said THOS. EDMONDSON & CONSTANT his wife now Dwells on beginning at a pussimon
tree in a bottom & running thence Easterly to the DEEP SWAMP thence down the said
Swmp to THOMAS BRYANTs line thence up to his Corner tree thence keeping the same
Course from said Corner to a small Branch that runs into the GLADE SWAMP thence
along the said Branch to WILLIAM GATEWOODs line thence along the said GATEWOODs
line up the GLADE SWAMP to another small branch thence up the said Branch to the
head thence to the Beginning together with all Timber Woods Swamps whatsoever & all
the title the said THOS. EDMONDSON & CONSTANT his Wife the said fifty acres of land To
Have and To Hold unto the said DANIEL TAYLOR his heirs and assigns forever. In Testi-
mony of the same we have set our hands & Seals
in presence of us THOS. **T** KIDD,   THOS. EDMONDSON
        ELIZA. **C** KIDD   CONSTANT **C** EDMONDSON
  At a Court held for Essex County on the 17th day of June 1729
THOS. EDMONDSON & CONSTANT his Wife (the sd CONSTANT being first privily examined)
acknowledged this their Deed Indented to DANIEL TAYLOR wch on his motion is admitted
to record
  Memorandum that the within land was delivered unto DANIEL TAYLOR by THOMAS ED-
MONDSON and CONSTANT his Wife by Turf and Twigg and the Kay to the door upon the
said Land
in presence of us THOS. **T** KIDD,   THOS. EDMONDSON
        ELIZA. **C** KIDD   CONSTNT **C** EDMONDSON
  At a Court held for Essex County on the 17th day of June 1729
THOMAS EDMONDSON and CONSTANT his Wife acknowledged this their livery and Seisin
of the lands & premises to DANIEL TAYLOR which is admitted to record

pp.   THIS INDENTURE made the Sixteenth day of June in the year of our Lord one
27-   thousand seven hundred and Twenty nine Between JAMES CROSBY and MARY
28   his Wife lately MARY BROWN of the Parish of St. Ann in the County of Essex of
        one part and MUNGO ROY of the Parish & County aforesaid of the other part Wit-
nesseth that the said JAMES CROSBY and MARY his Wife for the sum of Twenty five
pounds Currt. money of Virginia do hereby discharge the said MUNGO ROY to farm

letten One hundred acres of land where JAMES CROSBY now liveth runing from the
River up the Creek for breadth so on a straight line to the back line thence down to ye
River and so along the River to the beginning to include the aforesaid quantity of land
unto the said MUNGO ROY conform to a Deed granted for the said Land by CHARLES
BROWN JUNR. to CHARLES BROWN SENR. & MARY his Wife bearing date February the
Seventeenth in the year of our Lord one thousand Seven hundred & twenty three for
the Natural life of the said MARY with all houses & Tobacco houses & advantages any-
wise appertaining. To Have and To Hold all the premises dureing the natural life of the
said MARY CROSBY and further the sd JAMES CROSBY and MARY his Wife for themselves do hereby promise that they will keep MUNGO ROY his heirs in possession
dureing the term aforesaid. In Witness whereof the said JAMES CROSBY & MARY his
Wife have set their hands & Seals
in presence of us WM. NISBET,   JAMES **I** CROSBY
         M: BATTALEY   MARY **M** CROSBY
   At a Court continued & held for Essex County on the 18th day of June 1729
JAMES CROSBY and MARY CROSBY acknowledged this their Indented Lease of land to
DOCTR. MUNGO ROY which on his motion is admitted to record

pp.   TO ALL CHRISTIAN PEOPLE to whom this present Indentures shall come Know ye
28-   that I JOHN BILLUPS & DOROTHY my Wife of the Parish of St. Anns in the County
29   of Essex Daughter & heir Apparant of RICHD. AUBERY deced Son of HENRY
         AUBERY Deced do for diverse good causes but more especially for the sum of
three pounds currant mony of Virga. Building a sixteen foot House after the maner of
Comon Virga. Building that is to say only the outside work the said JOHN BILLUPS to find
the Jist & Nailes the consideration being in hand already reced hath released forever &
forever quit claimed unto JAMES GARNET of the Parish and County aforesaid in his full
possession all such Right Title whatsoever as we the said JOHN BILLUPS & DORITHY my
Wife had or ought to have in any part of a Track of land granted to Capt. SALVATOR
MUSCOE by PATTENT dated the Ninth day of July in the year one thousand seven hundred & twenty four for one hundred acres & by the said SALVATOR MUSCOE sold & conveyed unto the said JAMES GARNETT & in or to all the Land below the second Branch
above the CHURCH & of in or to all the Land above the Branch that lyeth within the
bounds hereater mentioned that is to say Beginning at a sasifigg on the uper or North
side of the Branch & runing down the said Branch to a red Oak & from the said red Oak
North East to a stake and from the said Stake West North to a small Maple on the side of a
large Branch next below Capt. SALVATOR MUSCOEs Dwelling Plantation by any ways or
means whatsoever To Have and To Hold the said parcell of land with all its appurtenances thereunto belonging unto the said JAMES GARNETT his heires & assignes wee
the said JOHN BILLIPS and DORITY my Wife shall be utterly excluded and barred forever
by these presents. In Wittness whereof we have set our hands and Seals this Eleventh
day of February in the year of our Lord one thousand seven hundred & twenty eight
nine
in presence of us JOSEPH SORRILL,   JNO. BILLIP,
         EDWARD WHITE, MARCK MORGAN   DOROTHY **δ** BILLIPS
    At a Court held for Essex County on the 17th day of June 1729
JOHN BILLUPS and DOROTHY his Wife acknowledged this Indented Release of land to
JAMES GARNETT Gent which on his motion is admitted to record

pp.   KNOW ALL MEN by these presents that I JACOB RICE of the County of MIDDLESEX
29-   do acknowledge my self to owe and stand indebted unto PITTMAN SCANDRETT
30   of Essex County the sum of Twenty pounds Sterling Mony of great brittain or

Virga. Currancy at Tenn p cent to be paid to the said PITTMAN SCANDRETT his heirs or assignes upon the Tenth day of September in the year 1729 for which payment truly to be made I bind myself in the penal sum of forty pounds of like Sterling or Virga. Currancy at Ten p cent of the like money firmley by these presents. In Wittness whereof I have set my hand & Seal this the Seventeenth day of May 1728
in presence of CHARLES STUART,   JACOB RICE
        DANIEL DAILY
    At a Court held for Essex County on the 17th day of June 1729
CHARLES STUART & DANIEL DAILEY made Oath that they did see JACOB RICE sign & deliver this his bond as his act and deed to PITTMAN SCANDRETT & then Mr. SCANDRETT made oath that he never had reced any thing in part of Satisfaction of the said bond but that it is at this time all due to him, which bond on his motion is admitted to record

pp.   THIS INDENTURE made this 28th day of March in the year of our Lord one thou-
30-   sand seven hundred twenty & Nine Between FRANCIS GOULDMAN of the Parish
31   of St. Ann in the County of Essex of the one part and THOMAS STHRASHLEY JUNR.
         & THOMAS STHRASHLEY & WILLIAM STHRASHLEY Sons of the aforesd THOS.
STHRASHLEY JUNR of the Parish of Southfarnham in the County aforesd of the other part Witnesseth that said FRANCIS GOULDMAN for the sum of Sixteen hundred pounds of good Tobacco convenient in the County aforesaid & forty Shillings Currant money of Virga. to him paid by these presents hath granted to farm lett & do grant unto said THOMAS STHRASHLEY JUNR & THOMAS STHRASHLEY & WILLIAM STHRASHLEY his Sons one parcel of land or wood land ground containing one hundred & forty acres being in the Parish of St. Ann in the County of Essex and bounded Begining at a marked ring Oak & Gum on the Middle Fork of OCCUPACY RUN from thence up a bottom & cross a Ridge to the head of a small Branch on the South Branch of OCCUPACY to two marked red Oakes & a black Oak thence down the said Branch to the main Swamp of OCCUPACY & down the said Swamp to a small Branch in an old field where formerley Collo. FRANCIS GOULD-MAN deced had a Quarter & where FRANCIS GOULDMAN party to these presents formerly lived thence up the said Branch to three marked persimon trees, from thence across to a small Branch on the uper side of sd old field to a marked Poplar thence down the said Branch to the Main Middle Fork of OCCUPACY RUN thence up the said Swamp to the plaice where it first began with all woods timber whatsoever thereunto belonging To Have and To Hold unto the said THOS. STHRESLY JUNR. & THOMAS STHRESHLEY & WILLIAM STHRESHLEY his Sons dureing the term of their natural lives and the live of the longer liver of them Successively one after the other as they are herein named paying yearly One pepper Corn on the Feast of Saint Michael the Arch Angel only if the same be lawfully demanded by said FRANCIS (the rents and services which from henceforth to our Soveraign Lord the King only excepted & foreprized). In Witness whereof the parties have set their hands and Seals
in presence of W. ROANE,   FRANCIS GOULDMAN
        EDWD. MORGIN
    At a Court held for Essex County the 17th day of June 1729
FRANCIS GOULDMAN acknowledged this Lease of land indented to THOMAS STHRESHLY JUNR which on his motion is admitted to record
    At a Court held for Essex County on the 17th day of June 1729
FRANCIS GOULDMAN acknowledged his livery & seizen of the land to THOS STHRESHLY JUNR. which is admitted to record

p.   TO ALL CHRISTIAN PEOPLE to whome these presents shall come Greeting. Now
32   Know ye that I NICHOLAS SMITH of Essex County do out of pure Love and Natural
        affection which I have and bear unto my Son FRANCIS SMITH do by these pre-
sents make over one Track of land to my said Son FRANCIS SMITH and to his heires forever, Begining at a Poplar tree in a line that parts me and JOHN GEORGE upon a Swamp
side and so down the Run of the said Swamp to the CHURCH SPRING BRANCH thence up
the said Branch to the CHURCH SPRING and so along the PATH from the CHURCH SPRING
to the CHURCH thence down the ROAD to the WHITE MARSH BRIDGE and so down the said
Swamp till it comes to the line between JAMES HIPKINS and me and along that line to a
Corner tree in HIPKINS tobacco ground and along the line that parts HIPKINGs, JOHN
GEORGE & me to a Mulberry tree thence to another Mulberry tree and so along a line to
a poplar on the Swamp side the begining place the said Land contains four hundred
acres the said land contains my Dwelling Plantation which I do except, I do acknowledge unto my loving Son FRANCIS SMITH the above tract of land unto him and his
heirs forever. In Wittness whereof I have hereunto set my hand and Seal this 14th day
of July 1729
in presence of us EMAL. WILLIAMS   NICHO. SMITH
        JOHN ⨍ SMITH
   At a Court held for Essex County on the 15th day of July 1729
NICHOLAS SMITH gent acknowledged this Deed of Gift to his Son FRANCIS SMITH which
is admitted to record

pp.   THIS INDENTURE made the Twelfth and Thirteenth day of June in the year of our
32-   Lord one thousand seven hundred twenty and nine Between LEONARD HILL of
35   the Parish of Southfarnham in the County of Essex Gent. of one part and
        ELEANER MEDLEY of the Parish & County aforesaid of the other part Witnesseth
that Whereas said LEONARD HILL by Indenture dated the day before the date hereof did
grant unto the said ELEANER MEDLEY her heirs and assignes a certain parsell of land
containing fifty acres bounded Beginning at a Corner tree of the land which was formerly BRIDGERs now belonging to the said LEONARD HILL standing on the upper side of
a branch which makes into the YORKER SWAMP runing from thence South South West
along a line deviding the said LEONARD HILLs land & the land which did formerly belong to JOHN SHARP now belonging to the Orphans of THOMAS HARWAR deced to the
YORKER SWAMP thence down the said Swamp to a Branch that makes into the YORKER
SWAMP thence up the said Branch to the begining tree standing near the plantation
belonging to the said ELEANOR MEDLEY and also all Tenements houses advantages whatsoever to the same belonging To Have and To Hold unto the said ELEANER MEDLEY
dureing the term of Six months from thence to the end that by Virtue thereof and of
the Statute for Transferring uses into possession the said ELEANER MEDLEY might be in
the actual possession & be enabled to make and accept of a grant and release of the
Same Now This Indenture Wittnesseth that the said LEONARD HILL for the sum of three
thousand five hundred pounds of good tobacco and cask clear by her the said ELEANER
MEDLEY to him in hand paid whereof the said LEONARD HILL doth hereby grant unto
the said ELEANER MEDLEY her heires and assignes all the aforesaid Tract and parsell of
land and all the Estate whatsoever of him the said LEONARD HILL To Have and To Hold
the said parsell of land with the appurtenances to the same belonging to the said
ELEANER MEDLEY her heirs and assignes forever. In Wittness whereof the said parties
have set their hands and Seals
in presence of JOS. ⨍ PATTERSON,   LEOD. HILL
        JAMES ⨉ DICKS

At a Court held for Essex County on ye 15th day of July 1729
LEONARD HILL gent acknowledged this his Release unto ELINOR MEDLEY which is admitted to record

p.   KNOW ALL MEN by these presents that we THOMAS HARDY, JOHN EDMONDSON
35   and JAMES JONES are held and firmly bound unto our Sovereign Lord GEORGE in
        the just sum of Ten thousand pounds of tobacco. Wittness our hands and seals
this 15th day of July 1729
    THE CONDITION of this obligation is such that Whereas THOMAS HARDY hath obtained a
Lycence to keep an ORDINARY at his Dwelling House if therefore the said THOMAS HARDY doth constantly find in his ORDINARY good wholesome & cleanly lodging & Dyet for
travellers and Stableage fodder and provender or Pasturage and provender as the Season shall require for their Horses for and during the Term of one whole year from the
day of the date hereof & shall not suffer any unlawfull gameing in his House or on the
Sabbath day suffer any to Tipple more then is necessary that then the above obligation
to be null & of none effect otherwise to remain in full force
                                        THOS. HARDY
                            JOHN EDMONDSON   JAMES JONES
    THOMAS HARDY, JNO. EDMONDSON & JAMES JONES acknowledged this bond to be their
act and deed in Essex County Court on ye 16th day of July 1729 which is ordered to be
recorded

pp.,   THIS INDENTURE made the twelve day of May in the year of our Lord one thou-
36-   sand seven hundred and Twenty nine in the Reign of our Sovereign Lord KING
38   GEORGE the Second over England Between HENRY YOUNG of South farnham
        Parish in Essex County in Virginia of one part and RICHARD TYLER JUNR. Gent
of the said County & Colony of the other part Wittnesseth that said HENRY YOUNG for an
in consideration of a piece parcell or Moyetye of Lands granted and surrendered and
delivered to the sd HENRY YOUNG by the said RICHARD TYLER that is due to the said
RICHARD TYLER by Marrying his present Wife KATRINE the Relique of WILLIAM
YOUNG deced, she the said KATRINE being the Mother of him the sd HENRY YOUNG, &
the said Land being in the said Parish & County and for and in consideration of the just
Sum of five shillings Sterling money and for divers other reasons he the said HENRY
YOUNG hath granted to farm letten unto the said RICHARD TYLER a parcel of land being
in the said Parish & County containing one hundred acres being part of a tract of land
and plantation the above said WILLIAM YOUNG lived on at the time of his decease being
bounded as followeth beginning at the Mouth of a Creek on the South side of the
RAPPA. RIVER which sd Creek runeth between this land & the land and plantation the
said WILLIAM YOUNG lived on at the time of his decease and the now Dwelling plantation of the said HENRY YOUNG at the time of the sealing and delivery of these presents
thence up the sd Creek its severall courses unto a tract of land formerly belonging &
held by WILLIAM SMITH of this Pish & County granted by PATENT unto one DOCTOR
GODSON & thence along the sd SMITHs line its severall courses Easterly to a stooping
Hiccory marked Corner this sd land & line now is due & belonging to WILLIAMSON
YOUNG given unto him by his Father WILLIAM YOUNG aforesd deced thence from the sd
Corner hiccory along a new marked line its severall courses Southerley through a Neck
of land and the head of a large MIRE PONN unto a marked corner pessimon tree standing in the line of JOHN EVANS he now dwells on thence along the said EVANS line and
land its severall courses unto a marked red Oak being an old corner on the end of a
point at the East end of said PONN thence Northerly by another new marked line now
made toward the sd River and Plantation nigh to the old field of the sd plantation unto a

Branch to a corner Maple, and Willo Oake thence downe the said Branch unto a Creek along the Courses of the sd Run unto the said River this sd Creek being between this land and plantation (and the land & plantation formerly possessed by TIMOTHY DRIS-COLL deced) thence up the sd River to the beginning place Together and allso all the woods orchards feedings and appurtenances whatsoever thereunto belonging To Have and To Hold the sd one hundred acres of land with the premises unto the sd RICHARD TYLER his Exrs. and Assignes from the day of the date hereof to the full term of the Natural life of him the said RICHARD TYLER JUNIOR, the the sd RICHARD paying on the tenth day of October in every year the rent of one year of Indian Corn onley if lawfully demanded and allso the quitrents that shall become due to our aforesaid Majesty. In Witness whereof the partys have set their hands and Seals
in presence of JOHN EVANS,   HENRY YOUNG
     JOHN GREENSMITH, JOHN HAYES
  At a Court held for Essex County on the 19th day of August 1729
HENRY YOUNG acknowledged this his Lease indented to RICHARD TYLER JUNR. gent which on his motion is admitted to record
  Memorandum that livery & Seizin by Turff and Twigg of said Land and allso quiet possession of the Dwelling houses by the keys & doors thereof on the sd land was delivered to RICHD. TYLER and to his assignes with warranty the sd HENRY YOUNG for himselfe his heirs this 12th day of May 1729
Test   JOHN EVANS,   HENRY YOUNG
    JOHN GREENSMITH, JOHN HAYES
  At a Court held for Essex County on the 19th day of August 1729
HENRY YOUNG acknowledgeld his livery & seisin of the lands to RICHARD TYLER JUNR. Gent wch is admitted to record

pp.   THIS INDENTURE made the fourteenth day of July in the year of our Lord one
39-   thousand seven hundred & twenty nine Between JAMES GARNETT of Essex
40   County in the Parish of St. Anns of one part and JOHN ROWZEE of the County &
      Parish aforesd of the other part Witnesseth that the said JAMES GARNETT for the sum of fifteen pounds Current money of Virginia doth hereby sell unto the said JOHN ROWZEE his heirs & Admintrs. & every of them forever one parcell of land containing fifteen acres being in the Pish & County aforesd above a Creek called LITTLE OCCUPA-TION & adjoyning on the South side the MAIN OCCUPATION CREEK it being all the land now claimed by the said JAMES GARNETT above the before mentioned LITTLE OCCUPA-TION CREEK which land was purchased by sd JAMES GARNETT of JOHN HINES which sd JOHN HINES purchased of ROBERT PAYNE Deced with all and singular the Houses, buildings, trees growing & other appurtenances whatsoever thereunto belonging To Have and To Hold the said land unto the sd JOHN ROWZEE (he the said JOHN ROWZEE & his heirs paying the rents & performing the services which shall hereafter become due in the premises aforesd unto the King only excepted) and said JAMES GARNETT for himself will warrant & forever defend. In Witness whereof the partyes have set their hands & Seals
in presence of THOMAS JONES,   JAMES GARNETT
     ELLINOR ROY, ANN BRONAUGH
  At a Court held for Essex County the 19th day of August 1729
JAMES GARNETT acknowledged this his Deed indented to JOHN ROWZEE which on his motion is admitted to record
  Memorandum that full possession was delivered by JAMES GARNETT to JOHN ROWZEE by Turff & Twigg the fourteenth day of July in the year of our Lord one thousand seven hundred & twenty and Nine in the presence of

Testes FRANCIS •𝒰 STEALL,   JAMES GARNETT
       THOS. JONES
  At a Court held for Essex County the 19th day of August 1729
JAMES GARNETT acknowledged his livery & seizen to JOHN ROWZEE which on his motion
is admitted to record

p.   KNOW ALL MEN by these presents that wee JAMES GRIFFIN, ROBERT PARKER &
41   JAMES RENNOLDS are held and firmly bound unto our Sovereign Lord GEORGE
       the Second in the full sum of Tenn thousand pounds of Tobacco this 19th day of
August 1729.
  THE CONDITION of the above obligation is such that Whereas JAMES GRIFFIN hath obtained a license to keep an ORDINARY at his House at TAPPA. if therefore said JAMES
GRIFFIN doth constantly provide in his ORDINARY good cleanly lodgeing & dyet fitt for
travellors, stableage fodder & provender or pasturage and provender as the Season
shall require for their Horses during the term of one year from the date of the day
hereof & shall not permit any unlawfull gameing in his House nor on the Sabath allow
any to tipple more than is necessary that then this obligation to be void Ellse to remain
in full power
in presence of W. BEVERLEY   JAMES GRIFFIN
                RO: PARKER   JAMES RENNOLDS
  At a Court held for Essex County on the 19th day of August 1729
This bond was acknowledged by JAMES GRIFFIN, ROBERT PARKER & JAMES RENNOLDS to
be their act and deed & ordered to be recorded

pp.   THIS INDENTURE made the fifteenth day of September in the year of our Lord
41-   one thousand seven hundred & Twenty Nine Between WILLIAM VAWTER of the
44   County of NORTHAMPTON in the Collony of Virginia of one part and HUGH CAREY
      of the County of Essex in the sd Collony of the other part Witnesseth that sd WIL-
LIAM VAWTER for the sum of thirty pounds Current money doth grant unto the said
HUGH CAREY his heirs & assigns forever a parcell of land containing seventy and five
acres lyeing in the sd County of Essex on the North side of POPOMAN SWAMP and
bounded begining at the head of a small Branch of the aforesd Swamp and so along a
line of marked Trees which devides JAMES BOULWAREs land from the aforesd piece of
land thence along the sd line to a Corner tree standing in a line of WILLIAM GOLDENs
land and thence along the sd line to a Corner Tree of THOMAS RAMSEYs land, and
thence along the sd RAMSEYs line to a Corner Tree standing in the line which was made
for a division between WILLIAM VAWTER party to these presents and his Brother
DAVID VAWTER & thence along the sd division line to the aforementioned Branch and
so up the said Branch to the first beginning together with all ways water courses &
appurtenance whatsoever thereunto belonging To Have and To Hold to him the sd HUGH
CAREY and to his heirs & assigns forever. In Witness whereof the party first
mentioned hath set his hand and Seal
in presence of THO: RAMSEY   WILLIAM VAWTER
       ROBT. PARKER
  At a Court held for Essex County on the 16th day of September 1729
WILLIAM VAWTER acknowledged his Deed to HUGH CAREY and on his motion is admitted
to record
  Also the same day - MARGARET VAWTER the Wife of the said WILLIAM VAWTER freely
relinquished her right of Dower in the land and premises to the aforenamed HUGH
CAREY which is admitted to record

At a Court held for Essex County on the 16th day of Septr. 1729
WILLIAM VAWTER acknowledged his livery & seizen of the lands to HUGH CAREY wch is
admitted to record

pp.   THIS INDENTURE made the fifteenth day of September in the year of our Lord
44-   one thousand seven hundred & Twenty Nine Between JOHN BEAZLEY of CARO-
46   LINE COUNTY of one part and HENRY BEAZLEY of Essex County of the other part
       Witnesseth that sd JOHN BEAZLEY for the sum of fifteen hundred pounds of Tobo
& Cask doth grant unto sd HENRY BEAZLEY his heirs & assigns all that parcell of land
which was given to the sd JOHN BEAZLEY by WILLIAM BEAZLEY late of Essex County
deced scituate in the County of Essex being fifty acres, and adjacent to the sd HENRY
BEAZLEY own land together with all & singular the ways, woods all other the profits
belonging (onely the sd BEAZLEY doth except halfe an acre of land conveniently ad-
joying and includeing the BURYING PLACE) To Have and To Hold the said fifty acres of
(land) with all its rights unto him the sd HENRY BEAZLEY his heirs and assigns forever.
In Witness whereof the parties have set their hands & Seals
in presence of SAMLL. BISWELL,   JOHN 𝄐 BEAZLEY
       RICHARD BILLUPS, NICHOLAS 𝐗 ADKINSON   WINEFRED ✝ BEAZLEY
At a Court held for Essex County on the 16th day of September 1729
JOHN BEAZLEY acknowledged this his Deed indented to HENRY BEEZLEY wch on his
motion is recorded
  Allso the same day - WINIFRED BEEZLEY came into Court & freely relinquished her
right of Dower in the land & premises conveyed by this Deed to HENRY BEEZLEY which
is admitted to record
  At a Court held for Essex County on the 16th day of September 1729
JOHN BEEZLEY acknowledged this livery & Seizen of the lands to HENRY BEEZELEY & was
admitted to record

pp.   THIS INDENTURE made the tenth and Eleventh day of September in the year of
47-   our Lord God according to the Computation now used in the Church of Great
52   Britain Seventeen hundred Twenty and Nine Between WILLIAM MARSH of
       Southfarnham Parish in County of Essex Cordwainer of one part and RICHARD
CAWTHORNE of the Parish & County aforesaid Boatwright of the other part Witnesseth
that said WILLIAM MARSH for the sume of Sixteen hundred pounds of good sound and
merchantable sweet scented Tobbo. paid hath granted unto said RICHD. CAWTHORNE in
his actuall possession now being by Virtue of Indenture made for one whole year and
of the Statute for the transferring of uses into possession and to his heirs and assigns
forever all that parcell of land which WILLIAM JOURNEY formerly sold unto one THO-
MAS WOOD and was by the sd WOOD given & bequeathed unto sd WILLIAM MARSH (being
part of a dividend of land wch sd WILLIAM JOURNEY sometime since sold unto Capt.
REUBEN WELCH deced) conteyning Seaventy acres bounded beginning at a Spanish Oak
corner thence running South East to a white Oak corner thence North East to a scrubby
black Oak Corner thence North East to a Hickory by a PATH side, thence North East to a
white Oak corner thence South to a hiccory a Corner tree in Mr. MERIWETHER's line
thence to the place of beginning all levell land all which premises being in the Parish
aforesd and adjoyning to the lands of MR. MERIWETHER, YOUNG, BROWN & others And
all houses, Timber, commodities whatsoever belonging To Have and To Hold ye sd Seaventy acres of land unto the sd RICHARD CAWTHORNE his heirs & assignes forever. In
Witness whereof the parties first named have sett their hands and Seals
in presence of THOMAS EDMONDSON JUNR.,   WILLIAM 𝐖 MARSH
       JOHN MEGGS

At a Court held for Essex County on the 16th day of September 1729
WILLIAM MARSH acknowledged this his Release Indented to RICHARD CAWTHORNE
which on his motion is admitted to record

pp. THIS INDENTURE made the fifteenth day of September in the Second year of the
53- Reign of our Sovereign Lord GEORGE the Second, and in the year of our Lord one
56   thousand seven hundred & Twenty Nine Between HANNAH UPSHAW of the
Parish of South farnham in the County of Essex of one part and JEREMIAH UP-
SHAW of the Parish and County aforesd of other part Witnesseth that said HANNAH UP-
SHAW for the sum of Tenn pounds Sterling hath sold unto said JEREMIAH UPSHAW his
heirs and assigns forever all that Plantation and tract of land where now sd JEREMIAH
UPSHAW Dwelleth being in the Parish of South farnham in the County of Essex containing Two hundred and Twenty acres of land which sd land the sd HANNAH UPSHAW
purchased of ROBERT SMITH by Indentures of Bargain and Sale relation being had to
the record where it doth appear And is bounded beginning where a Stake formerly
stood between the Hickorys corner of THOMAS TODDs land & comeing thence North West
to a white Oak by a Branch of HOSKINSES CREEK thence South West to the sd Branch and
crossing it to a great white Oak, thence North West to a red Oak on a hill, thence South
West to a Stone and a white Oak marked by it thence South East to the land which was
formerly one JOHN BRUSHWOODs to a Stake by a red Oak, thence by his line North East to
a white Oak, a chesnut Oak in a Branch thence South East to the land of the sd TODD to a
stake by a redd Oak, and lastly thence by his line North East to the place it begun the
said land lying between the MAIN SWAMPS of PISCATAWAY & HOSKINSES CREEKS but
touchetts nor butts on neither of the sd main Swamps and all houses Tobacco houses and
appurtenances wtsoever belonging To Have and To Hold the said Tract of land & all premises hereby granted unto the sd JEREMIAH UPSHAW his heirs and assigns. In Witness
whereof the parties have set their hands & Seals
in presence of THOS. STHRESHLY,   HANNAH ℎ UPSHAW
  WM. UPSHAW, W. ROANE
  At a Court held for Essex County on ye 16th day of September 1729
MRS. HANNAH UPSHAW acknowledged this her Deed Indented to JEREMIAH UPSHAW
wch on his motion is admitted to record
  At a Court held for Essex County on the 16th day of September 1729
MRS. HANNAH UPSHAW acknowledged her livery & Seizen of the lands within men-
tioned to JEREMIAH UPSHAW to be her act and deed which is admitted to record

pp. THIS INDENTURE made the fifteenth day of September in the Second year of the
56- Reign of our Sovereign Lord GEORGE the Second and in the year of our Lord one
59   thousand seven hundred & Twenty Nine Between JEREMIAH UPSHAW of the
Parish of South farnham in the County of Essex of one part and HANNAH UP-
SHAW of the Parish & County aforesd Widow of other part Witnesseth that said JERE-
MIAH UPSHAW for the Sum of Tenn pounds Sterling money doth fully release unto the
said HANNAH UPSHAW her heirs and Administrators all that Plantation tract of land
whereon sd HANNAH UPSHAW now Dwelleth being in the Parish of South farnham in
the County of Essex and the sd Plantation contains three hundred and fifty acres of land
which sd Plantation & tract of land is the proper Estate of sd JEREMIAH UPSHAW &
given to him the said JEREMIAH UPSHAW by his Father Capt. WILLIAM UPSHAW deced
by his Last Will and Testament and is part of a tract of land of one thousand acres of
land which sd WILLIAM UPSHAW purchas'd of Mr. HENRY BEVERLEY relation being had
to the record where it doth appear and all houses outhouses Tobo houses and appurtenances whatsoever thereunto belonging of him the sd JEREMIAH UPSHAW To Have and

To Hold to the onley use & behoofe of sd HANNAH UPSHAW her heirs & assigns forever.
In Witness whereof the parties have set their hands & Seals
in presence of us THOS. STHRESHLY,   JER. UPSHAW
        W. ROANE, WM. UPSHAW
  At a Court held for Essex County on the 16th day of September 1729
JEREMIAH UPSHAW acknowledged this his Deed indented to HANNAH UPSHAW to be his
act and deed which on her motion is admitted to record
  At a Court held for Essex County on the 16th day of September 1729
JEREMIAH UPSHAW acknowledged his livery & Seizen of the lands to Mrs. HANNAH UP-
SHAW which is admitted to record

pp.   THIS INDENTURE made the fifteen and Sixteenth day of September in the year of
59-   our Lord one thousand Seven hundred Twenty & Nine Between SAMUELL BAR-
65   BER & ANN his Wife Daughtr. & Heir of JOHN FOSTER deced of the Parish of North
        farnham in the County of RICHMOND of one part and WILLIAM DAINGERFIELD of
the Parish of Southfarnham & County of Essex Gent of other part Witnesseth that said
SAMUELL BARBER & ANN his Wife Daughter & Heir of JOHN FOSTER deced for sum of
Forty pounds Sterl. money hath bargained & sold unto the sd WILLIAM DAINGERFIELD
in his actual possession now being by virtue of Indenture for one year and by force of
the Statute for Transferring uses into Possession and to his heirs forever all that plantation or parcell of land which JOHN FOSTER Father of ANN BARBER the Wife of
SAMUELL BARBER aforesaid Daughter & heir of JOHN FOSTER deced purchased from
WILLIAM NORTH deceased by Deed bearing date the Eight day of May Seventeen hundred & five (be the same more or less) being in the Parish of Southfarnham & County of
Essex and bounded that is beginning at the mouth of a Creek called GELSONS CREEK ad-
joyning to a Tract of land granted by PATENT to BARTHOLOMEW HODGKINSON runing
thence S: W: along the line of the said HODGKINSON to the foot of the hill above Mr.
DAINGERFIELDs Plantation from thence N: W: to a deep gulley or branch down the said
Gulley or Branch to a piece of Marsh formerly sold by ANTHONY NORTH SENR. to THO-
MAS BUTTIN, & so along the side of the sd Marsh to the said GELLSONS CREEK where it
first begins (the BURYING PLACE of JOHN FOSTER and JOHN FOSTER JUNR. his Son only
Excepted) to the said WILLIAM DAINGERFIELD and all ways trees and appurtenances
whatsoever thereunto belonging and the reversions of every part of the said land To
Have and To Hold unto the said WILLM. DAINGERFIELD his heirs & assigns forever. In
Witness whereof the parties have set their hands and Seals
in presence of JAMES GARNETT,   SAMLL. BARBER
        THOS. MERRIWETHER, FRANS. SMITH   ANN BARBER
  At a Court held for Essex County on the 16th day of September 1729
SAMUEL BARBER & ANN BARBER (the said Ann being first privately examined by Mr.
ALEXANDR. PARKER) acknowledged this their Release Indented to WILLIAM DAINGER-
FIELD gent which on his motion is admitted to record
  Also the same day Came into Court SUSANNA METCALF the Wife of GILBERT METCALF &
freely relinquished her Dower of & in the lands & premises within mentioned to WM.
DAINGERFIELD Gent which on his motion is admitted to record

p.   KNOW ALL MEN by these presents that we JAMES GARNETT Sherriffe of Essex
66   County & BENJAMIN WINSLOW are held and firmly bound unto our Sovern. Lord
        the King his heirs in the Sum of Eighty two thousand, seven hundred pounds of
lawfull Merchantable Tobacco this 16th day of Septembr. 1729
  THE CONDITION of the above obligation is such that whereas JAMES GARNETT is admitted COLLECTOR of the County of Essex Now if the said JAMES GARNETT shall well &

faithfully collect & duely pay the Sum of Forty one thousand, three hundred & fifty pounds of Tobacco this day proportioned by the Court of the aforesd County of Essex to the respective Creditors therein mentioned that then the above obligation to be void else to remain in force

in presence of W. BEVERLEY   JAS. GARNETT
                                                               BENJA. WINSLOW

At a Court held for Essex County on the 16th day of Septembr. 1729
JAMES GARNETT gent & BENJA. WINSLOW acknowledged this bond to be their act and deed which is ordered to be recorded

pp.   TO ALL PEOPLE to whom these presents shall come I ROBERT GEORGE SENIOR of
66-   MIDDLESEX COUNTY send Greeting. Know ye that I the sd ROBERT GEORGE in
67   consideration of the naturall affection & fatherly love which I bear to my
        Loveing Son JOHN GEORGE of Essex County as allso for other goods causes have granted & by these presents do give unto my sd Son JNO. GEORGE & his heirs for ever all & Singular one track of land lyeing in Southfarnham Parish in Essex County containing two hundred & seventy acres Together with all houses, barns, Meadows & commodities whatsoever to the said land belonging To Have and To Hold unto my said Son JOHN GEORGE his heirs & assigns forever freely without any demand of me the said ROBERT GEORGE SENR. or any other person in my name. In Witness whereof I have hereunto set my hand & Seal this 18th day of November 1729

in presence of us NICHO. SMITH,   ROBERT R GEORGE
        SAMLL. CLAYTON

At a Court held for Essex County the 18th day of November 1729
ROBERT GEORGE acknowledged this Deed Poll to his Son JOHN GEORGE which on his motion is admitted to record

pp.   THIS INDENTURE made the Sixteenth and Seventeenth day of November in the
67-   third year of the Reign of our Sovereign Lord GEORGE the Second Anno Dom one
73   thousand seven hundred Twenty & Nine Between JAMES ALDERSON of St. Anns
        Parish in the County of Essex & ANN his Wife of one part and WILLIAM BROOKE Churchwarden of the sd Parish of St. Ann in the County aforesd for and on behalfe of himselfe & the rest of the Parishioners of the said Parish & by and with the advice & consent of the VESTRY MEN thereof of the other part Witnesseth that JAMES ALDERSON & ANN his Wife for the sum of Eleven thousand pounds of Merchantable Tobacco to him already secured to be paid have granted & sold unto the said WILLIAM BROOKE & his Successors Churchwardens of the Parish aforesd (for & on behalfe of themselves & the Vestry Men & Parishioners thereof as an Adition to the present GLEBE) and (now in his actual possession being of the dividet of land herein aftermentioned by virtue of an Indenture for one year & of the Statute for transferring uses into possession) & to his Successors for ever All that parcell of Woodland & cleared ground containing Sixty acres being in the Parish of St. Anns aforesd and bounded beginning at a Stake two poles from a red Oak by a PATH that divides this and the land of ROBERT BROOKE and running thence along an old marked line that divides this & the GLEBE land, North East to a corner white Oak, thence North West to two red Oaks, thence South West to the beginning and all ways fences comodities & appurtenances whatsoever thereunto belonging and all the Estate as well in Equity as at Law of the said JAMES ALDERSON & ANN his Wife To Have and To Hold unto the said WILLIAM BROOKE Churchwarden for himselfe & the rest of the Vestry Men Parishioners and Successors as an addition to the GLEBE of the sd Parish of St. Anns forever for enlargeing the GLEBE for the reception & better Entertainment of such Minister or Ministers as shall officiate in the sd Parish

Successively for evermore, and to no other use or purpose whatsoever. In Witness whereof the parties first named have set their hands and Seals
in presence of SALVATOR MUSCOE,   JAS. ALDERSON
        HUM. BROOKE, WILLIAM HANKIN   ANN ALDERSON
    At a Court held for Essex County on the 18th day of November 1729
JAMES ALDERSON & ANN ALDERSON (the sd ANN being first privily examined by
ALEXANDR. PARKER gent) acknowledged this their Indented Release to WILLIAM
BROOKE which on his motion is admitted to record

pp.   KNOW ALL MEN by these presents that I SARAH SMITH of the County of Essex and
73-   Parish of Saint Anns do constitute and appoint my friend RICHARD COVINGTON
79   to be my Lawfull Attorney to acknowledge my right of dower of a certain tract
        of land unto BENJAMIN WINSLOW or to his assigns. Witness my hand & Seale this
18th day of Novr. 1729
in presence of JOHN WILCOX,   SARAH SMITH
        FRANCIS COVINGTON, THOMAS COVINGTON
    At a Court held for Essex County on the 18th day of November 1729
This Power of Attorney from SARAH SMITH to RICHARD COVINGTON was proved by the
oaths of JOHN WILCOX & FRANCIS COVINGTON & admitted to record

        THIS INDENTURE made the fifteenth and seventeenth day of November in the
year of our Lord one thousand seven hundred and Twenty Nine Between JOHN SMITH
and SARAH his Wife of the Parish of St. Ann in the County of Essex of one part and BEN-
JAMIN WINSLOW of the aforesd Parish & County of the other part Witnesseth that the sd
JOHN SMITH and SARAH his Wife for the sum of Forty pounds Currt. Money of Virga.
hath granted unto the sd BENJA. WINSLOW (in his actual possession now being by virtue
of a bargain & sale to him made for one year and of the statute for transferring uses
into possession) and to his heirs and assigns forever all that pcell of land or Woodland
ground containing Ninety three acres, and forty two perches of land, being in the
Parish and County aforesd. and bounded begining at a wt. & red Oak corner trees to
SMITH & WINSLOW and thence along their lines S: E: to the mouth of a small Branch
thence down the Main Branch to the mouth of anothr. small Branch thence up that to
the sd SMITHS MILL PATH thence by a line of mark't trees North West to another
Branch thence up the same to three corner red oak Saplins a little below the MAIN
ROAD thence South West to the head of a ( ) call'd COVETIONS DEED thence down the
same to a corner Ash & Maple in the line that divides this and GRAYSONs land thence
along that line South East to WARINGs Corner Spanish Oak, thence along that line of
WARINGs North East to the sd WINSLOWs Corner white & Spanish Oak by a Branch
thence along the sd WINSLOWs line to the beginning and all houses, outhouses, gardens
and Trees and appurtenances whatsoever belonging To Have and To Hold unto the sd
BENJAMIN WINSLOW his heirs and assigns forever. In Witness whereof the parties
have set their hands and Seals
in presence of JOHN WILCOX,   JOHN SMITH
        FRANCIS COVINGTON, THOMAS COVINGTON   SARAH SMITH
    At a Court held for Essex County on the 18th day of Novr. 1729
JOHN SMITH acknowledged this Indented Release to BENJAMIN WINSLOW which on his
motion is admitted to record
    Also the same day SARAH SMITH the Wife of the sd JOHN SMITH by RICHARD COVING-
TON her Attorney came into Court & freely relinquished her right of dower of & in the
land conveyed by this Deed to BENJA. WINSLOW which is admitted to record

p.   KNOW ALL MEN by these presents that wee JAMES COLEMAN & NATHANIEL SAN-
79   DERS are held & firmly bound unto our Sovereign Lord GEORGE the Second in
      the sum of Ten thousand pounds of Tobacco. Witness our hands & Seals this 16th
day of December 1729
THE CONDITION of the above obligation is such that Whereas JAMES COLEMAN hath obtained a licence to keep an ORDINARY at SANDER's ORDINARY if therefore the sd JAMES
COLEMAN doth constantly find & provide in his ORDINARY good wholesom & cleanly
lodgeing & diet for Travellers & Stableage fodder & provender or pasturage and provender as the Season shall require for their Horses dureing the term of one whole year
from the day of the date hereof & shall not suffer any unlawfull gameing in his House
nor on the Sabbath day permit any to Tipple more than is necesary Then the above
obligation to be void else to remain in force
in the presence of us W. BEVERLEY,   JAMES COLEMAN
                                                              NATHLL. SANDERS
     This Bond was acknowledged by JAMES COLEMAN & NATHL. SANDERS in Essex County
Court on the 16th day of December 1729 & ordered to be recorded

p.   KNOW ALL MEN by these presents that I JANE SARJANT Wife of WILLIAM SAR-
80   JANT of the Citty of BRISTOLL have made and in my place putt and deputed THO-
      MAS WAREING of Essex County in the Collony of Virginia Gent my true & lawfull
Attorney for me to relinquish my right of Dowry to all Lands & Tenements which my
husband is now possessed of in KING GEORGE's County or any other County in the
Collony of Virginia which my said Husband shall make sale of, and for me to make seale
and deliver all other acts whatsoever concerning the premises as fully as I my selfe
might do. In Wittness whereof I have hereunto sett my hand and Seale this fourteenth
day of July in the year of our Lord one thousand seven hundred and Twenty Nine 1729.
in presence of WILLM. LLOYD,   JANE SARJANT
        JOSEPH SMITH
  At a Court held for Essex County the 16th day of December 1729
This Power of Attorney was in due form proved by the Oaths of the Witnesses therunto
& admitted to record

pp.   THIS INDENTURE made the third day of December in the year of our Lord one
80-   thousand seven hundred and Twenty Nine Between TOBIAS INGRAM of the
82   County of Essex of one part and ROBERT BROOKE of the County aforesd of the
      other part Witnesseth that sd TOBIAS INGRAM for & in consideration of the sum
of Six pounds Two shillings & Six pence current money of Virginia hath granted to
farm lett unto the said ROBERT BROOKE his heirs & Admrs. a parcell of land containing
Six acres & twenty five perches in St. Anns Parish in ye County aforesd bounded begining at a white Oak stump near the LANDING commonly called INGRAMS LANDING
and running thence South West along the line of sd BROOKE to a stake thence North
West to a Corner Hickory then North East to a corner Spanish Oak by the side of a Creek
called WASSANENSEN thence down the same to the begining with all the woods under-
woods & all other profitts with their appurtenances unto said ROBERT BROOKE his heirs
and Admrs. from day of the date of these presents dureing the term of three naturall
lives (to wit) the naturall live of the REVD. MR. ROBERT ROSE of St. Anns Pish & County
aforesd & the naturall lives of SUSANAH & WILLIAM BROOKE (Daughter & Son of the sd
ROBERT BROOKE & PHEBE his Wife) paying yearly the sum of Six shillings & three pence
Currt money of Virginia unto the sd TOBIAS INGRAM & the heires of his body lawfully
begotten to be paid yearly on ye twenty fifth day of March & if unpaid the space of
thirty days it shall be lawfull unto TOBIAS INGRAM and all other persons to whom the

right belong into the sd land and all the premises to have again. In Witness whereof
the parties have set their hands and Seals
in presence of W. BEVERLEY,   TOBIAS INGRAM
        JOHN FRAZER, ROBERT GIBSON **X**
    At a Court held for Essex County on the 16th day of Decembr. 1729
TOBIAS INGRAM acknowledged this his Lease indented with the livery and Seizin thereon endorsed to ROBERT BROOKE gent wch on his motion are recorded

pp.   THIS INDENTURE made the Seventeenth day of Septembr. in the year of our Lord
83-   one thousand seven hundred Twenty and Nine Between THOMAS MUNDAY of the
85   Parish of St. Ann in the County of Essex Planter of one part and JAMES MUNDAY
         of the aforesd Pish & County of the other part Witnesseth that I the said THO-
MAS MUNDAY as well for the naturall affection and Brotherly Love which I have unto
my well beloved Brother JAMES MUNDAY as well as other good causes have granted and
do give to my sd Brother JAMES MUNDAY one piece of land or wood land ground containing fifty acres being in the Pish & County aforesd and bounded beginning at a
Maple and white Oak standing in a Branch known by the name of GRAVES SPRING
BRANCH from thence up the sd Branch to the line that divides the land of the aforesd
THOMAS MUNDAY and the land of GRAVES, thence along the sd line to a Corner Hickory
of Mr. XPHER BEVERLEYs, and a red Oak saplin at the head of a Branch from thence to a
Corner Hickory by a Branch side then down the sd Branch to a large Swamp known and
called by the name of the DESART SWAMP from thence down the Water Course of the sd
Swamp to the Maple and white Oak where it first began with all houses, Orchards and
appurtenances whatsoever belonging which sd fifty acres of land is part of a tract of
land given by THOMAS MUNDAY of the aforesd Pish & County deced Gransfather to THO-
MAS MUNDAY party to these presents by his last Will and Testament to THOMAS MUN-
DAY of the Pish and County aforesaid deced Father to the aforesd THOMAS MUNDAY
party to these presents relation being had may appear To Have and To Hold the aforesd
pcell of land with all the premises unto the sd JAMES MUNDAY his heires and assigns
forever. In Witness whereof the parties have set their hands and seals
in presence of SALVATOR MUSCOE   THOMAS **T** MUNDAY
        JOHN MUNDAY, THOMAS MARRITT
    At a Court held for Essex County on the 16th day of Decembr. 1729
THOMAS MUNDAY acknowledged this Deed indented to JAMES MUNDAY and his livery &
Seizen of the premises within mentioned to JAMES MUNDAY and admitted to record

p.   VIRGINIA SS. TO ALL TO WHOM these presents shall come JOHN CARTER Esqr. his
85   Majestys SECRETARY of Virginia sendeth Greeting. WHEREAS application hath
         been made to me by WILLIAM BEVERLEY Gent. CLERK of the County of Essex to
appoint RICHARD TUNSTALL to be DEPUTY CLERK under him in the sd Office dureing his
absence or Indisposition KNOW YE therefore that I the sd JOHN CARTER do hereby appoint RICHARD TUNSTALL DEPUTY CLERK of the sd Court giveing and hereby granting
unto him full power & authority to perform & execute the sd Office dureing the absence
or indisposition of the sd WILLIAM BEVERLEY hereby revoking all former Comissions
given for the sd purpose. In Witness whereof I have set my hand & Seal this fifteenth
day of January One thousand seven hundred & Twenty Nine in the third year of his
Maties Reign   JOHN CARTER
    At a Court held for Essex County at Tappa. on the 17th day of February 1729
By virtue of the above Common. the above named RICHARD TUNSTALL having taken the
Oaths appointed by Act of PARLIAMENT & subscribed the Test was sworn DEPUTY CLERK
of this County

pp.   THIS INDENTURE made the twenty fifth and twenty sixth day of August in the
85-   year of our Lord one thousand seven hundred Twenty & Nine Between TIMOTHY
88   CONNER of the County of KING & QUEEN Planter of one part and ROBERT BROOKE
of the County of Essex Gentleman of other part Witnesseth that sd TIMOTHY CON-
NER for the sum of five pounds Currant money & two thousand pounds of Tobacco hath
granted and confirmed unto the sd ROBERT BROOKE (in his actual possession by virtue
of a bargain and sale for one year and by force of the statute for transferring uses into possession) and to his heirs and assigns forever a certain tract of land containing
One hundred & seventy five acres being the Moiety or half part of a Tract of land formerly belonging to TIMOTHY HAY late of the sd County of Essex and by Virtue of a Writ
of Extent bearing date the Twenty Sixth day of May in the year One thousand seven
hundred and Thirteen the sd Land was delivered by RICHARD COVINGTON Gent. then
SHERIFF of the sd County to sd TIMOTHY CONNER being divided by a line beginning at a
red Oak by a Branch called ASSAGES, and standing in a line of the sd ROBERT BROOKEs
land from the Outward line of Mr. CHRISTOPHER BEVERLEYs twelve hundred acres and
runing South East to the line of JOHN HART between two Hiccorys wch sd moyety or half
part is adjoyning to the land called & known by the name of BURTONS RANGE Together
with all houses, outhouses & tobacco houses and all claims whatsoever of him the sd
TIMOTHY CONNER to the same To Have and To Hold unto the sd ROBERT BROOKE his heirs
and assigns forever. In Witness whereof the sd TIMOTHY CONNER hath set his hand &
Seal in presence of us R. TUNSTALL,
   P. BIRD, JOHN BRYANT,   TIMOTHY T CONNER
   HUM. BROOKE

At a Court held for Essex County at Tappa. on the 17th day of February 1729
This Release indented from TIMOTHY CONNER to ROBERT BROOKE was proved by the Oaths
of RICHARD TUNSTALL, PHILEMON BIRD & HUMPHRY BROOKE three of the witnesses
thereto & admitted to record

p.   KNOW ALL MEN by these presents that I WINIFRID GOULDMAN of the County of
88   Essex doe nominate & appoint Majr. WM. DAINGERFIELD my true & lawfull Atturney to relinquish my right of Dower to a track of land sold & conveyed by my
husband FRANCIS GOULDMAN by Deed bearing date the thirtieth day of Decr. one thousand seven hundred & Twenty Nine unto JAMES GARNETT. As Witness my hand & Seal
this Sixteenth day of February 1729/30.
   THOS. LAWSON,   WINIFRID ✝ GOULDMAN
   SALVATOR MUSCOE, THOS. COVINGTON

At a Court held for Essex County on the 17th day of February 1729
This Power of Attorney from WINIFRED GOULDMAN to Majr. WM. DAINGERFIELD was
proved by the Oaths of SALVR. MUSCOE & THOMAS COVINGTON & admitted to record

pp.   THIS INDENTURE made the thirtieth day of Decr. in the year of our Lord Christ
88-   one thousand seven hundred & Twenty Nine Between FRANCIS GOULDMAN of
91   the Pish of St. Anns & County of Essex Gent. of one part and JAMES GARNETT of
the Pish & County aforesd of other part Witnesseth that said FRANCIS GOULDMAN
for sum of one hundred & Seventy six pounds Currt money of Virginia doth sell unto
the said JAMES GARNETT his heirs & assigns forever all his right & Title to a certain
parcell of land or Woodland ground being in the County of Essex & KING & QUEEN
bounded begining at a white Oak a Corner tree of BOUGHANs & FISHERs & runing along
their line across the land North to another white Oak thence West Norwest to an Ash
standing by or nigh a Run in a Main Branch of MATTAPONY being a Corner mentioned
in the Original PATENT of the sd Land finally North East to its begining containing by

Estimation Eleaven hundred and twenty two acres being formerly granted by PATENT dated the twenty fifth day of Aprill one thousand seven hundred & four unto RICHARD COVINGTON, JAMES BOUGHAN & WM. WILLIAMS the sd WILLIAM WILLIAMS his part being sold & conveyed unto ED. GOULDMAN deced as by a Deed of Division between RICHARD COVINGTON & JAMES BOUGHAN & ED. GOULDMAN bearing date the 9th day of August one thousand seven hundred & Eight being had from the Essex Record will & may more at large appear the sd FRANCIS GOULDMAN the Son & heirs at law of the sd ED. GOULDMAN deced hath fully confirmed unto the sd JAMES GARNETT his heirs & assigns forever all his right & title to the aforesd land. To Have and To Hold unto the said JAMES GARNETT his heirs and assigns forever. In Witness whereof FRANCIS GOULDMAN hath set his hand and Seal

in presence of EDWARD MORGIN,   FRANCIS GOULDMAN
        MARK MORGIN, AMEY **Q** PHRAIZIER,
        AGNESS **✝** NALL

At a Court held for Essex County on the 17th day of Febry., 1729
FRANCIS GOULDMAN acknowledged this Deed Indented to JAMES GARNETT gent & WINIFRED the Wife of the sd FRANCIS by WILLIAM DAINGERFIELD gent her Attorney freely relinquished her right of dower in the land conveyed by the Deed which are admitted to record.
This livery & Seizen acknowledged by FRANCIS GOULDMAN to JAMES GARNETT in Essex County Court the 17th day of February 1729 & admitted to record

pp.   THIS INDENTURE made the thirteenth and Seventeenth day of February in the
91-   year of our Lord Christ one thousand seven hundred & Twenty Nine Between
94   ROBERT GRESHAM of the County of Essex Planter of one part and EDMUND BAGGE
        of the same County Planter of other part Witnesseth that sd ROBERT GRESHAM
for the sum of thirty pounds Currt. money of Virginia doth grant unto the said EMUND BAGGE (in his actual possession now being by virtue of one Indenture for term of one year & of the Statute for transferring uses into possession) & to his heirs & assigns all that tract of land in the Pish of St. Anns in the County of Essex containing two hundred acres of land & bounded Beginning at the old Corner red Oak stump on the North East side of the COUNTY ROAD & runing thence South West to a corner red Oak that devides this & the land of MONCASTER thence along his line West to an old corner red Oak thence North East along the old line to three corner Red Oake sapplins near the old Corner Stump (by the ROLEING ROAD) wch devides this & the land of JOHN SMITH thence along the sd SMITHs irregular mark't line which if it were straite would be forty three degrees East to the beginning being the land whereon CHARLES GRESHAM Father to the sd ROBERT late deced lived & which sd ROBERT enjoys in right of his Mother FRANCES who had the same given to her by the WILL of her Father ROBT. PARKER as may appear Together with all houses, gardens, grounds & appurtenances whatsoever belonging To Have and To Hold to the onely use & behoofe of the sd EDMUND BAGGE his heirs and assigns forever. In Witness whereof the parties above named have hereunto set their hands and Seals

in presence of ROBT. ROSE,   ROBT. GRESHAM **ℛ** his mark
        THOMAS LLOYD
At a Court held for Essex County on the 17th day of February 1729
ROBERT GRESHAM acknowledged this Release indented to EDMOND BAGGE which on his motion is admitted to record
        KNOW ALL MEN by these presents that I ROBERT GRESHAM am held and firmly bound unto EDMUND BAGGE of the same County in the sum of two hundred pounds Currt.

money of Virginia this Seventeenth day of February in the year of our Lord one thousand seven hundred Twenty & Nine

THE CONDITION of this obligation is such that if ROBERT GRESHAM shall at all times keep all the conditions mentioned in Deeds of Lease and Release wch on his part ought to be kept and also shall at all times defend all such Controversies, Disputes wch shall be brought against the sd EDMUND BAGGE his heirs & assigns on account of the land conveyed That then this obligation to be void otherwise to remain in force

in presence of ROBT. ROSE,   ROBERT   **R**   GRESHAM
      THOMAS LLOYD

At a Court held for Essex County on the 17th day of Febry. 1729
ROBERT GRESHAM acknowledged this bond to EDMOND BAGGE which is admitted to record

p.   KNOW ALL MEN by these presents that We JOHN VAWTER & WILLIAM GRAY both
95   of Essex County are held and firmly bound unto our Sovern. Lord GEORGE the
     2d. in the full sum of Ten thousand pounds of Tobacco this XVIIth day of March
Anno Dom MDCCXXIX

THE CONDTION of the above obligation is that whereas JOHN VAWTER hath obtained a Licence to keep an ORDINARY at his own House in St. Anns Pish if therefore the said JOHN VAWTER doth provide in his ORDINARY good wholesome & cleanly lodging & dyet for Travellers & Stableage fodder & provender or pasturage & provender as the Season shall require for their Horses dureing the term of one whole year from the day of these presents & shall not permit unlawfull gameing in his House nor on the Sabbath day suffer any to Tipple or drink more then is necessary that then this obligation to be void else to remain in force

                              JNO. VAWTER
                              WM. GRAY

At a Court held for Essex County on Tuesday the XVIIth day of March MDCCXXIX
JOHN VAWTER & WILLIAM GRAY acknoweldged this bond which is admitted to record

pp.   KNOW ALL MEN by these presents that We FRANCIS CRANE, JNO. FARGUSON &
95-   JOHN EDMONDSON are held & firmly bound unto our Sovrn. Lord GEORGE the Se-
96   cond in the full sum of Ten thousand pounds of Tobacco this XVIIIth day of
     March MDCCXXIX

THE CONDITION of this obligation is that Whereas FRANCIS CRANE hath obtained a Licence to keep an ORDINARY in TAPPAHANNOCK TOWN Therefore if said FRANCIS CRANE doth provide in his Ordinary good wholesome & cleanly lodging & dyet for Travellers & Stableage fodder & provender or pasturage & provender as the season shall require for their Horses dureing the term of one whole year from the date hereof & shall not permit unlawfull gameing in his House nor on the Sabbath day suffer any to Tipple or drink more then is necessary that then this obligation to be void else to remain in force
                          FRANCIS CRANE
            JNO. FARGUSON   JOHN EDMONDSON

At a Court held for Essex County on Wednesday the XVIIIth day of March MDCCXXIX
FRANCIS CRANE, JOHN FARGUSON & JOHN EDMONDSON acknowledged this bond which is admitted to record

p.   KNOW ALL MEN by these presents that we FRANCIS CRANE, SAMUEL CLAYTON &
96   JOHN FARGUSON of the County of Essex are held and firmly bound unto our
     Sovrn. Lord GEORGE the Second in the full sum of Twenty pounds Sterling dated
the XVIIth day of March MDCCXXIX

THE CONDITION of this obligation is such that Whereas the above bound FRANCIS

CRANE is by the Court of Essex County licenced to keep the FERRY at TAPPAHANNOCK to NAYLORS HOLE Now if the sd FRANCIS shall constantly keep two sufficient boats (to wit) a foot boat & an Horse boat with two able hands to attend the same, and allso give passages without delay to such publick messages & expresses as be mentioned (in and by an Act of Assembly Entituled an act for the regulation and settlement of Ferrys and for the dispatch of Publick expresses to be Ferry free) pform all & whatsoever the Law enjoyns and requires and truly & faithfully comply wth the daily Business of a FERRY KEEPER that then the above obligation to be void otherwise to remain in force

FRANCIS CRANE

SAMLL. CLAYTON   JOHN FARGESON

At a Court held for Essex County the XVIIth day of March MDCCXXIX FRANCIS CRANE, SAMUEL CLAYTON & JOHN FARGUSON acknowledged this bond which is admitted to record

pp.   THIS INDENTURE made the seaventh day of March in the year of our Lord one
97-   thousand seven hundred & Twenty nine Between ANN BARWICK of the Parish
98   of Southfarnham in the County of Essex Widw. of one part and PITTMAN SCAN-
          DRETT of the same Parish and County Mercht. of other part Witnesseth that the
sd ANN BARWICK for the sum of Sixteen pounds, Nineteen shillings and Two pence hath sold unto sd PITTMAN SCANDRETT his heirs and assigns forever for & dureing the Naturall life of the sd ANN BARWICK her thirds or right of dower of two hundred acres of land being the Plantation whereon she now lives being in the Parish & County aforesd and is part of a tract of land sold by JOHN GRIFFING late of the aforesd County to WILLIAM AYRES by Deed dated the Tenth day of December 1696 To Have and To Hold the sd third part or right of Dower of the said Two hundred acres of land unto the sd PITTMAN SCANDRETT his heirs and assigns for & dureing the life of the sd ANN BARWICK. In Witness whereof the sd ANN BARWICK hath hereunto set her hand and Seal
in presence of PT. GODFREY,   ANN BERRICK

        JAS. ALDERSON, BENJA. WINSLOW

At a Court continued and held for Essex County on the XVIIIth day of March MDCCXXIX ANN BERRICK acknowledged this her Deed to PITTMAN SCANDRETT which on his motion is admitted to record

Memorandum That on the Eighteenth day of March in the year 1729 livry and Seisen of the within land was given to PITTMAN SCANDRETT by ANN BERWICK in presence of ELIZABETH GAMES, ELIZABETH E FOGGE, ELIZABETH + PARSONS

At a Court continued & held for Essex County the XVIIIth day of March MDCCXXIX This Livery & Seisen was acknowledged by ANN BERRICK to PITTMAN SCANDRETT and is admitted to record

pp.   THIS INDENTURE made the fourteenth day of February in the year of our Lord
98-   one thousand seven hundred & Twenty Nine Thirty Between HUGH CARY of the
99   County of Essex of one part and WILLIAM RAMSEY of the same County of the
          other part Witnesseth that sd CARY for the sum of ffourty pounds Sterl. hath
sold unto sd WILLIAM RAMSEY his heirs and assigns forever fifty acres of land in the sd County and being that tract of land whereon the sd CARY doth now dwell which said land he the said CARY bought of SAMUEL WARREN Together with all and Singular the ways, waters, Trees thereunto belonging To Have and To Hold the sd Fifty acres of land to the sd WILLIAM RAMSEY his heirs and assigns forever. In Witness whereof the parties to these presents have set their hands and Seals
in presence of WILLIAM LANDRUM,   HUGH H CARY

        MARTHA M LANDRAM. SAMUEL BIZWELL

At a Court held for Essex County on Tuesday the XVIIth day of March MDCCXXIX
HUGH CARY acknowleged this his Deed to WILLIAM RAMSEY wch on his motion is admitted to record

pp.
100-
101
THIS INDENTURE made the fourteenth day of February in the year of our Lord one thousand seven hundred & Twenty Nine Thirty Between THOMAS RAMSEY of the County of Essex of one part and HUGH CAREY of the same County of the other part Witnesseth that THOMAS RAMSEY for the sum of thirty pounds Sterl. hath sold unto the said HUGH CAREY his heirs & assigns a certain parcel of land being fifty acres in the sd County and bounded Beginning on the North side of POPOMON SWAMP in the line of DANIEL NOEL runing West to the upper Corner tree divideing the sd THOMAS RAMSEYs land from the land of WM. GOLDEN thence along the sd GOLDENs line to the sd Swamp thence the several courses of the sd Run to our first menconced begining Together with all other profitts and appurtenances thereunto belonging To Have and To hold unto him the sd HUGH CARY his heirs and assigns forever. In Witness whereof the partys have set their hands & Seals
in presence of us SAMLL. BIZWELL,   THO: RAMSEY
        WILLIAM RAMSEY, WILLIAM LANDRUM
At a Court held for Essex County on Tuesday the XVIIth day of March MDCCXXIX
THOMAS RAMSEY acknoweldged his Deed to HUGH CARY which on his motion is admitted to record
At a Court held for Essex County the XVIIth day of March MDCCXXIX
This Livery & Seizen was acknowledged by THOMAS RAMSEY to HUGH CARY and is admitted to record

p.
101
KNOW ALL MEN by these presents that I CLEMENT NICHOLSON of WHITEHAVEN in the County of CUMBERLAND Merchant for good causes have made WILLIAM PEARSON Commander of the Ship called *THE GLOBE OF WHITEHAVEN* aforesd and JOHN WALKER of WTHAVEN Merchant my true and Lawfull Attorneys and assigns in my name & to my use to ask for recover and receive by all lawfull ways from all and every person in Virginia and MARYLAND whom it doth concern all sums of money or other debts are to me in any wise due giving and by these presents my said Attorneys joyntly & Severally all my power concerning the premises generally to do such Lawfull Acts as fully and effectually as I my self in my own person could do allowing for firm & Valid whatsoever my said Attorneys shall Lawfully do. In Witness whereof I the sd CLEMENT NICHOLSON have set my hand and seal this Thirteenth day of October in the Second year of the Reign of our Sovereign Lord GEORGE the Second Anno Dom 1728
Sealed and delivered on paper three
        Six penny Stamps hereon   CLEMT. NICHOLSON
in presence of JNO PECK, GEORGE CROSBY
At a Court held for the County of Essex at Tappa. on the XIXth day of May MDCCXXX
This Letter of Attorney from CLEMENT NICHOLSON to WILLIAM PEARSON & JOHN WALKER was proved by the Oaths of the Witnesses & admitted to record

pp.
101-
105
THIS INDENTURE made the Six day of Aprill in the year of our Lord one thousand thousand seven hundred and thirty Between FRANCIS GOULDMAN of the Parish of St. Ann in the County of Essex of one part and THOMAS STHRESHLY JUNIOR of the Pish of Southfarnham in the County aforesaid of other part Witnesseth that FRANCIS GOULDMAN for the sum of Sixteen hundred pounds of good Tobacco convenient in the County aforesd and forty Shilling Curt. money of Virginia hath granted to farm let unto the sd THOMAS STHRESHLY JUNIOR and his heirs One peice of land or Woodland

containing One hundred and forty acres being in the Pish of St. Ann in the County aforesaid and bounded beginning at a marked Ring Oak & Gum on the Middle Fork of OCCUPACY RUN from thence up a bottom and across a Ridge to the head of a small Branch on the South Branch of OCCUPACY to two marked red Oaks and a black Oak thence down the sd Branch to the Main Swamp of OCCUPACY and down the sd Swamp to a small Branch in an old field where formerly Colo. FRANCIS GOULDMAN deced had a Quarter, thence up the sd Branch to the main Middle Fork of OCCUPACY RUN, thence up the sd Swamp to the place where it first begun with all woods, swamps, marshes, Trees growing and Emoluments whatsoever belonging To Have and To Hold unto the sd THOMAS STHRESHLY JUNR. and to his heirs & assigns for ever & dureing the Natural lives of THOMAS STHRESHLEY and WILLIAM STHRESHLEY Sons of the said THOMAS STHRESHLY JUNIOR party to these presents and TAMMASEN STHRESHLY his Daughter and the life of the longer liver of them paying yearly dureing the lives aforesaid unto the sd FRANCIS GOULDMAN and his heirs of his body lawfully begotten on the twenty fifth day of March and if it shall happen that the yearly rent of three Shillings be behind by the space of thirty days sd FRANCIS GOULDMAN into the parcell of land to reenter and the same to have again. In Witness whereof the ptys have set their hands and Seals
in presence of JOHN HUNT,   FRANCIS GOULDMAN
          JAMES *F* HOLDER
  At a Court held for Essex County the XIXth day of May MDCCXXX
FRANCIS GOULDMAN acknowledged this Lease & Livery & Seizen of the land mentioned to THOMAS STHRESHLY JUNIOR which on his motion is admitted to record

          KNOW ALL MEN by these presents that I FRANCIS GOULDMAN am held and firmly bound unto THOMAS STHRESHLY JUNR. in the sum of fifty pounds Currt. money of Virginia this Six day of Aprill in the year of our Lord one thousand seven hundred and thirty. THE CONDICON of the above obligation is that if FRANCIS GOULDMAN at all times hereafter keep all the covenants mentioned in Indenture for three lives between sd FRANCIS GOULDMAN and THOMAS STHRESHLY JUNR. that then this obligation to be void else to stand
in presence of JAMES *I* HOLDER,   FRANS. GOULDMAN
          JOHN HUNT
  At a Court held for Essex County the XIXth day of May MDCCXXX
FRANCIS GOULDMAN acknowledged his bond to THOMAS STHRESHLY JUNR. which is admitted to record

p.   KNOW ALL MEN by these presents that wee JOHN SMITH, FRANCIS GOULDMAN
105   & ROBERT PARKER are held and firmly bound unto our Soveraign Lord GEORGE
        the 2d in the just sum of Ten thousand pounds of Tobacco this 19th day of May
1730. THE CONDITION of the above obligation is such that Whereas JOHN SMITH hath obtained a Licence to keep and ORDINARY at his Dwelling House in St. Anns Pish if therefore sd JOHN SMITH doth constantly provide good wholesom & cleanly Lodgeing & dyet for Travellers & Stableage fodder & provender for their horses for & dureing the term of one whole year from the day hereof & shall not suffer any unlawfull gameing in his House nor on the Sabbath day suffer any to Tipple more then is necessary then the above obligation to be void else to remain in force
in presence of MARK WEEKES   JOHN SMITH
                                        RO: PARKER   FRANS. GOULDMAN
  At a Court held for Essex County on the 19th day of May 1730
JOHN SMITH, ROBERT PARKER & FRANCIS GOULDMAN acknowledged this bond to be their act & deed which is ordered to be recorded

pp.   THIS INDENTURE made the ninth day of May in the year of our Lord one thou-
106-   sand seven hundred & thirty between FRANCIS GOULDMAN of the Pish of St. Ann
108   in the County of Essex of one part and WILLIAM ROANE of the Parish of South-
        farnham in the County aforesaid of other part Witnesseth that said FRANCIS
GOULDMAN for the sum of Twenty pounds Current money of Virga. doth demise, grant &
to farm let unto sd WILLIAM ROANE & his heirs one percel of land woodland ground &
premises containing two hundred acres being in the Parish of Southfarnham in the
County of Essex and bounded beginning at the percoson near the mouth of a small
Branch which leads to the Main Run of HOSKINSES CREEK thence South East to a Corner
on a level near GOULDMANS PLANTACON thence South East crossing a Branch that
issueth out of SOUTH SWAMP, thence to an other Corner on a level some distance from
the Swamp, thence North West to a Corner of Mr. JOHN GATEWOODs land & thence to the
place it begun Together with all Woods, Swamps, Marshes and Trees and all other profits
belonging To Have and To Hold unto the said WILLIAM ROANE & to his heirs & assigns
dureing the natural lives of SARAH ROANE his Wife and the sd WILLIAM ROANE and
likewise during the lives of THOMAS STHRESHLY & WILLIAM STHRESHLY Sons of Mr.
THOMAS STHRESHLY JUNIOR and dureing the life of the longer liver of them paying
yearly unto sd FRANCIS GOULDMAN & the heirs of his body lawfully begotten & for default of such issue to the Right heirs inheritable to the premises the yearly rent of
three Shillings currt. money of Virginia to be paid on the five & Twentieth day of
March & if it so happen that the yearly rent be behind by the space of thirty days next
the day after the day it ought to be paid (provided same be lawfully demanded) that
from thence it shall be lawfull for the said FRANCIS GOULDMAN into the said parcel of
land & the same to have again. In Witness whereof the parties have set their hands &
Seals
in presence of us THOS. STHRESHLY,   FRANS. GOULDMAN
        JOHN GRIGGS
    At a Court held for Essex County on the 19th day of May 1730
FRANCIS GOULDMAN acknowledged this his Lease indented with the livery & Seizen
thereon endorsed to WILLIAM ROANE which on his motion is admitted to record
        KNOW ALL MEN by these presents that I FRANCIS GOULDMAN am held and firmly
bound unto WILLIAM ROANE in the sum of forty pounds Currt. money of Virga. this
Ninth day of May in the year of our Lord Christ one thousand seven hundred & Thirty
  THE CONDICON of the above obligation is such that if FRANCIS GOULDMAN truely fulfill
all articles on part of sd FRANCIS GOULDMAN which ought to be fulfilled in Indenture
according to the purport of the same Indenture that then this obligation to be void or
else to remain in force
in presence of THOS. STHRESHLY,   FRANCIS GOULDMAN
        JOHN GRIGGS
    At a Court held for Essex County this 19th day of May 1730
FRANCIS GOULDMAN acknowledged this bond to WILLIAM ROANE to be his act and deed
which is ordered to be recorded

pp.   THIS INDENTURE made the 19th day of May in the year of our Lord God one thou-
108-   sand seven hundred & thirty Between CHARLES TRAINUM & LIDIA his Wife of
109   the County of CAROLINE in the Parish of Drisdale of one part and JOHN RUSSELL
        of the County of Essex in the Pish of Southfarnham of the other part Wittnesseth
that sd CHARLES TRAINAM & LIDIA his Wife for the sum of Twelve pounds Current
money of Virginia doth sell unto the aforesd JOHN RUSSELL his heirs or assigns all that
tract of land being in the County of Essex in the Pish of Southfarnham and bounded
Beginning at a Spanish Oak a Corner of EVAN DAVISes by the MILL ROAD Side runing

South West to a white Oake thence South West to a Hickory thence West by South to a
stooping red Oake, thence South West to a pick Hickory by the MAIN ROAD side thence
North West into the MAIN ROAD side, thence East to a white Oak on a hill side by a
Branch, thence East South to a forked red Oak by a PATH, thence south East to the beginning, containing Eighty acres of land which sd land or woodland ground with all
the houses, Orchards, watters and all other things thereon being To Have and To Hold
unto the said JOHN RUSSELL his heirs and assigns forever. In Witness whereof the said
parties have set their hands and Seals
in presence of MARY X WEBB,   CHARLES   TRANUM
       WM.COVINGTON   LIDIA W TRANUM
   At a Court held for Essex County on the XIXth day of May MDCCXXX
CHARLES TRAINUM & LYDIA his Wife (the sd LYDIA being first privily examined by
ALEXANDER PARKER Gent) acknowledged this their Deed indented with the livery &
Seizen thereon endorsed to JOHN RUSSELL which on his motion are admitted to record

pp.   THIS INDENTURE made the Six day of April in the year of our Lord Christ one
109-   thousand seven hundred & Thirty between FRANCIS GOULDMAN of the Pish of
112   St.Ann in the County of Essex of one part and JOHN HUNT of the Pish of South-
        farnham and in the County of Essex of the other part Witnesseth that the sd
FRANCIS GOULDMAN for the sum of Sixteen hundred pounds of good Tobo. convenient
in the County aforesd and for forty Shillings Currt. money of Virginia to him paid doth
grant and to farm let unto the sd JOHN HUNT and his heirs one Plantacon and woodland
ground containing One hundred & Sixty acres being in the Prish of St. Ann within the
County aforesd and on the branches of OCCUPACY CREEK Commonly called by the name
of COLO. GOULDMANS QUARTER and bounded Beginning at a large Popler on the West
side of a Branch it being the beginning Corner tree of the sd FRANCIS GOULDMAN and
EDWARD CLARK from thence to include all the land belonging to sd FRANCIS GOULDMAN
that lies between the lands of THOMAS STHRESHLY JUNR. JOHN BARBEE, EDWARD
CLARK, THOMAS COVINGTON and THOMAS WARREN Together with all the houses, out
houses, Swamps, Marshes Trees and all Comodities whatsoever belonging To Have and To
Hold unto the sd JOHN HUNT and to his heirs and assignes for & dureing the natural
lives of GEORGE HUNT & WILLIAM HUNT Brothers of the sd JOHN HUNT and likewise for
the life of JOHN HUNT Son of the aforesd WILLIAM HUNT and the life of the longer liver
of them paying unto the sd FRANCIS GOULDMAN & heirs of his body lawfully begotten
the yearly rent of three Shillings Currt. money of Virga. to be paid yearly on the five
and Twentieth day of March and if it happen the yearly rent be behind the space of
thirty days next after it ought to be paid (provided it be lawfully demanded) that then
and henceforth it may be lawfull for the sd FRANCIS GOULDMAN into the sd Plantacon
wth the appurtenances to reenter & the same to have again. In Witness whereof the
partys have set their hands and Seals
in presence of THOS. STHRESHLY,   FRANCIS COULDMAN
       JAMES I HOLDER
   At a Court held for Essex County on the XIXth day of May MDCCXXX
FRANCIS GOULDMAN acknowledged this his Lease indented with the Livery & Seizen
thereon endorsed to JOHN HUNT which on his motion are admitted to record
        KNOW ALL MEN by these presents that I FRANCIS GOULDMAN do hereby acknow-
ledge to have Reced of JOHN HUNT the full sum of Sixteen hundred pounds of Tobacco
and forty Shillings Currt. money of Virginia being the consideration to be paid by the
within Indenture, and I doe further acknowledge to have reced from the within named
JOHN HUNT three Pounds Currt. money it being the yearly Rent for Twenty and One
years as Witness my hand the Seventh day of April in the year of our Lord Christ one

thousand seven hundred and thirty
        THOS. STHRESHLY,   FRANS. GOULDMAN
        JAMES **I** HOLDER
This Receipt was acknowledged by FRANCIS GOULDMAN to JOHN HUNT in Essex Court on
the XIXth day of May MDCCXXX
        KNOW ALL MEN by these presents that I FRANCIS GOULDMAN am held and firmly
bound unto JOHN HUNT in the sum of fifty pounds Current money of Virginia dated the
Six day of April in the year of our Lord one thousand seven hundred and Thirty
    THE CONDITION of the above obligation is such that if FRANCIS GOULDMAN keep all the
Covenants wch on the part of sd FRANS. GOULDMAN ought to be observed menconed in
one pair of Indentures in all things according to the meaning of the said Indenture
that then this obligation to be void else to be in full force
in presence of THOS. STHRESHLY,   FRANS. GOULDMAN
        JAMES **I** HOLDER
    At a Court held for Essex County on the XIXth day of May MDCCXXX
FRANCIS GOULDMAN acknowledged this bond to JOHN HUNT to be his act and deed which
is admitted to record

pp.   BY THIS PUBLICK INSTRUMENT of Procuration be it Known and Manifest unto
112-   all People that on this day being the Eleventh day of February Anno Dom One
113   thousand seven hundred Twenty Nine before me GEORGE MORE Notary & Tabel-
         lion by Lawfull Authority admitted & Sworn dwelling in DUBLIN in IRELAND
personally appeared Mr. ROBERT STEWARD of the City of DUBLIN aforesd Merchant
which apprr. declared that by Virtue of a Power or Letter of Attorney to him given by
MRS. DOROTHY MORGAN Widw. and Admrx. of EVAN MORGAN deceased, he the sd ROBERT
STEWART hath made, and appointed & in his stead, and place put Collo. HENRY ARMI-
STEAD of Virginia to be his true and lawfull granting unto him full power for him the
sd Apprr. but in the Name and to the use of the sd DOROTHY MORGAN to ask and receive
of all and every person whatsoever resideing in the Province of Virginia in AMERICA
(whom it may concern) all debts, dues, sums of money, goods and other Specialtys
which were due or belonging to the sd EVAN MORGAN at the time of his decease on any
account whatsoever, and which are belonging to the said DOROTHY MORGAN as Admrx.
or other wise howsoever and to settle the premises and to take all lawfull ways whatsoever for the recoverey by Suite, arrest, action, attachment or otherwise according to
the Laws, and Customs of the Country and to that end for the sd DOROTHY MORGAN to
appear and represent in all or any Court, and before all or any Lords or Judges and on
Receipt of the premises give any acquittances that shall be requisite, and if need be to
depute one or more attorneys under him in the premises to do all lawfull things whatsoever which shall be necessary about the premises as fully in all respects as the sd
appearer by Vertue of the said Power of Attorney might or could do if personally present. In Witness whereof the sd Apprr. hath set his hand and seal in the presence of
me the sd Notary and other the Witnesses hereunto subscribing the day, Month and
year first written
in presence of us JOHN SAVAGE,   ROBT. STEWARD
        JOHN YOUNGER   GEO: MORE Not Publ
    At a Court held for Essex County on the XIXth day of May MDCCXXX
This Power of Attorney from ROBT. STEWARD to Collo. HENRY ARMISTEAD was proved by
the Oaths of JOHN SAVAGE & JOHN YOUNGER Witnesses thereto & admitted to record

pp.   THIS INDENTURE made the Eighteenth day of Aprill in the year of our Lord one
114-   thousand seven hundred and Thirty Between EDWARD CLARK of the Parish of
115   St.Anns in the County of Essex of one part and JOHN ONEALL of the Parish and
County aforesaid of the other part Witnesseth that the sd EDWARD CLARK for
divers good causes but more espetially for the love good will and Affection which he
hath and doth bear to sd JOHN ONEALL and MARY his Wife hath by these presents doth
give unto sd JOHN ONEALL and MARY his Wife and to the heirs of their body lawfully
begotten for ever One hundred and five acres of land being in the Parrish and County
abovesaid, It being part of the tract of land where the sd EDWARD CLARK now lives (the
sd One hundred and five acres of land being in the actuall possession of the sd JOHN
ONEALL) bounded beginning at a Marked Maple standing in a line that devideth this
land from COVENTONs land on a Branch thence with the sd line North West to a marked
Maple standing in a Branch, thence up the same South West to a live Oak standing near
the head of the sd Branch thence South West to a red Oak standing on a hill side thence
South East to a live Oak standing on the first above mentioned Branch thence down the
same binding thereon to the beginning with all the appurtenances whatsoever belonging To Have and To Hold the said One hundred and five acres of land unto the sd
JOHN ONEALL and MARY his Wife and the heirs begotten for ever, And the sd EDWARD
CLARK shall warrant and forever defend the same. In Witness whereof the above parties have set their hands & Seals

in presence of JNO. VAWTER,   EDWARD **E** CLARK
     WM. THOMAS, SAMLL. BROWNE

At a Court held for Essex County on the XIXth day of May MDCCXXX
EDWARD CLARK acknowledged his Deed indented to JOHN ONEAL to be his act and deed
which is admitted to record

pp.   THIS INDENTURE made the Twentieth and Twenty First day of Aprill in the year
115-   of our Lord one thousand seaven hundred and Thirty Betweene RICHARD COLE-
118   MAN of GLOSTER COUNTY of one part and NATHANIEL FOGG of County of Essex of
other part Witnesseth that sd RICHARD COLEMAN for sum of fifty pounds Currt.
money of Virginia doth sell unto the sd NATHANIEL FOGG his heirs & assigns (in his
actuall possession by virtue of Indenture for one year and of the Statute for Transferring uses into possession) and to his heirs & assignes for ever, one certain parcell of
land containing Two hundred Ninety three acres and ninety one pole situate lying and
being on the head Branches of COCKELLSHELL CREEKE in Essex County and on a Swamp
knowne by the name of the MUDDY BRANCH in KING and QUEEN COUNTY the sd Land
crossing the Ridge bounded as followeth, beginning at a red Oake standing in REN-
NOLDS line Corner tree to FRANCIS GRAVES land thence North West to three red Oakes
corner to Mrs. ANN THACKERs land thence with the sd THACKERS line West to a white
Oake corner to the sd THACKER thence South West to a Maple standing in the sd MUDDY
BRANCH thence down the saime it's severall Courses, South East to a Maple standing on
the sd Swamp, thence South East to a live Oake standing in the abovesaid GRAVES line,
thence with the sd line North East to the first above mentioned red Oake, Together with
all and singular the profitts and appurtenances whatsoever belonging To Have and To
Hold the sd Two hundred Ninety three acres and ninety one pole of land unto the sd
NATHANIEL FOGG his heirs and assignes forever. In Witness whereof the abovesd
partys have set their hands and Seals

in presence of JNO. VAWTER,   RICHD. COLEMAN
     RO. PARKER, THOS. STHRESHLY,
     SALVATER MUSCOE, MUNGO ROY

At a Court held for Essex County on the XIXth day of May MDCCXXX
This Indenture from RICHARD COLEMAN to NATHANIEL FOGG was proved by the oaths of
Mr. THOS. STHRESHLY JUNR., DOCTR. MUNGO ROY and ROBERT PARKER and admitted to
record

pp.   THIS INDENTURE made the 15th and 16th day of June in the year of our Lord
118-   Christ one thousand seven hundred and Thirty Between THOMAS BLANTON and
121   ANN BLANTON his Wife of the County of SPOTSILVANIA Planter of one part and
        THOMAS STHRESHLY of the County of Essex of other part Witnesseth that sd THO-
MAS BLANTON and ANN his Wife for sum of fifteen pounds Sterling hath granted unto
sd THOMAS STHRESHLY his heirs & assigns forever (in his actual possession) one Plantacon or parcell of Woodland ground by virtue of an Indenture for one year and of the
Statute for the transferring of uses into possession and to his heirs & assigns forever
One Plantacon or percel of land containing one hundred and fifty acres in the Parish
of Southfarnham in the County of Essex and is part of a PATTEN of Two hundred acres of
land formerly granted unto THOMAS BLANTON Father of the sd THOMAS BLANTON and
dated by the sd PATTEN April the twentyeth in the year of Christ one thousand six hundred & Eighty Two relation being had to sd PATTEN and is bounded beginning at a dead
white Oak near THOMAS GRAVES Corner red Oak thence running North East to a bent in
an old line thence North East to the Mouth of BEACH SWAMP & on GILSONS MAIN SWAMP
thence up the sd GILSONS SWAMP to Mr. JAMES RENNOLDs Corner on the sd GILSONS
SWAMP thence South West to Mr. JAMES RENNOLDs Corner on the sd GILSONS SWAMP
thence South West to a Corner Hickory of DANIEL SULLIVANTs & THOMAS GRAVES
thence to a Corner red Oak of the said THOMAS GRAVES thence to the beginning Together with all houses, out houses, Tobo houses, Comodities belonging unto the sd premises and all the right of them the sd THOMAS BLANTON and ANN his Wife to the same To
Have and To Hold unto the sd THOMAS STHRESHLY his heirs and assigns forever. In Witness whereof the parties first named have set their hands & Seals
in presence of JEREMIAH UPSHAW,   THOMAS *T B* BLANTON
        THOMAS MARRITT
   At a Court held for Essex County on the XVIth day of June MDCCXXX
THOMAS BLANTON acknowledged this his release of land indented to THOMAS STHRESH-
LY and ANN the Wife of the sd THOMAS BLANTON freely relinquished her Dower in the
sd Land which on motion of the sd THOMAS STHRESHLY are admitted to record

p.   KNOW ALL MEN by these presents that I JOHN McCULLOCH now of the County of
122   Essex Merchant have made in my place & stead putt WILLIAM BEVERLEY of the
        County of Essex Gent my true and lawfull Attorney to sue for recover & receive
from any person whatsoever all such debts, sums of money which now are or any time
hereafter shall become due unto me either in my own right or as Factor or Agent for
Messieurs JAMES CORNE & COMPANY Merchants in DUMFRIES in North Britain or by any
other ways or means whatsoever and upon receipt thereof Releases or other discharges
for me to make and upon neglect or refusall of payment to prosecute such actions as
shall seem necessary to be done and generally to do every other lawfull acts in as full &
ample manner as I my self could do if I was personally present by these presents ratifying whatsoever my sd Attorney shall lawfully do. In Witness whereof I have set my
hand & Seale the third day of June in the year of our Lord one thousand seven hundred
& thirty and in the third year of the Reign of our Sovereign Lord GEORGE the Second
in presence of ROBERT JONES,   JOHN McCULLOCH
        EDW. BARRADALL

At a Court held for Essex County on the XVIth day of June MDCCXXX
JOHN McCULLOCH Mercht. ackowledged this his Power of Attorney to WM. BEVERLEY
gent to be his act and deed which is admitted to record

pp.   THIS INDENTURE made this 16th day of June in the year of our Lord God one
122-   thousand seven hundred and Thirty Between WILLIAM GATEWOOD and KATHE-
124   RIN his Wife of the County of Essex and Parish of Southfarnham of one part and
       THOMAS WILLIAMSON JUNER of the aforesd County and Parish of the other part
Witnesseth that the sd WILLIAM GATEWOOD and KATHERINE his Wife for the sum of two
thousand foure hundred pounds of lawfull Sweet Sented Tobacco and Cask to them paid
hath granted and sold unto him the said THOMAS WILLIAMSON JUNER his heirs &
assigns forever all that percell of land in the Parish of Southfarnham within the
County of Essex and bounded begining at a red Oak a Corner of THOMAS COOPERs in the
line of BENJA. FISHER by the MILL ROAD side, runing thence South Easterly along a line
of marked trees over the GLEADY SWAMP to a Scrubby Oake standing in THOS. EDMOND-
SONs line thence along his line to THOMAS KIDDs line thence including all the upper
part of the sd Devident of land according to the several courses of the PATTENT to the
place where it begun containing Seventy five acres Together with all Timber & Trees
likely to become Timber, Swamps, and Appurtenances whatsoever to the said land
appartaining and all the Estate right of the sd WILLIAM GATEWOOD and KATHERINE his
Wife To Have and To Hold the sd land unto him the said THOMAS WILLIAMSON JUNER his
heirs and assigns forever, which sd land is part of one hundred and fifty acres given
by WILL to RICHARD CARTER by Mr. PHILLIP PARR deced and the sd RICHARD CARTER
being dead without disposeing of the same it doth now of right belong unto the aforesd
KATHERIN GATEWOOD Sister to the sd RICHARD CARTER deced and the said WILLIAM
GATEWOOD and KATHERIN his Wife granted the sd Parcell of land and every part unto
the sd THOMAS WILLIAMSON his heirs and assigns forever. In Witness whereof the
parties first menconed have set their hands and Seals
in presence of THOMAS DILLON,   WM. GATEWOOD
     RO. PARKER   KATHERINE ✗ GATEWOOD
  At a Court held for Essex County on the XVIth day of June MDCCXXX
WM. GATEWOOD & KATHERINE GATEWOOD (the sd KATHERINE being first privily Examined by ALEXR. PARKER Gent) acknowledged their Indenture to THOMAS WILLIAMSON
JUNR. which on his motion is admitted to record

p.   KNOW ALL MEN by these presents that We SALVATOR MUSCOE & JAMES GARNETT
124   & THOMAS STHRESHLY JUNR. Gent are held and firmly bound unto our Soveraign
       Lord GEORGE the 2d. in the sum of one thousand pounds Sterling this 21st day of
July Anno Dom 1730
  THE CONDITION of the above obligation is such yt if the above bound SALVATOR MUSCOE
Gent SHERIFF of the County of Essex shall render unto the Auditor & Receiver General
of his Matys Revenue a particular true account of all his Matys Rents & Dues ariseing
within the sd County and also due payment of all other Publick dues & fees put into his
hands to Collect within the sd County unto the severall persons to whom the same shall
be due & payable & true performance to make of all matters and things relating to his
Office dureing his Continuance therein, then ye above obligation to be null & of none
effect else to remain in full force
                        SALVATOR MUSCOE
                  JAS. GARNETT   THOS. STHRESHLY
  At a Court held for Essex County on the XXIst day of July MDCCXXX
SALVATOR MUSCOE, JAMES GARNETT & THOMAS STHRESHLY JUNR. Gent acknowledged

this bond to be their acts and deeds which is ordered to be recorded

pp.   THIS INDENTURE made the twenty Sixth day of January in the forth year of the
125-   Reign of our Sovereign Lord GEORGE Anno Domini 1729 Between JOHN BOUGHAN
127   of Essex County of one part and JOSEPH MAN of the same County of other part
          Witnesseth that said JOHN BOUGHAN for sum of Twenty pounds Current money of
Virginia have sold unto said JOS: MAN in his actual possession now being by virtue of a
bargain and sale for one year and by force of the Statute for transferring uses into possession his heirs and assigns forever all that track of land in the Parish of Southfarnham in County of Essex containing one hundred acers and bounding Beginning at two
Beaches on ye Swamp side that runs down to the MAIN SWAMP and from then runing
Easterly on a line that binds upon Capt. RUBIN WELCH to a white Oak on the head of a
Branch and from thence down the sd Branch its several Courses to the Main Swamp and
from thence up the sd Main Swamp to a Lesser Swamp that parts the said BOUGHANs
land that he now lives upon from this land and from thence up the sd Swamp to the
place where it first begun togeather with all houses, buildings and appurtinances
whatsoever belonging allso all the actual right of said JOHN BOUGHAN To Have and To
Hold unto the said JOS. MAN his heirs and assigns forever. In Witness whereof the
partys first written have set their hands & Seals
in presence of THOS. BARKER,   JOHN X BOUGHAN
         AMBE: JONES; FRANCIS JONES
    At a Court held for Essex County on the 21st day of July 1730
JOHN BOUGHAN acknowledged this his Release indented to JOSEPH MAN to be his act &
deed which on his motion is admitted to record

pp.   THIS INDENTURE made the 18th day of July in the year of our Lord God one thou-
127-   sand seven hundred and thirty Between JOSEPH MAN of the Parish of Southfarn-
131   ham in the County of Essex of one part and JOHN FARGESSON and JOHN CROXTON
          both of the Parish and County aforesd of the other part Witnesseth that the sd
  JOS. MAN for the sum of Thirty four pounds Current money of Virginia doth grant to
them the said JOHN FARGESSON and JOHN CROXTON their heirs and assigns for ever all
the right which is or shall hereafter become due to sd JOSEPH MAN to a certain parcell
of land in the Parish and County aforesaid containing Sixty Eight acres of land being
part of a tract formerly belonging to FRANCIS BROWN deceasd. and bounded begining at
a Corner red Oak and white Oak standing by the side of the Main Branch called the
MIDDLE BRANCH being the Corner between the sd JOSEPH MAN and JOHN FARGESSON
from thence along the dividing line to two corner Maples and Gum standing in the
Mouth of a Small Branch being the Corner between the said JOSEPH MAN, JOHN FAR-
GESSON and JOHN CROXTON from thence along the divideing line between sd JOSEPH MAN
and JOHN CROXTON to a Corner Hickory from thence along the divideing line between sd
JOSEPH MAN and FRANCIS BROWN to a Corner red Oak and Poplar standing by the side of
the Main Branch called the MIDDLE BRANCH being the Corner between sd JOSEPH MAN
and FRANCIS BROWN from thence downthe sd Branch to the place where it began and
all houses, building, Water & appurtenaces to the same belonging and all the Estate
right of the sd JOSEPH MAN to the same To Have and To Hold the sd land unto JOHN FAR-
GESSON and JOHN CROXTON their heirs and assigns for ever. In Witness whereof JOSEPH
MAN hath set his hand and Seal
in presence of us THOMAS BARKER,   JOS: MAN
         THOMAS YOUNGER, ANN CROXTON   MARY X MAN
    At a Court held for Essex County on the 21st day of July 1730
JOSEPH MANN acknowledged his Deed Indented with the livery and Seizen thereon en-

dorsed to JOHN FARGUSON & JOHN CROXTON which on their motion are admitted to record

Also the same day MARY MANN came into Court & freely relinquished her right of Dower in the land convey'd by this Deed from her Husband to JOHN FARGUSON & JOHN CROXTON which is admitted to record

KNOW ALL MEN by these presents that I JOSEPH MAN am held and firmly bound unto JOHN FARGESSON and JOHN CROXTON both of them in the penal Sum of Sixty Eight pounds Currt. money of Virga.

THE CONDITION of the above obligation is such that if the above JOSEPH MAN his heirs or Administrators shall at all times forever keep all the Covenants mentioned in the Indentured Deed of Sale and also cause that MARY his Wife do relinquish all her right of sd Land that then this Obligation to be void or otherwise to stand. In Witness whereof the sd JOSEPH MAN hath set his hand and seal this 18th day of July one thousand seven hundred and thirty

in presence of us THOMAS BARKER,   JOS. MAN
            THOMAS YOUNGER, ANNE CROXTON

At a Court held for Essex County the 21st day of July 1730
JOSEPH MAN acknowledged this Bond to JOHN FARGUSON & JOHN CROXTON to be his act and deed which is admitted to record

KNOW ALL MEN by these presents that I JOHN FARGESSON am held and firmly bound unto JOHN CROXTON in the sum of Thirty Four pounds Currt. money of Virga.

THE CONDITION of the above obligation is such that Whereas the above bounded JOHN FARGESSON and JOHN CROXTON having jointly bought a tract of land of JOSEPH MAN containing sixty eight acres the sd land as aforesd being seperated and divided by them the sd JOHN FARGESSON and JOHN CROXTON by their own joint Will Consent and agreement by a line of division through the sd tract of land which sd dividing line to begin at two corner Maples and a Gum standing in the Mouth of a small branch from thence to the Main Branch called the MIDDLE BRANCH all that part or moiety lying on the one side of the dividing line to belong to the sd JOHN CROXTON and to his heirs forever and all the other part lying on the other side to belong to the sd JOHN FARGESSON and to his heirs and assigns forever. If therefore the above bounden JOHN FARGESSON will at all times hereafter quietly and peaceably suffer JOHN CROXTON his heirs and assigns to possess all that part lying on that side of the sd Dividing line without the trouble of him the sd JOHN FARGESSON or his heirs or any other person whatsoever that then this obligation to be of none effect or otherwise to stand in force. In Witness whereof the sd JOHN FARGESSON hath set his hand and Seal this 18th day of July in the year of our Lord one thousand seven hundred and thirty

in presence of us THOMAS BARKER,   JOHN FARGESSON
            THOMAS YOUNGER, ANN CROXTON

At a Court held for Essex County on the 21st day of July 1730
JOHN FARGUSON ackowledged this bond to JOHN CROXTON to be his act and deed which is admitted to record

KNOW ALL MEN by these presents that I JOHN CROXTON stand held and firmly bound unto JOHN FARGESSON in the sum of thirty four pounds of Current money of Virginia. THE CONDITION of the above obligation is such that whereas JOHN CROXTON and JOHN FARGESSON haveing jointly bought a certain tract of land of JOSEPH MANN and aforesd being seperated and devided by them by their own joint consent and agreement If therefore the sd JOHN CROXTON & his heirs shall at all times forever suffer JOHN FARGESSON his heirs and assigns to occupy all that part on that side of the sd Dividing line without any trouble of him the sd JOHN CROXTON or his heirs that then this obligation to be void otherwise to stand and remain in force

in presence of us THOMAS BARKER,   JOHN CROXTON
              THOMAS YOUNGER, ANN CROXTON
At a Court held for Essex County on the 21st day of July 1730
JOHN CROXTON acknowledged this bond to JOHN FARGESSON to be his act & deed which is
admitted to record

pp.   THIS INDENTURE made the 21 day of July 1730 Anno Dom 1730 Between THOMAS
131-   STAPLETON & MARY his Wife of CAROLINE COUNTY of one part and ALEXANDER
133   GRAVES of MIDDLESEX COUNTY of the other part Witnesseth that sd THOMAS
          STAPLETON for the sum of fifty pounds Currt. money of Virginia hath sold unto
said ALEXANDER GRAVES in his actual possession now being by bargain and sale for one
year and by force of the statute for transferring uses into possession and to his heirs
and assigns all that tract of land containing two hundred acres being in the County of
Essex bounded on the South East side by the land of THOMAS CROWs, Southwest by the
land of WILLIAM CHANEY, North West by the land of WILLIAM JEFFERIES and on the
North East side by the land of DANIEL DOBBINS including the aforesd quantity of two
hundred acres To Have and To Hold the sd land with all the appurtenances thereunto
belonging unto him the sd ALEXANDER GRAVES his heirs and assigns forever. In Witness whereof they have set their hands and Seals
in presence of THOS. STHRESHLY,   THOMAS STAPLETON
          JAMES SKELTON, JOHN BRYANT
At a Court held for Essex County the XXIst day of July MDCCXXX
THOMAS STAPLETON acknowledged this his Release indented to ALEXR. GRAVES which
on the motion of JOHN BRYANT is admitted to record
Allso the same day came MARY STAPLETON the Wife of the sd THOMAS STAPLETON and
freely relinquished her right of dower in the land conveyed by this Release to ALEXR.
GRAVES which is admitted to record

pp.   VIRGINIA SS. BY HIS MATYS LIEUT. GOVR. and Commander in Chief of the
134   of this Dominion
135   A PROCLAMATION NOTIFYING THE PEACE AND CESSATION OF HOSTILITIES BETWEEN
          HIS MAJESTY AND THE KING OF SPAIN
Whereas I have reced his Majestys Commands to make known to all his good Subjects of
this Colony that a TREATY OF PEACE is happily concluded between his Majesty and the
Most Christian King of the one part and the King of Spain on the other to which the
State General of the United Provinces have since acceded and that in consequence of
the said Treaty all acts of hostilities are to cease on the one part, and the other all Prizes
which have been taken on either side since the arrival of the King of Spains Orders for
a Cessation of Arms at CARTAGENA the 11/22 of June 1728 are to be punctually restored
upon a application to the Governors of the respective places to which such prizes were
carried or in default thereof to the Just Value of the sd Prizes and their Cargoes at the
time when they were taken and reparation according to Justice also give for any further damage occasioned by the detention thereof till the time of their being delivered
up Excepting Seizures made on account of illegal trade in the places and Limits pro-
hibited by the Laws and Treatys of peace and Comerce. I have therefore in Obedience to
his Majestys Commands thought fitt to issue this Proclamation hereby in his Majestys
name charging and requiring all officers and other his Majesties Subjects within this
Colony that they forbear all acts of hostilities against the Subjects of the King of Spain
their Ships Vessells or Effects and to the end his Matys Subjects of this Colony whose
Vessells or Effects have been taken by any of the Subjects of Spain since the said 11/22
of June 1728 may be the better enable to seek and obtain reparation for the losses and

damages sustainted thereby I do hereby notify and make known that an authentic Copy
of the schedule sent by the King of Spain to the Viceroyes of PERU and NEW SPAIN and
others the Governors and Officers of the Spanish Dominions of America for the pur-
poses aforementioned is now in my hands of which any of his Matys Subjects haveing
occasion to make use thereof in any of the Spanish Governments in the WEST INDIES
may be furnished with attested Transcripts and for the better Notification of this his
Matys. Pleasure I do hereby order and required the Sheriffs of the several Counties that
they cause publication hereof to be made at their respective COURT HOUSES. Given at
the COUNCILL CHAMBER in WILLIAMSBURGH the twenty ninth day of May 1730 in the
Third year of our Reign
               GOD SAVE THE KING   WILLIAM GOOCH
To the Sheriff of the County of Essex
                    Copias Test   R. HICKMAN
  July 22d 1730 This Proclamation publishd. by WM. GRAY SSEC

pp.   THIS INDENTURE made the 15th day of September in the year of our Lord
135-   MDCCXXX Between RICHARD TAYLOR JUNR. and CATHERINE his Wife of one part
136   and PETER RICHESON of the other part WHEREAS WILLIAM YOUNG and the sd
         CATHERINE his Wife and ROBERT RANSONE and FRANCES his Wife were seized in
fee in the right of sd CATHERINE and FRANCES of and in a certain Plantation and Tract
of land with the appurtenances being in the Parish of Southfarnham upon the DRAGON
SWAMP in the County of Essex containing three hundred & six acres of land comonly
called & known by the name of THOMAS's QUARTER and so being thereof Seized by their
certain Indentures of Lease and Release bearing date the 20th and 21st days of February in the year of our Lord MDCCXV did convey the sd Plantacon & premises for a valuable consideration, and all their Estate right to the same, unto the sd PETER RICHESON
his heirs and assigns forever and did acknowledge the sd Indentures before the County
Court of Essex at a Court held the 21st day of February in the year MDCCXV aforesd the sd
CATHERINE and FRANCES being first privily examined and thereupon the sd Indentures were recorded but by the Omission and Negligence of the Clerk of the sd Court the
private Examination of the said CATHERINE and FRANCES was not recorded, Now This
Indenture Witnesseth that the sd RICHARD TAYLOR and CATHERINE his Wife for sum of
Forty Two shillings Sterling to the sd RICHARD by the sd PETER paid do ratifye and confirm to the sd PETER RICHESON his heirs and assigns being in his full and peaceable
possession & Seisin and all the Estate Right and interest that the sd RICHARD TAYLOR
and CATHERINE his Wife have in the Lands with the appurtenances aforesaid To Have
and To Hold to the sd PETER RICHESON his heirs and assigns forever. In Witness whereof the parties have set their hands and seals
in presence of JOHN HAYES,   RICHD. TYLER JUNR.
    CHARLES PAIN, WILLIAM RICHESON   CATHARINE TYLER
  At a Court held for Essex County on the 15th day of September 1730
RICHARD TYLER & CATHERINE his Wife (the sd CATHERINE being first privily Examined
by NICHOLAS SMITH Gent) acknowledged this their Deed indented to PETER RICHESON
which on his motion is admitted to Record
  ESSEX SS. THOMAS WARING Gent. Justice of the Peace of the sd County makes Oath that
in February Court 1715 in the sd County he did privily Examine FRANCES RANSOME &
KATHERINE YOUNG to certain Deeds for land from the sd FRANCES & KATHERINE & their
husbands WM. YOUNG and ROBERT RANSONE to PETER RICHESON, and they confessed
they did the same freely voluntarily and without Compulsion.
Sworn to in Essex Court this   T. WARING
15th day of Septr. 1730 & recorded

pp.   KNOW ALL MEN by these presents that I JAMES CORBET of DUMFRIES in Great
136-   Brittain for divers good causes have made and appointed my trusty friend
137   SAML. CLAYTON of Essex County in Virginia my true and lawfull Atturney for me
        and in my name to demand and receive from ELIZABETH HUDSON Widw., and
ELIZABETH HUDSON JUNR. the sums of L 2:16:6 & L 3:14:5 current mony as by these
accounts will appear giveing to my said Atturney my sole & full power to persue such
legall courses for the recovering and obtaining the same as I my selfe might or could
doe were I personally present and upon receipt of the same acquittances and other suf-
cient discharges to give for me and in my name ratifieing & confirming what my sd
Atturney shall lawfully do in the premises. As Witness my hand & Seale this 6th day of
July 1730
in presence of ROBT. GREAVES,   JAS. CORBET
       SUSAN CLAYTON
   At a Court held for Essex County on the 15th day of September 1730
This Power of Attorney from JAMES CORBETT to SAMUEL CLAYTON was proved by the
Oath of ROBERT GRAVES a Witness thereto and admitted to record

pp.   THIS INDENTURE made the fourteenth day and fifteenth day of September in the
137-   year of our Lord God according to the Computation now used in the Church of
143   Great Brittain Seaventeen hundred and thirty Between SAMUEL GREEN of the
        Parish of Southfarnham in the County of Essex Sonne and heir of DANL. GREEN
late of the sd County deced of one part and JAMES WEBB of the sd Pish and County of the
other part Witnesseth that sd SAMUEL GREEN for the sum of three thousand pounds of
good sound and merchantable tobacco to him paid by the sd JAMES WEBB he doth grant
and confirm unto the sd JAMES WEBB his heirs and assigns for ever the land, Plantation
and premises hereafter mentioned in his actual possession now being by virtue of Indenture of bargain & Sale for one whole year and of the Statute for transferring uses
into possession All that tract of land conteyning One hundred and eighty acres with all
and singular its rights together with all houses, Edifices, Orchards, Feedings and appurtenance wtsoever belonging being in the Parish aforesd on the South side of the
RAPPA. RIVER and on the North side of the DRAGON SWAMP formerly bought by one
SAMUEL GREEN Grandfather to the sd SAMUEL GREEN party to these presents and one
CHARLES CHAIR of one HENRY CREATON being part of a tract of two hundred and twenty
acres of land formerly granted by PATTENT to one THOMAS PADDINSON and bounded as
follows begining at an old OAK SWAMP by the Main DRAGON SWAMP and running up a
Branch thereof North East over the sd Branch to a Corner Chesnut thence North East to
a white Oak on a hill side by an other Branch thence North East to a great Oal Corner
white Oak belonging to THOMAS CROW and WM. CHAYNY thence East to a white Oak in
THOMAS CROWs and THOMAS HINES's lines now markt for a Corner of the deviding line
between one BREDGAR and this land of GREENs thence South West to the DRAGON
SWAMP again to a markt Popler thence up the DRAGON SWAMP again the sevll. Courses
to the beginning place being the land and Plantation whereon SARAH CUFFE now
liveth and the revertions and remainder and also all the Estate right whatsoever To
Have and To Hold unto the sd JAMES WEBB his heirs and Assignes forever. In Witness
whereof the parties have set their hands and Seals
in presence of PT.GODFREY,   SAMLL. GREEN
       JOHN REEVES
   At a Court held for Essex County the 15th day of Septr. 1730
SAMUEL GREEN acknowledged this his Release indented to JAMES WEBB which is admitted to record

KNOW ALL MEN by these presents that I SAMUEL GREEN stand justly indebted unto JAMES WEBB in the sum of Six thousand pounds of good sound and Merchantable Tobacco this fifteenth day of September Anno Dom 1730

THE CONDITION of this obligation is such that if JAMES WEBB shall at all time peaceably and quietly have all that one hundred and Eighty acres of land sold by SAMUEL GREEN to the sd JAMES WEBB and if the above bounden SAMUEL GREEN do truely save harmless the sd JAMES WEBB his heirs and assigns from all manner of troubles at any time made or done contrary to the tenor and meaning of the sd Indentures that then this obligation to be void or else to remain in force

in presence of PT. GODFREY,   SAMLL. GREEN
       JOHN REEVES

At a Court held for Essex County on the 15th day of Septr. 1730
SAMUEL GREEN acknowledged bond to JAMES WEBB to be his act & deed which is admitted to record

pp.   THIS INDENTURE made the 14th and 15th day of September in the year of our
143-   Lord one thousand seven hundred and Thirty Between JOSEPH ADCOCK and
147   ELIZABETH his Wife of Essex County of one part and RICHARD CUMTON of the aforesd County Carpender of the other part Witnesseth that the aforesd JOSEPH ADCOCK and ELIZABETH his Wife for the sum of Twelve pounds Current money have sold unto the sd RICHARD CUMTON and to his heirs and assigns Seventy five acres of land lying in the Parish of Southfarnham in the County of Essex being part of two hundred acres of land that formerly belonged to JOSEPH BELAND deceased Grandfather of the sd JOSEPH ADCOCK by the Mothers Side the sd Land is bounded on the lands of JOHN HAILL and THOMAS GATEWOOD and all the Estate right whatsoever of the sd JOSEPH ADCOCK and ELIZABETH his Wife all which premises are now in the actual possession of him the sd RICHARD CUMTON by Virtue of one Indenture for one whole year and by Virtue of the Statute for the transferring of uses into possession. In Witness whereof the sd JOSEPH ADCOCK and ELIZABETH his Wife have set their hands and Seals

in presence of PT. GODFREY,   JOSEPH ADCOCK
       JOHN REEVES   ELIZABETH Ⓐ ADCOCK

At a Court held for Essex County the 15th day of Septr. 1730
JOSEPH ADCOCK & ELIZABETH ADCOCK acknowledged this Indenture to RICHARD CUMTON to be their act and deed which on his motion is admitted to record

p.   KNOW ALL MEN by these presentss that We JAMES GRIFFIN & JAMES RENNOLDS
147   are held and firmly bound unto our Sovrn. Lord GEORGE the 2d. in the just sum of Ten thousand pounds of Tobacco this 15th dy of Septr. Ano. Dom 1730

THE CONDITION of the above obligation is such that Whereas the above bound JAMES GRIFFIN hath obtained a Licence to keep an ORDINARY at his House in TAPPA. TOWN if therefore sd JAMES GRIFFIN doth constantly provide in his ORDINARY good wholesome and cleanly lodging and diet for Travellers & Stableage fodder & provender or pasturage and provender as the Season of the year shall require for their Horses for the term of one whole year from the date hereof and shall not suffer any unlawefull gameing in his House nor on the Sabbath day to permit any to Tipple or drink more then is necessary that then the above obligation to be void or else to remain in force

                            JAMES GRIFFING
                            JAMES RENNOLDS

At a Court held for Essex County on the 15th day of Septr. 1730
JAMES GRIFFING & JAMES RENNOLDS acknowledged this bond to be their act and deed which is ordered to be recorded.

p.   KNOW ALL MEN by these presents that We SALVATOR MUSCOE Sheriff of Essex
148   and THOMAS WARING Gent are held and firmly bound unto our Sovrn. Lord the
        King in the sum of Seventy seven thousand Eight hundred & Nine pounds of
Lawfull Tobo this 20th day of October 1730
THE CONDITION of the above obligation is such that Whereas SALVATOR MUSCOE is admitted COLLECTOR of the Publick & County levys for this present year of 1730 Now if sd
SALVATOR MUSCOE shall faithfully Collect & duely pay the sum of thirty eight thousand
nine hundred & four and an half pounds of lawfull Tobo. being this year proportioned
by this Court & the late General Assembly of this Colony to the severall Creditors therein mentioned that then the above obligation to be void else to remain in force
                                             SALVATOR MUSCOE
                                             T. WARING
    At a Court held for Essex County the 20th day of October 1730
SALVATOR MUSCOE and THOMAS WARING Gent acknowledged this bond to be their act
and deed which is admitted to record

pp.   THIS INDENTURE made the Sixteenth and Seventeenth day of October in the year
148-   of our Lod One thousand Seven hundred and Thirty Between GEORGE ANDREWS
153   of the Parish of St. Anns in the County of Essex Planter of one part and BLOOM-
        FIELD LONG of the Parish of Hanover in the County of KING GEORGE Black Smith
of the other part Witnesseth that the sd GEORGE ANDREWS for the sum of Sixty pounds
Currant money hath sold to the sd BLOOMFIELD LONG (in his actual possession now by
Virtue of a bargain and Sale for one whole year & by force of the Statute for the transferring of uses into possession) and to his heirs all that parcell of land containing Two
hundred acres being in the ffreshes of RAPPAHANNOCK & on the South side the River
adjacent to the land sold by ROBERT PAYNE JUNIOR to Mr. JAMES SCOTT & to the land of
MR. GAINES begining at a white Oak corner tree to MR. GAINES and extending thence
along the sd GAINES line South East to a small Hickory thence along another line of
GAINES East South East to a small black Oak on a hill side near a great Run thence crossing the sd Run South West to a Stake thence North West to a Stake in the line of Mr.
JAMES SCOTT thence along the sd SCOTTs line to the first menconed Station being part of
a Tract of land Granted unto ROBERT PAYNE SENR. for three thousand one hundred and
forty one acres by PATENT bearing date the 27th day of Aprill 1668 which sd Land on
the Decease of the aforesd ROBERT PAYNE SENR. descended to ROBERT PAYNE Son of the
aforesd ROBERT PAYNE, and by ROBERT PAYNE JUNR. sold by Deed of Feofment to GEORGE
ANDREWS SENR. & GEORGE ANDREWS JUNR. & now on the decease of the aforesd GEORGE
ANDREWS SENR. and GEORGE ANDREWS JUNR. the sd land descended to GEORGE ANDREWS
(Son of the aforesd GEORGE ANDREWS JUNR.) party to these presents Together with all
houses, fences, gardens and appurtenances whatsoever belonging to the said land To
Have and To Hold unto the sd BLOOMFIELD LONG his heirs and assigns forever. In Witness whereof the sd GEORGE ANDREWS hath set his hand and seal
in presence of W. THORP,   GEORGE ⟨mark⟩ ANDREWS
        CORNELES. REYNOLDS, JOHN LONG,
        JOHN MILLER
    At a Court held for Essex County on the 20th day of October 1730
GEORGE ANDREWS acknowledged this his Release indented to BLOOMFIELD LONG to be his
act and deed which is admitted to record
    Allso the same day Came into Court ANN the Wife of the sd GEORGE ANDREWS and freely
relinquished her right of dower in the land conveyed by this Deed to BLOOMFIELD LONG
which is admitted to record

pp.
153-
157

THIS INDENTURE made the twenty second and twenty third day of September in the year of our Lord one thousand seven hundred and Thirty Between JONA-THAN HAILE of the Pish of Southfarnham in County of Essex Blacksmith of one part and THOMAS DAVIS of the Pish and County aforesaid Planter of other part Witnesseth tht the sd JONATHAN HAILE for the sum of Twenty one pounds Two shillings and Six pence Currt. money of Virginia doth sell unto the sd THOMAS DAVIS his heirs and assignes all that parcell of land containing Seventy acres being in the Parish and County aforesd being part of the tract of land whereon he the sd JONATHN. now dwells and now in the possession of him the sd THOMAS DAVIS by Virtue of Indenture for one year and of the Statute for the tranferring of uses into possession and bounded begining at the lower end of a Small ISLAND in the Marsh on the South West side of GILLSONS CREEK otherwise called the MILL CREEK and at the mouth of a Swamp called the OLD PLANTATION SWAMP thence up the Southwest side thereof the severall courses of the sd Swamp to a Stake in the sd JONATHAN HAILEs pasture thence N. E. to the sd Creek side thence up the sd Creek the severall Courses thence to the begining and all ways waters woods and appurtenances whatsoever appertaining and all the Estate right of the sd JONATHAN HAILE To Have and To Hold unto the sd THOMAS DAVIS his heirs and assigns. In Witness whereof the partys have set their hand and seal

in presence of T. WARING,   JONATHAN HAILE
        THOS. LOYD, TIMOTHY DALY

At a Court held for Essex County the 20th day of October 1730
JONATHAN HAILE acknowledged this his Release indented to THOMAS DAVIS to be his act and deed which is admitted to record

pp.
157-
160

THIS INDENTURE made the nineteenth day of October in the year of our Lord Christ One thousand seven hundred and Thirty Between FRANCIS GOULDMAN of the Parish of St. Anns in the County of Essex of one part and NICHOLAS PAM-PLIN of the Parish of Struten Major in KING & QUEEN COUNTY of the other part Witnesseth that the sd FRANCIS GOULDMAN for the sum of thirty pounds Curt. money of Virga. doth fully acquit sd NICHOLAS PAMPLIN his heirs and Admrs. forever and for other considerations hereafter mentioned hath demised to farm let unto the sd NICHO-LAS PAMPLIN one piece of land plantation & Wood land ground containing three hundred acres being in the Parish of Southfarnham in the County of Essex and bounded Joyning on the land of Majr. WILLIAM TODD and on the land of JOHN ROBERTS and on the land of JOHN GATEWOOD and on the land formerly leased unto WM. ROANE together with all the houses Orchards Comodities whatsoever appertaining To Have and To Hold the aforesd land unto the sd NICHOLAS PAMPLIN for and during the natural lives of SARAH PAMPLIN Wife of the sd NICHOLAS PAMPLIN, and WILLM. PAMPLIN & NICHOLAS PAMPLIN JUNER Sons of the abovesd NICHS. PAMPLIN dureing the life of the longer liver of them paying during the lives aforesd unto the sd FRANCIS GOULDMAN and heirs of his body lawfully begotten the yearly rent of Six shillings Current money of Virginia to be paid yearly on the five & twentyeth day of March and if it shall happen that the rent be unpaid in the space of thirty days next the day after it ought to be paid (Provided same be lawfully demanded) that then it shall be lawfull for FRANCIS GOULD-MAN & persons to whom the right belong the aforesd land to have again. In Witness whereof the parties have set their hands and seals

in presents of us THOS. STHRESHLY,   FRANS. GOULDMAN
        W. RENNOLDS, W. ROANE

            KNOW ALL MEN by these presents that I FRANCIS GOULDMAN do hereby acknow-ledge to have reced from NICHOLAS PAMPLIN the full sume of thirty pounds current money of Virginia it being the consideration to be paid to me by the Indenture and I do further acknowledge to have reced Six pounds Six shillings Current money it being the yearly rent within mentioned for Twenty & one years. As Witness my hand this Nineteen day of October in the year of our Lord Christ one thousand seven hundred and thirty

Test   THOMS. STHRESHLY,   FRANS. GOULDMAN
         W. RENNOLDS, W. ROANE
     At a Court held for Essex County on the 20th day of October 1730
FRANCIS GOULDMAN acknowledged this his Lease indented wth the livery and Seizen & receipt thereon endorsed to Mr. NICHOLAS PAMPLIN which are admitted to record

         KNOW ALL MEN by these presents that I FRANCIS GOULDMAN am held and firmly bound unto NICHS. PAMPLIN in the sum of Sixty pounds Current money of Virginia the nineteenth day of October one thousand seven hundred and Thirty

     THE CONDITION of the above obligation is such that if FRANCIS GOULDMAN shall hereafter observe all the Covenants which on the part of the sd FRANCIS GOULDMAN his heirs ought to be performed that then this obligation to be void or else to stand
in presence of THOS. STHRESHLY,   FRANS. GOULDMAN
         W. RENNOLDS, W. ROANE
     At a Court held for Essex County on the 20th day of October 1730
FRANCIS GOULDMAN acknowledged this bond to Mr. NICHOLAS PAMPLIN to be his act and deed which is admitted to record

pp.   THIS INDENTURE made the 19th day of October in the year of our Lord God one
161-   thousand seven hundred and Thirty between JOHN RUSSELL of County of Essex
162   in Parish of Southfarnham of one part and EDWARD HARPER of the County of
         KING & QUEEN in Drizdell Parish of the other part Witnesseth that sd JOHN RUS-
SELL for sum of twenty three pounds good and lawfull Currant mony of Virginia hath sold unto sd EDWARD HARPER his heirs and assigns all that parcell of land being in the County of Essex in the Parish of Southfarnham and on the Branches of PISCATAWAY CREEK and bounded Begining at a Spanish Oak Corner of EVEN DAVISes runing thence South West to a white Oak, thence South West to a marked Hickory, thence W: by S: to a Stooping red Oake by a PATH thence S: by W: to a marked red Oak by a Pyne, thence N: W: into the MANE ROAD thence East North to a white Oake saplin by the MANE ROADE, thence East North to a white Oake on a hill side thence E. South to a forked red Oake standing by the PATH near the old field of ARTHUR HODGES thence South East to the Begining containing eighty acers of land according to the platt togeather with all Timber trees likely to become timber, woods swamps and emmolements whatsoever belonging unto him the said EDWARD HARPER his heirs and assigns forever. In Witness whereof the sd party hath set his hand and Seal
in presence of THO: EDWARDS,
         RICHARD 介 COOPER   JOHN 介 RUSSELL
     At a Court held for Essex County on the 20th day of October 1730
JOHN RUSSELL acknowledged this his Deed indented to EDWARD HARPER to be his act & deed which is admitted to record

pp.   KNOW ALL MEN by these presents that wee THOMAS HARDY & JOHN EDMONDSON
162-   both of Essex County are held and firmly bound unto our Soveraign Lord
163   GEORGE the 2d. in the just sum of Ten thousand pounds of Tobo. this 17th day of
         November Ano Dom 1730
     THE CONDITION of the above obligation is such that Whereas the above bound THOMAS HARDY hath obtained a Licence to keep an ORDINARY at his House if therefore sd THO-MAS HARDY doth constantly provide in his said ORDINARY good wholesome and cleanly

lodgeing and diet for Travellers & Stableage fodder & provender or pasturage and provender as the Season of the year shall require for their Horses for the term of one whole year from the date hereof, and shall not suffer any unlawfull gameing in his House nor on the Sabbath day to permit any to Tipple or drink more then is necessary that then the above obligiation to be void otherwise to remain in full power
in presence of MARK WEEKES   THOS. HARDY
                                                             JNO. EDMONDSON

At a Court held for Essex County the XVIIth day of November MDCCXXX
THOMAS HARDY & JOHN EDMONDSON acknowledged this bond to be their act and deed which is admitted to record

pp. 163-169

THIS INDENTURE made this fourteenth and fifteenth day of November in the year of our Lord Christ one thousand seven hundred and Thirty Between EDWARD MURROUGH of the Parish of St. Anns in the County of Essex Taylor and MARTHA his Wife, Surviving Daughter of ISAAC FLOWERS of the Parish of St. Anns within the County aforesd deced, of one part and WILLIAM BROOKE of the Parish of St. Anns in the County aforesd of the other part Witnesseth that sd EDWARD MURROUGH and MARTHA his Wife for the sum of Forty pounds Current money of Virginia do hereby sell unto sd WILLIAM BROOKE (in his actual possession now being of the tract of land hereinafter mentioned by virtue of Indenture for one year and by Virtue of the Statute for the transferring of uses into possession) and to his heirs and assignes forever our Estate right claim and demand whatsoever to all that tract of land and plantation whereon we now live containing one hundred seventy acres and fifty six perches being in the Parish of St. Anns and County of Essex aforesd being the land granted to ISAAC FLOWERS deced by PATTENT dated the second day of November in the year of our Lord one thousand seven hundred and five, part of which One hundred and seventy acres and fifty six perches being purchased of JOHN BUTLER and ROBERT BEIZWELL deced by the sd ISAAC FLOWERS deced both parcels of land sold by the sd BUTLER and BEIZWELL deced being part of one PATTENT granted to RICHARD COLEMAN deced bearing date in the year of our Lord Sixteen hundred and fifty beginning at the Corner of the sd COLEMANs PATTENT & running West to a ditch bounding according to PATTENT farther South running along the sd Ditch to a BEVERDAM on a Creek thence down the sd Creek to the North line of the PATTENT thence North to the beginning place and all houses buildings Orchards woods and advantages whatsoever To Have and To Hold the sd Tract of land to the sd WILLIAM BROOKE his heirs and assigns forever. In Witness the parties have set their hands and seals
in presence of THOS. PLUMMER,   EDWARD E MURROUGH
      J. FOSTER, DANIELL DISKIN   MARTHA + MURROUGH
At a Court held for Essex County the XVIIth day of November MDCCXXX
MARTHA MURROUGH being first privily examined by ALEXR. PARKER Gent acknowledged this her Release indented (perfected by her self and her husband EDWARD MURROUGH) to WILLIAM BROOKE and the perfection thereof by the sd EDWARD & MARTHA to the sd WILLIAM BROOKE being also proved by the Oaths of all the Witnesses thereto was on the sd WILLIAMs motion admitted to record

pp. 169-170

KNOW ALL MEN by these presents that we JAMES COLEMAN, RICHARD WILTSHIRE & ROBERT GREAVES are held and firmly bound unto our Soveraign Lord GEORGE the 2d. in the just sum of Ten thousand pounds of Tobacco this 15th day of December Ano Dom 1730
THE CONDITION of the above obligation is that Whereas JAMES COLEMAN hath obtained a Licence to keep and ORDINARY at SAUNDERS's ORDINARY if therefore the sd JAMES

COLEMAN doth constantly provide in his said ORDINARY good wholesome and cleanly lodgeing and diet for Travellers and Stableage, fooder & provender or pasturage and provender as the Season shall require for their Horses, for the term of one whole year from the date hereof, and shall not suffer any unlawfull gameing in his house nor on the Sabbath day permit any to Tipple or drink more then is necessary that then the above obligation to be Void else to remain in force

                                                    JAMES COLEMAN
                                    RICHARD WILTSHIRE   ROBERT GREAVES
   At a Court held for Essex County on the 15th day of December 1730
JAMES COLEMAN, RICHARD WILTSHIRE & ROBERT GREAVES acknowledged this bond to be their act and deed which is admitted to record

pp.   KNOW ALL MEN by these presents that I JOHN MOTLEY of the County of Essex doth
170-   by these presents oblidge my self and my heirs for the consideration of fifty
173   acres of land lying in the County of Essex given and granted from ELIZABETH
        WHEATON unto me and my heirs bearing date with these presents for the sd fifty
acres of land which in consideration I do bind my self and my heirs to maintain and keep the abovesd ELIZABETH WHEATON and find and allow her sufficient meat drink cloathes and lodging during her natural life Provided she will stay and abide and dwel and live with me or my heirs as Witness my hand and Seal this Elevinth day of December 1730
Testis   JNO. NANCE,   JOHN ⏀ MOTLEY
        JOHN BOULLER, THOMAS ⸿ COOK,
        EDMD. Ɛ CARELL
   At a Court held for Essex County on the XVth day of December MDCCXXX
JOHN MOTLEY acknowledged the within Obligation to be his act & deed which is ordered to be recorded
        THIS INDENTURE made this Eleventh day of Decemr. in the year of our Lord Christ one thousand seven hundred and Thirty By and Between ELISBETH WHETEN Wido. of the County of Essex in Parish of St. Anns of one party, and JOHN MOTLEY of the same County & Parish of the other party Witnesseth that is to say for divers good causes Espeatualy for and in consideration of the keeping and maintaining of the said ELIZBETH WHETEN dureing her natural life the recit whereof I do hereby acknowledge and hold my self satisfied have bargained and sold unto the sd JOHN MOTLEY and his heirs forever all that tract of land containing fifty acres cityated in County of Essex and Parish of St. Ann bounded on the land of JOHN MOTLEY and on the land of JOHN BOWLER and on a Corner tree of JOHN ROWZEE togeather with all the houses Orchards Plantation whatsoever belong to the same To Have and To Hold unto the sd JOHN MOTLEY his heirs and assigns forever. In Witness whereof the sd ELIZBETH WHEATEN hath set her hand and Seale
in presence of JNO. NANCE,   ELIZBETH ✝ WHEATON
        JOHN BOULLER, THOMAS COOK,
        EDMOND Ɛ CARELL
   At a Court held for Essex County the XVth day of December MDCCXXX
ELIZABETH WHEATON acknowledged this her deed of land indented to JOHN MOTLEY to be her act and deed which on his Motion is admitted to record
        KNOW ALL MEN by these presents that I ELIZABETH WHEATON am justly indebted unto JOHN MOTLEY in the sum of Sixty pounds Sterling this Eleventh day of Decr. 1730
   THE CONDITION of ye above obligation is such that sd ELIZABETH WHEATEN hath sold unto sd JOHN MOTLEY parcle of land in the County of Essex and if the sd ELIZTH. WHEATEN from time to time and forever make a good title to the sd JOHN MOTLEY and his

heirs from any claims of persons whatsoever that then the above obligation to be void
or els to stand in force

Testis   JNO. NANCE, JNO. BOULLER   ELIZLBETH ✚ WHEATEN
          EDMD. Ɛ CARELL, THOMAS COOK

At a Court held for Essex County on the XVth day of December MDCCXXX
ELIZABETH WHEATEN acknowledged this bond to be her act & deed which is admitted to
record

pp.   THIS INDENTURE made the eighteenth and nineteenth day of January in the
174-   year of our Lord Christ according to the computation now used in the Church of
179   Great Brittain one thousand seven hundred and Thirty between JOHN MOSS of
         the County of WESTMORELAND Carpenter of one part & SALVATOR MUSCOE of the
County of Essex of the other part Witnesseth that sd JOHN MOSS for sum of Sixteen
pounds Currt. money of Virginia doth sell unto the said SALVATOR MUSCOE (in his
actual possession now being by virtue of Indenture for one year and of the Statute for
transferring uses into possession) and to his heirs and assigns forever all the Estate
right in one Devident of land whereon his Father ROBERT MOSS dwelt containing five
hundred acres being in the Parish of St. Ann & County of Essex and adjoyning to the
land whereon Majr. ROBERT BROOKE now lives, which land was given by the aforesd
ROBERT MOSS to his five Sons THOMAS, WILLIAM, ROBERT, RICHARD and JOHN MOSS to be
equally divided between them as by the sd ROBERT MOSS last Will and Testament relation
being had to the records of Essex County Court may at large appear and all houses gardens trees and appurtenances whatsoever belonging and all the Estate Right To Have
and To Hold unto the said SALVATOR MUSCOE his heirs and assigns forever. In Witness
whereof the parties have set their hands and Seals

in presence of JAMES SHEPPEY,   JNO.   MOSS
         ELIZA. MUSCOE, MARY MUSCOE

At a Court held for Essex County on the XIXth day of Janry. MDCCXXX
JOHN MOSS acknowledged his release indented to SALVATORE MUSCOE to be his act and
deed which on his motion is admitted to record

pp.   THIS INDENTURE made the nineteenth and Twentieth day of January in the year
179-   of our Lord God one thousand seven hundred and Thirty Between JOHN WEBB of
184   the County of Essex of one part and SAMUEL CLAYTON of the County aforesaid of
         the other part Witnesseth that Whereas the sd JOHN WEBB by Indenture bearing
date the day before the date hereof for the consideration herein mentioned (five shillings) did sell unto sd SAMUEL CLAYTON two hundred acres of land and likewise all my
whole right & title to the whole PATENT formerly granted to JOHN BIBBEY as will appear
being in Southfarnham Parish in the County of Essex joyning on PISCATAWAY CREEK
on the lower side thereof joyning on the land of the sd CLAYTON and allso all waies
waters comodities and advantages belonging To Have and To Hold the said land therein
mentioned unto the sd SAMUEL CLAYTON his heirs during the term of Six months to the
end that by Virtue thereof and by Virtue of the Statute for transferring uses into possession the said SAMUEL CLAYTON might be in the actuall possession of the premises
and be enabled to accept Release for the same. Now This Indenture Witnesseth that sd
JOHN WEBB for the consideration of sd SAMUEL CLAYTON giveing unto him the sd JOHN
WEBB fifty acres of land out of the aforesd Two hundred and laid of according to a bond
given by the sd SAMUEL CLAYTON to him the sd JOHN WEBB bearing date the fourth day
of October 1729 the receipt whereof he doth hereby acknowledge and for divers other
good causes hath granted unto him the said SAMUEL CLAYTON his heirs and assigns all
the aforesd two hundred acres of land and all his right & title to the PATENT formerly

granted to JOHN BIBBY and every part thereof To Have and To Hold the sd land and other the premises unto the sd SAMUEL CLAYTON his heirs and assigns. In Witness whereof the parties have set their hands and Seals

in presence of JOHN GRIFFING,   JOHN WEBB
        WM. FRAZER, OWIN *QQ*OWINGS

At a Court held for Essex County on the XVIth day of February MDCCXXX
JOHN WEBB acknowledged this his release indented to SAMUEL CLAYTON to be his act and deed which on his motion is admitted to record

        KNOW ALL MEN by these presents that I JOHN WEBB am held and firmly bound unto SAMUEL CLAYTON in the sum of one hundred & fifty pounds Sterl. dated this twentieth day of January 1730

THE CONDITION of this present obligation is such that JOHN WEBB hath sold unto the sd SAMUEL CLAYTON two hundred acres of land and all his right to a PATENT granted to JOHN BIBBEY if therefore the above named SAMUEL CLAYTON his heirs & assigns shall at all time forever hereafter peaceably occupy and enjoy the sd parcell and kept harmless from all manner of titles committed or done by JOHN WEBB or any other persons & execute other and more effectual assureing and sure making of the sd land granted to the sd SAMUEL CLAYTON and further that sd JOHN WEBB hath a bond from the sd SAMUEL CLAYTON to him the sd JOHN WEBB for the acknowledgmt. of fifty acres of land to be laid of according to the sd Bond and further the sd JOHN WEBB doth oblige himself that ever he do sell the sd fifty acres of land that the sd SAMUEL CLAYTON or his heirs shall have the same giveing as much as any other person whatsoever that then this obligation to be void otherwise to remain in force

in presence of JOHN GRIFFING,   JOHN WEBB
        WM. FRAZER, OWIN *Q O.* OWINGS

At a Court held for Essex County on the XVIth day of February MDCCXXX
JOHN WEBB acknowledged this bond to be his act and deed which is admitted to record

pp.   THIS INDENTURE made the fifteenth and 16th day of March in the year of our
185-   Lord God one thousand seven hundred and Thirty Between ALEXANDER GRAVES
188   of the County of MIDDLESEX of one part and DANIEL DOBBINS of the County of
         Essex of other part Witnesseth that sd ALEXANDER GRAVES for the sum of Twenty
six pounds of good and lawfull currant mony of Virginia hath granted unto the sd
DANIEL DOBYNS in his actuall possession now being by Virtue of a bargain and Sale for
one year and by force of the Statute for transferring uses into possesion and to his
heirs and assigns forever all that Plantacon parcell of land containing two hundred
acres being in the County of Essex and bounded beginning on the South East side by the
land of JOHN GEORGE South West by the land of WILLIAM CHEANEY, Norwest by the land
of THOS. FITZ JEFFRIS and North East on the land of DANIEL DOBYNS including the aforesd quantety of Two hundred acres this sd land did formerly belong to GRIFFING
ROBARDS of this County and by his heirs sold to ALEXANDER GRAVES above menconed To
Have and To Hold the said land with all appurtenances thereunto belonging to the sd
DANIEL DOBYNS and his heirs and assigns forever. In Witness whereof the party first
abovementioned hath set his hand and fixed his Seal

in presence of us JAMES GATEWOOD,   ALEXR. GRAVES
        WM. COVINGTON

At a Court held for Essex County on the XVIth day of March MDCCXXX
ALEXANDER GRAVES acknowledged his Release of land Indented to DANIEL DOBYNS &
MARY the wife of the said ALEXANDER relinquished her right of dower in the lands
conveyed by this Release to the sd DANIEL DOBYNS & on his mocon the same is admitted
to record

KNOW ALL MEN by these presents that I ALEXANDER GRAVES am held and firmly bound unto DANIEL DOBYNS in the sum of fifty two pounds of good and lawfull mony of Virginia this (blank) day of (blank)

THE CONDITION of this above obligation is such that Whereas certain Deeds made between ALEXANDER GRAVES and DANIEL DOBYNS bearing equal date now if said ALEXANDER GRAVES his heirs shall truely keep all agreements which on his part ought to be kept in the above Deeds that then this obligation to be void else to stand in full power

in presence of JAMES GATEWOOD,   ALEXR. GRAVES
          WM.COVINGTON

At a Court held for Essex County on the XVIth day of March MDCCXXX
ALEXANDER GRAVES acknowledged his bond to DANIEL DOBYNS to be his act & deed which is admitted to record

pp.   THIS INDENTURE made the twenty sixth day and twenty seventh day of Novem-
188-   ber MDCCXXX Between JOHN GETAR of the one part and WILLIAM HENRY TER-
191   RETT of the other part Witnesseth that sd JOHN GETAR for the sum of thirty
pounds Sterling hath granted unto the sd WILLIAM HENRY TERRETT (in his actual possession now being by Virtue of an Indenture for one year and by force of the Statute for transferring uses into possession) and to his heirs & assigns forever one hundred and fifty acres of land in Essex County being the moiety or half part of a PATTENT formerly granted to RICHARD WEST & ROGER CLOTWORTHY lying on the upper side of the line of markd trees that devides the sd land in two parts & the sd CLOTWORTHY conveyed to NICHOLAS CATLETT and by the sd CATLETT conveyed to WILLIAM GIBSON who by his Last Will and Testament bequeathed the same to ELIZA. GIBSON Mother of MARY POWELL and also the moiety or half part of one hundred acres of land situated in the County aforesd which was bequeathed by the sd WILLIAM GIBSON to JAMES BARTLETT & for want of issue descended to ELIZABETH GIBSON Mother of the aforesaid MARY POWELL who with her Husband THOMAS POWELL conveyed the same to the aforesaid JOHN GETAR party to these presents (relation being had to the records of Essex County doth more fully appear) and all the Estate right whatsoever belonging of him the said JOHN GETAR unto the premises To Have and To Hold unto the said WILLIAM HENRY TERRETT his heirs & assigns. In Witness whereof the party to these presents hath set his hand and Seal

in presence of us THOS. ROY,   JOHN ✝ GETAR
          JOHN STEVINS

At a Court held for Essex County on the XVIth day of March MDCCXXX
JOHN GETAR acknowledged his Release of land Indented to WILLIAM HENRY TERRETT which on his mocon is admitted to record

pp.   THIS INDENTURE made the XXth day of March in the fourth year of the Reign of
192-   our Soveraign Lord GEORGE & in the year of our Lord God one thousand seven
195   hundred and Thirty Between WILLIAM HENRY TERRETT of the Parish of St.
Marys & the County of CAROLINE of one part and THOMAS PLUMMER of the Parish of St. Anns in the County of Essex of the other part Witnesseth that sd WILLIAM HENRY TERRETT for the quantity of three thousand pounds of Tobo and cask doth confirm unto the sd THOMAS PLUMMER (in his actual possession now being by Virtue of an Indenture made for one year and by force of the Statute for transferring uses into possession) and to his heirs and assigns forever one hundred and fifty acres of land in Essex County being the moiety or half part of a PATENT formerly granted to RICHARD WEST and ROGER CLOTWORTHY lying on the upper side the line of marked trees that divides the sd land in two parts & by the sd CLOTWORTHY conveyed to NICHOLAS CATLETT &

by the sd CATLETT conveyed to WILLM. GIBSON who by his Last Will & Testament bequeathed the same to ELIZABETH GIBSON Mother to MARY VIRGIL and allso the Moiety or half part of one other hundred acres of land in the Parish and County aforesaid adjoyning to the abovesaid land which was bequeathed by the sd WILLIAM GIBSON to JOHN BARTLET and for want of issue decended to ELIZABETH GIBSON Mother of the aforesd MARY VIRGIL which MARY maried with THOMAS POWELL who with the sd MARY conveyed the sd land to JOHN GEATER & by the sd GEATER conveyed to WILLIAM HENRY TERRETT party to these presents relation being had to the records of Essex County will appear and all right title and demand whatsoever of him the sd WILLIAM HENRY TERRETT To Have and To Hold unto the sd THOMAS PLUMMER his heirs and assigns forever. In Witness whereof the party to these presents hath set his hand and Seal

in presence of MUNGO ROY,   WM. HENRY TERRETT
          THOS. COLEMAN

At a Court held for Essex County on the XVIth day of March MDCCXXX
WILLIAM HENRY TERRETT acknowledged this his Release to THOMAS PLUMMER which on his motion is admitted to record

pp.   THIS INDENTURE made the XXth day of January in the year of our Lord MDCCXXX
195-   Between CHRISTOPHER BEVERLEY of KING & QUEEN COUNTY Gent of one part and
196   PETER DUDLEY of RICHMOND COUNTY Planter of the other part Witnesseth that
          sd CHRISTOPHER BEVERLEY for the sum of Ten pounds fifteen shillings Current
money to him paid or secured to be paid doth demise sett & to farm lett unto the sd PETER DUDLEY the house & Tenement where JAMES BYROM late lived together with eighty acres of land thereto adjoyning in the Parish of South farnham & County of Essex To Have and To Hold unto the sd PETER DUDLEY his Exrs. & assigns for the full time & term of twenty & one years from day of these presents paying therefore yearly on the feast day of St. Michael the Archangel the royal Quitrent of the sd land & one ear of Indian Corn and the sd PETER DUDLEY shall not comit waste and if sd rent be unpaid by space of thirty days in any year that then sd CHRISTOPHER BEVERLEY to reenter & the same to have again and the sd CHRISTOPHER BEVERLEY for himself doth warrant the sd land to the sd PETER DUDLEY. In Witness whereof the parties have sett their hands and Seals
in presence of BENJA. WINSLOW,   CHR. BEVERLEY
          BENJA. WAGGENER, RICHARD DUDLEY

At a Court held for Essex County on the XVIth day of March MDCCXXX
CHRISTOPHER BEVERLEY Gent acknowledged this Lease indented to PETER DUDLEY which is admitted to record

pp.   THIS INDENTURE made the Second day of March in the year of our Lord Christ
197-   one thousand seven hundred and Thirty Between FRANCIS COVINGTON of the
199   Parish of Southfarnham in County of Essex Planter of one part and JAMES BOOTH
          of the Parish of St. Ann within County of Essex Husbandman of other part Witnesseth that said FRANCIS COVINGTON for the sum of Sixty pds Current money of Virginia doth sell unto sd JAMES BOOTH his heirs and assignes forever in his actual possession now being one Plantacon or tract of land in the Parish of Southfarnham in the County aforesd containing Two hundred acres and is the plantation and premises whereon the sd FRANCIS COVINGTON lately dwelt and adjoying unto the land of CHRISTOPHER BEVERLY and unto the land of HENRY TANDY and also the land of THOMAS MERIWEATHER To Have and To Hold to him the sd JAMES BOOTH his heirs and assigns forever and moreover I the sd FRANCIS COVINGTON do for my self my heirs have put and made my trusty & well beloved friends Major WILLIAM BEVERLEY and Mr. JAMES GARNETT of

this County to be my lawfull Attorneys in my name and place to execute and acknowledge in the sd County Court of Indicature or General Court of record in WILLIAMS-
BURGH when thereunto required by sd JAMES BOTH his heirs or assigns in as full manner as I could do was I present. In Witness whereof I the sd FRANCIS COVINGTON have
set my hand and Seal

in presence of THOS. COVINGTON,   FRANCIS COVINGTON
        WILLIAM COVINGTON, ROBT ℞ GRISANE

   At a Court held for Essex County on the XVIth day of March MDCCXXX
This Deed of bargain and sale of land indented with livery & Seizin therein endorsed
from FRANCIS COVINGTON to JAMES BOOTH was proved by the oaths of THOMAS COVING-
TON, WILLIAM COVINGTON & ROBERT GRESHAM witnesses thereto & on the motion of the
said JAMES was admitted to record

pp.   KNOW ALL MEN by these presents that wee WILLIAM DUNN JUNR. & EDWARD
199-   HARPER & WILLIAM GRAY are held and firmly bound unto our Sovrn. Lord
200   GEORGE the 2d. in the ffull sum of ten thousand pounds of tobacco this XVIth day
        of March 1730
THE CONDITION of the above obligation is that Whereas the above bound WM. DUNN
JUNR. hath obtained a Licence to keep an ORDINARY at PERKINS's ORDINARY if therefore said WM. DUNN JUNR. doth constantly provide in his said ORDINARY good wholesome and cleanly lodgeing and diet for Travellers & Stableage fodder & provender or
pasturage & provender as the Season of the year shall require for their Horses for the
term of one whole year from the date hereof and shall not suffer any unlawfull gaming
in his House nor on the Sabbath day permitt any to Tipple more than is necessary that
then the above obligation to be void else to stand
                              WM. DUNN JR.
                    EDWD. HARPER   WM. GRAY
   At a Court held for Essex County on the XVIth day of March MDCCXXX
WILLIAM DUNN JR., EDWARD HARPER & WILLIAM GRAY acknowledged this bond to be
their act & deed which is admitted to record

pp.   THIS INDENTURE made the 17 day of May in the year of our Lord God one thou-
200-   sand seven hundred and Thirty One between FRANCIS BROWN of the Parish of
201   Southfarnham in County of Essex of one part and HENRY BOUGHAN JUNIOR of
        the Parish and County aforesaid of other part Witnesseth that sd FRANCIS
BROWN for the sum of one thousand pounds of tobacco & cask hath sold unto the sd
HENRY BOUGHAN JUNR. his heirs and assigns forever all the right which is or shall
hereafter become due to the sd FRANCIS BROWN to a certain parcell of land in the
Parish and County aforesaid containing fifty acres bounded begining at the BRIDGE
called HENRY BROWNS BRIDGE by the mouth of a Branch thence up the sd Branch to a
Spring in THOMAS WOODS old field now belonging to JOHN CROXTON thence North Wes-
terly along the dividing line between the sd JOHN CROXTON and FRANCIS BROWN and
from thence along the dividing line to the main Branch called the MIDDLE BRANCH
thence up the sd Branch to the begining and all Houses, buildings, Orchards and Commodities whatsoever to the same belonging To Have and To Hold unto him the said
HENRY BOUGHAN JUNR. his heirs and assignes forever. In Witness whereof I the sd
FRANCIS BROWN have set my hand and Seale

in presence of us THOMAS BARKER,   FRANCIS ✗ BROWN
        JOHN BOUGHAN, HENRY ℬ BROWN

   At a Court held for Essex County on the XVIIIth day of May MDCCXXXI
FRANCIS BROWN acknowledged this his Deed of land indented with livery & seizen

thereon endorsed to HENRY BOUGHAN JUNR. which is admitted to record

pp. 202-206 THIS INDENTURE made the eleventh and twelfth day of May in the year of our Lord one thousand seven hundred and Thirty One Between THOMAS REYNOLD of the County of Essex of one part and JOHN CLEMENT of the same County of the other part Witnesseth that said THOMAS REYNOLD for the sum of Fifteen pounds Sterling money of England hath granted unto the sd JOHN CLEMENT his heirs and assigns forever one parcel of land one hundred and fourty acres being all that tract of land of which the sd THOMAS REYNOLD bought of RICHARD LONG in the County aforesd lying on a Branch of BLACKBURNS CREEK bounded begining at a marked Beech by a Branch side thence East to a red Oak Corner tree to Capt. JOHN HAWKINS and also to the land of SAMUELL STALLARD thence binding on the sd STALLARDs line South East to a red Oak Corner tree to the sd STALLARD and to ROBERT PARKER, thence with the sd PARKERs line and the line of DAVID PITTS South West till it cometh to a white Oak standing in the line of the sd DAVID PITTS Corner Tree to TIMOTHY SWILLAVAN thence with the sd SWILLAVANs line to the Branch aforementioned, thence down the sd Branch binding on the run till it comes to the first mentioned beginning and all the Estate, Right & demand of him the said THOMAS REYNOLDS in the sd land which land and premises now are in the actual possession of him the sd JOHN CLEMENT by Virtue of one Indenture of bargain and sale for one year and by Virtue of the Statute for transferring uses into possession To Have and To Hold the said Seat or Parcell of land unto the sd JOHN CLEMENT his heirs and assigns forever. In Witness whereof the parties have set their hands and Seals

in presence of us SAMLL. BIZWELL,   THOMAS REYNOLDS
JAMES DANIELL JUNR., SAMLL. BROWNE

At a Court held for Essex County on the XVIIIth day of May MDCCXXXI
THOMAS REYNOLDS acknowledged this his Release of land Indented to JOHN CLEMENT which on his motion is admitted to record
Allso the same day MARY the Wife of the sd THOMAS REYNOLDS came into Court and freely relinquished her right of dower in the land conveyed by this Release to JOHN CLEMENTS which is admitted to record

pp. 206-207 KNOW ALL MEN by thesepresents that I JONATHAN LAMBERT Marriner of the City of BRISTOL have made in my place my beloved friend SIMON MILLER of the County of Essex and Parish of St. Ann my lawfull Attorney for me & in my name to recover and receive of all or every person all such debts of money or Tobacco which are due to me granting to my said Attorney my full authority about the premises and upon receipt to make acquittances and to perform in every respect as myself could doe if I were there in mine own person By Virtue of these presents have hereunto set my hand and seal this 12th day of Aprill Anno Dom 1731

in presence of us WM. BROOKE,   JONATHAN LAMBERT
THOS. PLUMMER

At a Court held for Essex County on the XVIIIth day of May MDCCXXXI
This Power of Attorney from JONATHAN LAMBERT to SIMON MILLER was proved by the oaths of the witnesses thereto & on the sd MILLERs motion is admitted to record

pp. 207-208 KNOW ALL MEN by these presents that We NICHOLAS SMITH, THOMAS WARING and WILLIAM COVINGTON of the County of Essex are held and firmly bound unto our Soveraign Lord GEORGE the 2d. in the sum of one thousand pounds Sterling this XVIIIth day of May Anno Dom MDCCXXXI

THE CONDITION of the above obligation is such that if the above bound NICHOLAS

SMITH Gent who is this day by Virtue of a Commission from the Honble the Governor admitted & Sworn SHERIFF of the County of Essex shall render unto the Auditor or Receiver General of his Majties Revenue a particular account of all his Majties Rents & dues ariseing within the sd County of Essex and due payment make of all Publick Dues of the said County & all fees put into his hands to collect unto the severall persons to whom the same shall be due and true performance make of all matters and things relating to his Office during the time of his Continuance therein that then this obligation to be void else to remain in force

in presence of W. BEVERLEY,   NICHO. SMITH
                          T. WARING   WM. COVINGTON

   At a Court held for Essex County on the XVIIIth day of May MDCCXXXI
NICHOLAS SMITH, THOMAS WARING & WILLIAM COVINGTON Gent acknowledged this bond to be their act and deed which is ordered to be recorded

pp. | KNOW ALL MEN by these presents that wee MARTIN WILLARD of Essex County &
208- | CHRISTOPHER BEVERLEY of KING & QUEEN COUNTY Gent are held and firmly
209 | Bound unto MARY PERRY her Exrs., Admrs. in the sum of thirty pounds Sterling
this XVIIIth day of May Anno Dom MDCCXXXI

THE CONDITION of this Obligation is such that whereas Judgment. being this day given in Essex County Court unto the sd MARY PERRY against the above bound MARTIN WILLARD in an action of debt depending between sd MARY PERRY Plt and sd MARTIN WILLARD Defendt. the sd MARTIN WILLARD had an appeal granted him to the Eight day of the next General Court giveing Security according to Law if therefore the sd MARTIN WILLARD Appellant as aforesd shall accordingly appear and prosecute the sd Appeal at the next General Court and perform the Judgment of the sd General Court and pay the damages of fifteen p cent which the Court gives upon the principal Debt damages and costs of the County Court this day recovered if cast upon the sd Appeal that then the above obligation to be void otherwise to stand

MARTIN /M\ WILLARD
CHR. BEVERLEY

   At a Court held for Essex County on the XVIIIth day of May MDCCXXXI
MARTIN WILLARD & CHRISTOR. BEVERLEY acknowledged this bond to be their act and deed which is admitted to record

p. | KNOW ALL MEN by these presents that we JOHN VAWTER & THOMAS HAWKINS of
209 | Essex County are held and firmly bound unto our Sovereign Lord GEORGE the 2d.
in the just sum of ten thousand pounds of Tobacco this XVIIIth day of May

MDCCXXXI. THE CONDTION of the above obligation is such that the above bound JOHN VAWTER hath obtained a Licence to keep and ORDINARY at his House, if therefore the sd JOHN VAWTER doth constantly find & provide in his ORDINARY good wholesome and cleanly lodgeing & diet for Travellers & Stableage fodder & provender or pasturage as the Season of the year shall required for their Horses during the term of one whole year from the date hereof & shall not suffer any unlawfull gaming in his house nor on the Sabbath day suffer any to Tipple more than is necessary that then the above obligation to be void else to remain in force

JNO. VAWTER
THOS. HAWKINS

   At a Court held for Essex County the XVIIIth day of May MDCCXXXI
JOHN VAWTER and THOMAS HAWKINS acknowledged this bond to be their act & deed which is admitted to record

pp. THIS INDENTURE made the twenty third and twenty fourth day of May in the
210- year of our Lord one thousand seven hundred and Thirty and One Between JOHN
215 BATES SENIOR of the Parish of Southfarnham & County of Essex of one part and
PITMAN SCANDRETT of the Parish and County aforesd of the other part Witnesseth that the sd JOHN BATES SENIOR for the sum of Twenty pounds Currency and Seven
hundred pounds of Tobacco and Cask hath sold unto the sd PITTMAN SCANDRETT his
heirs and assigns all that Sixty one acres of land being part of a greater tract of land
whereon RICHARD GREGORY did dwell and being formerly granted to WILLIAM JOHN-
SON scituate in the Parish of Southfarnham and County of Essex aforesd. and on the
North side of PISCATAWAY CREEK and bounded beginning at a Stake in the head of a
Valley on the MAIN ROAD near a Branch and runing down the several Courses thereof
to the MAIN ROAD and along the ROAD to the beginning And all the Estate right and demand of him the sd JOHN BATES all which said premises are now in the actual possession of the sd PITMAN SCANDRETT by virtue of one Indenture of Bargain and Sale to him
thereof made for the term of one year and by Virtue of the Statute for transferring uses
into possession and the reversion and profits of the premises To Have and To Hold unto
the said PITTMAN SCANDRETT his heirs and assigns forever. In Witness whereof the
parties have sett their hands and Seals
in presence of ALEXANDER PARKER,   JNO. BATES
       HENRY TANDY, JOHN REEVES
   At a Court held for Essex County the XVth day of June MDCCXXXI
JOHN BATES acknowledged this Release of land indented to PITTMAN SCANDRETT which
on his motion is admitted to record
       KNOW ALL MEN by these presents that I JOHN BATES am held and firmly bound
unto PITTMAN SCANDRETT in the sum of Sixty pounds Sterling this twenty fourth day of
May Seventeen hundred & thirty one
       THE CONDITION of the above obligation is such that if JOHN BATES shall at all times keep
all Covenants which on the part of the sd JOHN BATES ought to be kept mentioned in
Indenture that then this obligation to be void else to remain in force
in presence of us ALEXANDER PARKER,   JNO. BATES
       HENRY TANDY, JOHN REEVES
   At a Court held for Essex County on the XVth day of June MDCCXXXI
JOHN BATES acknowledged this bond to PITTMAN SCANDRETT which on his motion is
admitted to record

p. Essex Court House July 20th 1731
215 I do hereby appoint Coll. WILLIAM BEVERLEY of this County my Attornie in all
causes & actions I may have in the Countie particularly in a Cause now depending betwixt JAMES GATEWOOD, SAMUEL CLAYTON and my self. Witness my hand day
and date aforesd.
Test WIL ROBINSON   PAT. CHEAP
   At a Court held for Essex County on the XXth day of July MDCCXXXI
PATRICK CHEAP Mercht. acknowledged this his Powr. of Attorney to WILLIAM BEVER-
LEY which on his mocon is admitted to record

pp. THIS INDENTURE made the 30th and 31st day of May in the year of our Lord God
215- one thousand seven hundred and Thirty One Between WILLIAM KEMP of the
219 County of GLOUCESTER in the Parish of Ware of one part and THOMAS FITS JEF-
FRESS of the County of Essex in the Parish of Southfarnham of the other part
Witnesseth that the sd WILLIAM KEMP for the consideration of Twelve pounds of good
and lawfull money Currant of Virginia hath sold unto the sd THOMAS FITS JEFFRESS his

heirs and assigns in his actual possession now being by virtue of a bargain & sale for one year and of the Statute for transferring uses into possession and to his heirs all that plantation or tract of land containing One hundred acres in the County of Essex in the Parish of Southfarnham and on the North side of the Northermost Branch of the DRAGON SWAMP and bounded on the South East side by the land of WILLIAM CHEANEY late deced and by the land of ANNE COX and the land now belonging to Mr. ROBERT BAYLOR and opposite to the land WILLIAM COLE and binding upon the aforementioned DRAGON SWAMP including the aforesd Quantity of One hundred acres which sd land is aprt of a PATENT formerly granted to THOMAS WILLIAMSON of this County for Two hundred acres and since by divers Sales did belong on one ROGER BURGYNE deced and now it doth of right belong unto the aforesd WILLIAM KEMP as next heire unto the aforesd BURGYNE deced To Have and To Hold all the premises thereunto belonging unto him the said THOMAS FITS JEFFRESS and his heirs and assigns forever and sd WILLIAM KEMP and his Wife for themselves do hereby warrant and defend the said land. In Witness whereof the parties to these presents have set their hands & Seals
in presence of us PETR. KEMP,   WILLIAM KEMP
        JOHN MITCHELL
  At a Court held for Essex County the XXth day of July MDCCXXXI
WILLIAM KEMP acknowledged this his Release of land indented unto THOMAS FITS JEFFRESS which on his motion is admitted to record
        KNOW ALL MEN by these presents that I WILLIAM KEMP and held and firmly bound unto THOMAS FITS JEFFRESS in the sum of forty pounds of good and lawfull mony of Virginia this 31st day of May 1731
  THE CONDITION of this obligation is that Whereas certain Deeds made between WILLIAM KEMP of one part and THOMAS FITS JEFFRESS of the other part Now if the above bound WILLIAM KEMP shall truely keep all the agreements which on his part ought to be observed without fraud or Covin that then this obligation to be void otherwise to stand in force
in presence of PETR. KEMP,   WILLIAM KEMP
        JOHN MITCHELL
  At a Court held for Essex County the XXth day of July MDCCXXXI
WILLIAM KEMP acknowledged this bond to be his act and deed which is admitted to record

pp.   TO ALL CHRISTIAN People to whom these presents shall come I JOHN HALL send
219-   Greeting. Know ye that I ye sd JOHN HALL have made and in my stead by these
225   presents do ordain RICHARD BUSH of the Parish of Southfarnham in the County
        of Essex my true and lawfull Attorney to acknowledge in the Court held for Essex
County a certain tract of land in a pair of Indentures meaning that I the said JOHN HALL give RICHARD BUSH my lawfull Attorney full power to Release unto RICHARD BRIZENDINE of the Parish of Southfarnham in Essex County ratyfying whatseover my said Attorney shall do in my name. In Witness whereof I have sett my hand and Seal this 19th day of July 1731
in presence of ISAAC HUDSON,   JOHN f HALL
        JOHN GEORGE, EDWARD E BOMER
  At a Court held for Essex County the XXth day of July MDCCXXXI
This Power of Attorney from JOHN HALL to RICHARD BUSH was proved by the Oaths of all the witnesses thereto & is admitted to record

        THIS INDENTURE made the Twenininth day of April in the year of our Lord God one thousand seven hundred and Thirty One Between JOHN HALL of the Pish of St.

Peters in the County of NEW KENT of one part and RICHARD BRIZENDINE of the Parish of Sofarnham in the County aforesd of other part Witnesseth that JOHN HALL in consider-atin of three thousand pounds of lawfull tobacco to him in hand paid or secured to be paid doth fully grant unto RICHARD BRIZENDINE in his actuall possession by Virtue of a Bargain & Sale to him for one year and by Virtue of the Statute for transferring uses into possession all that parcell of land in Southfarnham Parish in County of Essex con-taining ninety acres lying and joyning on the land of NATHANIEL NEWBLE and SARAH CRUST which sd ninety acres of land was formerly sold by SAMEUL GREEN to JOHN GUNN by Sale bearing date the 28th day of July 1677 and by the Last Will & Testament of the sd JOHN GUNN given unto SARAH GREEN afterwards Wife of CHARLES HALL and so fall to me the sd JOHN HALL by inheritance To Have and To hold the said land with appurte-nances to use and behoof of the said RICHARD BRIZENDINE his heirs and assigns for-ever. In Witness whereof the said JOHN HALL hath set his hand & Seal
in presence of ISAAC HUDSON,   JOHN **I** HALL
       JOHN GEORGE, EDWARD **E** BOMER
   At a Court held for Essex County on the XXth day of July MDCCXXXI
JOHN HALL by RICHARD BUSH his Attorney acknowledged this his Release of land In-dented to RICHARD BRIZENDINE which on his motion is admitted to record
       KNOW ALL MEN by these presents that I JOHN HALL am held and firmly bound unto RICHD. BRIZENDINE in the penal sum of Six thousand pounds of legal Sweet scented Tobacco this twenty ninth day of April 1731
       THE CONDITION of this obligation is such that whereas if JOHN HALL at all times here-after shall keep all the articles mentioned in Indenture which on the part of the sd JOHN HALL ought to be observed that then this obligation to be void otherwise to remain in force
in presence of ISAAC HUDSON,   JOHN **F** HALL
       JOHN GEORGE, EDWARD **E** BOMER
   At a Court held for Essex County on the XXth day of July MDCCXXXI
JOHN HALL by RICHARD BUSH his Attorney acknowledged this his bond to be his act & deed which is admitted to record

pp.   THIS INDENTURE made the fifteenth day of May in the fourth year of the Reign
225- of our Soveraigne Lord GEORGE the Second & in the year of our Lord one thou-
228   sand seven hundred thirty and one Between THOMAS SHORT of the Parish of St.
       Anns in County of Essex of one part and JOHN NANCE of the Parish and County abovesd of the other part Witnesseth that sd THOMAS SHORT in consideration of the sum of sixty pounds Current mony of Virginia doth sell unto the sd JOHN NANCE his heirs and assignes forever one parcell of land containing one hundred and twenty and three acres it being the one half part of a tract of land granted to JAMES COGHILL by PATENT dated the Twenty Fourth day of March Anno Dom 1664/5 for two hundred and forty acres of land bounded as by the sd PATENT (the other part being now in the possession of Mr. DANIEL GAINES and CORNELIUS NOELL and all the right of Surplusage belonging to the sd Land) togeather with all the appurtenances whatsoever To Have and To Hold unto the said JOHN NANCE his heirs and assigns forever and also that the sd THOMAS SHORT will acknowledge this Deed in Essex Court and that his Wife CATHARINE will then and there relinquish her right of dower. In Witness whereof the parties have set their hands and Seals
in presence of HENERY MOTLEY,   THOMAS SHORT
       THOMAS TILLER, JNO. VAWTER
   At a Court held for Essex County on the XXth day of July MDCCXXXI

THOMAS SHORT acknowledged this his Deed indented to JOHN NANCE which on his
motion is admitted to record

Be it Remembered that on the fifteenth day of May Anno Dom 1731 full Seizen was
given and delivered by THOMAS SHORT to JOHN NANCE by Turf and Twigg in presence of
    HENERY MOTLEY,
    THOMAS TILLER JNO. VAWTER

At a Court held for Essex County on the XXth day of July MDCCXXXI
This Livery and Seizin of the land was acknowledged by THOMAS SHORT to JOHN NANCE
which on his motion is admitted to record

pp. KNOW ALL MEN by these presents that I SUSANA RUCKER the Wife of JOHN
228- RUCKER of St. Marks Parish in the County of SPOTSYLVANIA do appoint WIL-
233 LIAM BEVERLEY Gent to be my true and lawfull Attorney in my name to appear
    before the Court of Essex County and there in open Court to relinquish my right
of dower to land sould to EDWARD MURROUGH by PETER RUCKER, THOMAS RUCKER & my
sd Husband JOHN RUCKER by Deeds and I do hereby confirm whatsoever my sd Attorney
shall do. In Witness I have set my hand and Seal this 15th day of July 1731
Witness PETER **P** RUCKER,   SUSANA **J** RUCKER
    WILLIAM RUCKER

At a Court held for Essex County the XXth day of July MDCCXXXI
This Power of Atty. was proved by the witnesses thereto & is admitted to record

    THIS INDENTURE made the thirteenth day of March in the year of our Lord one
thousand seven hundred & Thirty Between PETER RUCKER, JOHN RUCKER and THOMAS
RUCKER of the County of SPOTSILVANIA Planters of the one part and EDWARD MUR-
ROUGH of the County of Essex Taylor of the other part Witnesseth that said PETER
RUCKER, JOHN RUCKER & THOMAS RUCKER for the sum of Thirty five pounds Currt.
mony of Virginia have sold unto EDWARD MURROUGH and his heirs forever all that
tenement of land and plantation being on the South side of the RAPPAHANNOCK RIVER
in the Parish of St. Anns in County of Essex being by estimation Fifty six acres begining
at two Maples standing in a Branch of COCKLESHELL CREEK and in WILLIAM SCOTTs line
thence running North with the sd line to a Stake in a glade Corner to JAMES COGHILLs
One hundred and fifty acres thence with his line North West to a Stake standing on the
Eastward side of a Hickory in the line of JAMES COGHILLs PATENT thence with the sd
line East to the place begun the land being part of a PATTENT of land granted to JAMES
COGHILL for one thousand and Sixty acres of land and the reversion and every part and
parcel thereof To Have and To Hold unto the said EDWARD MURROUGH and to his heirs
and assigns forever. In Witness whereof the parties have set their hands and Seals
in presence of D. GAINES,   PETER **P** RUCKER
    ISAAC **+** TINSLEY, STEPHEN **JM** MECORMICKS JOHN RUCKER
                  THOMAS RUCKER

At a Court held for Essex County on the XXth day of July MDCCXXXI
PETER RUCKER, JOHN RUCKER & THOMAS RUCKER acknowledged their Deed Indented &
livery & Seizen endorsed to EDWARD MURROUGH which on his motion is admitted to
record

Also the same day ELIZABETH the Wife of the sd PETER RUCKER & SUSANNA the Wife of
the sd JOHN RUCKER by WILLIAM BEVERLEY Gent her the sd SUSANNAs Attorney came
into Court & freely relinquished their rights of dower in the land conveyed by this
Deed from their sd Husbands PETER RUCKER & JOHN RUCKER which is admitted to record.

    KNOW ALL MEN by these presents that wee PETER RUCKERand JOHN RUCKER of
the County of SPOTSILVANIA do stand bound unto EDWARD MURROUGH of the County of

Essex in the sum of One hundred pounds Curt. mony this 13th day of March 1730.
THE CONDITION of the above obligation is such that Whereas PETER RUCKER and JOHN
RUCKER (togeather) with THOMAS RUCKER have sold unto EDWARD MURROUGH land in
Essex County Now if the above bound when required make such assurances and conveyances of the land to the only use and benefit of the sd EDWARD MURROUGH his heirs
without any disturbance from any person whatsoever that then this obligation to be
void otherwise to stand in force
in presence of us D. GAINES,   PETER P RUCKER
      ISAAC + TINSLEY, JNO. VAWTER   JOHN RUCKER
   At a Court held for Essex County on the XXth day of July MDCCXXXI
PETER RUCKER & JOHN RUCKER ackowledged this bond to be their act & deed which is
admitted to record

pp.   THIS INDENTURE made the nineteenth day of July in the year of our Lord Christ
233-   one thousand seven hundred and Thirty One Between ROBERT BROOKE of the
236   Parish of St. Anns in the County of Essex of one part and CORNELIUS SALE of the
         Parish and County aforesaid of other part Witnesseth that sd ROBERT BROOKE for
sum of Two thousand five hundred pounds of Tobo and Caske hath sold unto the said
CORNELIUS SALE his heirs and assigns forever one parcel of land containing one hundred and twenty five acres saving to himself his proportionable part of two acres for
the use of the CHURCH which sd one hundred and twenty five acres of land was last
purchased by the said ROBERT BROOKE from ABRAHAM MAYFIELD by Deeds dated the
Second day of January 1727 and bounded by the lands in possession of the sd CORNELIUS
SALE and lands in the possession of THOMAS JONES, and of Colo. JOSEPH SMITH's Exrs,
with all & singular its appurtenances To Have and to Hold unto the said CORNELIUS SALE
his heirs and assigns. In Witness whereof the parties have set their hands and seals
in presence of MICHAEL WHARTON,   RO: BROOKE
      THOS. SAMUEL, ABNER GRAY
   At a Court held for Essex County the XXth day of July MDCCXXXI
ROBERT BROOKE Gent acknowledged this Deed indented & livery and Seizin thereon endorsed to CORNELIUS SALE which on his motion is admitted to record

pp.   THIS INDENTURE made the Seventeenth and eighteenth day of June in the year
236-   of our Lord Christ one thousand seven hundred and Thirty One Between WIL-
242   LIAM KARNALL & MARY KARNALL of the Parish of St. Anns in the County of
         Essex Planter of one part and JOHN MERRITT of the Pish of St. Anns in the
County aforesaid Planter of other part Witnesseth that said WM. KARNALL & MARY
KARNALL for the sum of Thirteen pounds doth sell unto the said JOHN MERRITT (in his
actual possession) one Plantacon or parcel of land with the appurtenances (by virtue of
a bargain and Sale for one year and of the Statute for transferring uses into possession)
and to his heirs and assigns one tract of land containing One hundred acres being in
the Parish of St. Anns in the County of Essex and is the Plantation & Tenements whereon the sd WILLIAM KARNELL & MARY KARNELL his Wife now Dwelleth comonly called
or known by the name of Mr. KENNYS PLANTACON, and is adjoyning unto the land of
Mr. EDMUND BAGGE and unto the land of JOSEPH MUNDAY commonly called JACKSONs
together with the houses buildings water ways and appurtenances belonging to the sd
land To Have and To Hold unto the said JOHN MERRITT his heirs & assigns forever. In
Witness whereof the parties have set their hands and Seals
in presence of NATHAL. FOGG,   WILLIAM + KARNALL
      ℼ ROBERT WALSH, ROBERT ℼGRISUM,   MARY ⌐ KARNALL
      JOHN MERRITT

At a Court held for Essex County the XXth day of July MDCCXXXI
This Release of Land indented from WILLIAM KARNALL & MARY his Wfie to JOHN MER-
RITT was proved by the Oaths of all the Witnesses thereto & on his motion is admitted to
record

       KNOW ALL MEN by these presents that We WILLIAM KARNALL & MARY KAR-
NALL are held and firmly bound unto JOHN MERRITT in the sum of One hundred & fifty
pounds Sterling this Eighteenth day of June Anno Dom 1731

THE CONDITION of the above obligation is such that if said WILLIAM KARNALL & MARY
his Wife shall in all things keep all & singular the conditions in the Indenture which
ought to be kept that then this oblgiation shall be void otherwise to remain in force
in presence of NATHAL. FOGG,   WILLIAM KARNALL
      ROBERT WALCH, ROBERT GRISUM   MARY KARNALL
      JOHN MERRITT
    At a Court held for Essex County on the XXth day of July MDCCXXXI
The Pfection of this bond from WILLIAM KARNALL & MARY his Wife to JOHN MERRITT
was proved by the oaths of the witnesses thereto & on his motion is admitted to record

pp.   KNOW ALL MEN by these presents that I JNO. WALKER Mercht. of WHITEHAVEN
242- in the County of CUMBERLAND have for good considerations nominated RICHD.
243   TYLER Gent my true and lawfull Attorney for me to recover and receive all debts
       of mony and Tobacco that belong to me giving my sd Attorney my full power in
the premises in my name to perform all & singular such things as shall be necessary
touching the premises as fully as if I the sd JNO. WALKER was personally present ratti-
fying wtsoever my said Attorney shall do. In Witness whereof I have hereunto set my
hand and seal the 23d day of June in the year of our Lord 1731
in presents of JOHN TYLER,   JOHN WALKER
      HENRY YOUNG
    At a Court held for Essex County on the XXth day of July MDCCXXXI
This Powr. of Attorney from JOHN WALKER to RICHD. TYLER Gent was proved by the
Oaths of the witnesses thereto & is admitted to record

pp.   KNOW ALL MEN by these presents that we JOHN BATES, SAML. CLAYTON &
243- SAMUEL FARGUSON are held and firmly bound unto our Sovrn. Lord GEORGE the
244   2d. in the just sum of Ten thousand pounds of tobacco this XXIth day of July Anno
       Dom MDCCXXXI
THE CONDITION of the above obligation is such that whereas JOHN BATES hath obtained
a Licence to keep an ORDINARY at TAPPA. if therefore the sd JOHN BATES doth constantly find & provide in his ORDINARY good wholesome and cleanly lodgeing & diet for
travellers & Stableage fodder & provender or pasturage as the Season of the year shall
require for their Horses during the term of one whole year from the date hereof &
shall not suffer any unlawfull gaming in his House nor on the Sabbath day suffer any
to Tipple more than is necessary that then the above obligation to be void else to
remain in force
                              JOHN BATES
                SAMUEL CLAYTON   SAMLL. FARGUSON
    At a Court held for Essex County the XXIst day of July MDCCXXXI
JOHN BATES, SAMUEL CLAYTON & SAMUEL FARGUSON acknowledged this bond to be
their act & deed which is admitted to record

pp.   KNOW ALL MEN by these presents that we JOHN BOUGHAN and SUSANNA his Wife
244-   of the Parish of St. Anns in the County of Essex have for a valuable considera-
245   tion to us paid by JOHN MOTLEY of the Parish and County aforesd sold and de-
        livered unto the sd JOHN MOTLEY one negro girl called Beck being about nine
years of age, and do oblige our selves to defend the sd Negro girl from all persons whatsoever laying any claim thereunto. In Witness our hands and seals this 12th day of
June 1714.
in presence of THOMAS COOPER,   JOHN BOUGHAN
        WILLIAM WILSON   SUSANN ✝ BOUGHAN
    The above sd Negro girl was born the 20th day of April 1705.
    At a Court held for Essex County on the XVIIIth day of August MDCCXXXI
This Bill of Sale of a Negro girl with the age underwritten was on the motion of JOHN
BATES admitted to record

pp.   THIS INDENTURE made the twenty first day of September in the year of our Lord
245-   one thousand seven hundred and thirty one Between JOHN BRYANT and FRAN-
246   CES his Wife of the one part and PETER RICHESON of the other part Whereas
        WILLIAM YOUNG and the sd CATHERINE his Wife and ROBERT RANSONE and
FRANCES his Wife were seized in fee in the right of the sd CATHERINE and FRANCES of
and in a certain plantation and tract of land with the appurtenances being in the
Parish of Southfarnham upon the DRAGON SWAMP in the County of Essex containing
three hundred and Six acres of land commonly called by the names of THOMAS's QUAR-
TER and so being thereof seized by their certain Indentures of Lease and Release
bearing date the twentieth & twenty first day of February in the year of our Lord one
thousand seven hundred and fifteen did convey the said Plantation for a valuable consideration unto the said PETER RICHESON his heirs and assigns and did acknowledge the
Indentures before the County Court of Essex at a Court held the twenty first day of
February in the year of our Lord one thousand seven hundred and fifteen aforesd the
sd CATHERINE and FRANCES being first privily examined and thereupon the sd Indentures were recorded but by the Omission and negligence of the Clerk of the sd Court the
private Examination of the sd CATHERINE and FRANCES was not recorded
  Now This Indenture Witnesseth that the sd JOHN BRYANT and FRANCES his Wife for the
sum of three pounds Eighteen shillings Current mony of Virginia have confirmed to
the sd PETER RICHESON his heirs and assigns being in his full possession and Seizin of
all the Estate title that sd JOHN BRYANT and FRANCES his Wife have in the lands To Have
and To Hold to the sd PETER RICHESON his heirs and assigns. In Witness whereof the sd
partys have set their hands & Seals
in presence of RICHD. TYLER JUNR.,   JOHN BRYANT
        CHARLES PAIN, WILLIAM RICHESON   FRAS. BRYANT
    At a Court held for Essex County on the XXIst day of September MDCCXXXI
JOHN BRYANT & FRANCES his Wife (the said FRANCES being first privily examined by
JAMES GARNETT Gent) acknowledged their Deed indented to PETER RICHESON which on
his motion is admitted to record

pp.   KNOW ALL MEN by these presents that we BENJA. WINSLOW and SIMON MILLER
246-   of the County of Essex are held and firmly bound unto NATHANIEL FOGG in the
247   sum of Twenty pounds Sterl. this XXIst day of September MDCCXXXI
        THE CONDITION of the above obligation is such that Whereas Judgment being this
day given in Essex County Court unto the sd NATHANIEL FOGG against BENJA. WINSLOW
in an action of Debt depending between the sd NATHANIEL FOGG & the sd BENJA.
WINSLOW. the sd BENJA. WINSLOW had an Appeal granted him to the 8th day of the next

General Court giveing Security according to Law if therefore the sd BENJA. WINSLOW
Appellant as aforesd shall appear at the next General Court and prosecute the sd Appeal
and perform the Judgment of the sd Court and pay the damages of fifteen p cent which
the Law gives upon the principall Debt and costs of the County Court this day recovered
as aforesd if cast in the sd Appeal that then this obligation to be void otherwise to stand
in full force

BENJA. WINSLOW
SIMON MILLER

At a Court held for Essex County on the XXIst day of September MDCCXXXI
BENJAMIN WINSLOW & SIMON MILLER acknowledged this bond to be their acts and deeds
which is admitted to record.

pp.   KNOW ALL MEN by these presents that I WILLIAM WATTKINS of the Parish of
247   Hannover in the County of PRINCE WILLIAM do appoint Mr. THOMAS MOORE of
252   the Parish of Southfarnham in the County of Essex to be my lawfull Attorney in
my place to acknowledge to JOSEPH DIMILLO in the County Court of Essex Deeds
of Lease and Release bearing date the twelfth & thirteenth of November in the year of
our Lord one thousand seven hundred and Thirty and One. In Witness whereof I have
set my hand & seal the day and year above written

in the presence of JOHN HILTON,   WILLIAM X WATKINS
      WILLIAM (S) DELAYNEY

At a Court held for Essex County the XVIth day of November MDCCXXXI
This Power of Attorney from WILLIAM WATTKINS to THOS. MOORE was proved by the
Oaths of JOHN HILTON and WM. DELANEY Witnesses thereto and admitted to record

THIS INDENTURE made the twelfth & thirteenth day of November in the year of
our Lord God one thousand seven hundred thirty and One Between WILLIAM WATTKINS
and ALICE his Wife of the Parish of Hanover in the County of PRINCE WILLIAM of the
one part and JOSEPH DIMILLO of the Parish of Southfarnham in the County of Essex
Planter of the other part Witnesseth that the sd WILLIAM WATTKINS & ALICE his Wife
for the sum of nine hundred pounds of Lawfull tobacco to them in hand paid do hereby
sell unto the sd JOSEPH DIMILLO in his actual possession now being by virtue of Indenture for one year and by force of the statute for the transferring uses into possession
and to his heirs forever all that plantation tract of land containing three hundred
acres which said land is now adjoyning to or part of the sd Plantation & tract of land
whereon SAMUEL HALLEWRIN now Dwelleth being in the Parish of Southfarnham in
the County of Essex and all Orchards gardings advantages whatsoever To Have and To
Hold unto the sd JOSEPH DIMILLO his heirs and assigns forever. In Witness whereof the
partics above named have set their hands and Seals

in presence of JOHN HILTON,   WILLIAM † WATTKINS
      MILLECED (her M mark) HALLURING   ALICE X WATTKINS

At a Court held for Essex County the XVIth day of November MDCCXXXI
This Release of land indented from WILLIAM WATTKINS and ALICE his Wife to JOSEPH
DIMILLO was proved by the Oaths of all the Witnesses thereto and the sd ALICE being
first privily examined by THOMAS STHRESHLY JUNR. Gent. freely acknowledged the sd
Release to the sd JOSEPH DIMILLO which on his motion is admitted to record

pp.   THIS INDENTURE made the Second day of October in the year of our Lord one
252-   thousand seven hundred and thirty one Between WILLIAM MOSELEY of the
255   County of GOOCHLAND of one part and ROBERT BROOKE of the County of Essex of
the other part Whereas EDWARD MOSELEY late of the Parish of St. Anns in the

County of Essex aforesd Gent deced in and by his last Will and Testament in writting bearing date the twenty third day of January in the year one thousand seven hundred and Twenty Six among other things did declare his will to be "that after the decease of his loving Wife ELIZABETH MOSELEY all his land not before bequeathed except his part of the WHITE OAK SWAMP after in his sd Will disposed of shou'd be for WILLIAM MOSE-LEY" and did give and bequeath as aforesd the sd remainder except as aforesd to him the sd WILLIAM MOSELEY Son of BENJAMIN MOSELEY to him and his heirs lawfully begotten for ever "and for want of such heirs to his the sd Testators next heir at law" as by the the sd Will relation being had thereunto may more fully & at large appear And Whereas the sd WILLIAM MOSELEY the Son of the said BENJAMIN MOSELEY is since dead without issue of his body lawfully begotten whereby the reversion of the sd lands after the death of the sd Testators Wife ELIZABETH MOSELEY doth of right belong unto sd WIL-LIAM MOSELEY party to these presents as Nephew and heir at Law to the sd Testator EDWARD MOSELEY. Now This Indenture Witnesseth that in consideration of the sum of twenty two pounds Eight shillings Currt. money to the sd WILLIAM MOSELEY paid by ROBERT BROOKE he the sd WILLIAM MOSELEY doth confirm unto the said ROBERT BROOKE his heirs & assigns the reversion immediately when it shall happen after the death of the sd ELIZABETH MOSELEY the widow & Relict of the sd Testator EDWARD MOSELEY of all the land whatsoever so given by sd EDWARD MOSELEY to the sd WILLIAM MOSELEY Son of BENJAMIN MOSELEY after the decease of his the sd Testators Wife ELIZABETH MOSELEY in his last Will as aforesd and more especially to a certain parcel of land in the Parish of St. Anns in the County of Essex containing one hundred acres and next adjoyning to a certain tract of land formerly purchased by ROBERT BROOKE Father of the sd ROBERT BROOKE party to these presents of the sd EDWARD MOSELEY being part of the land given and devised by the sd EDWARD MOSELEY in his Last Will & Testament and all the Houses, Orchards, woods and appurtenances whatsoever belonging To Have and To Hold unto the sd ROBERT BROOKE immediately when it shall happen after the death of the sd ELIZA-BETH MOSELEY Widow of the sd Testator. In Witness whereof I have set my hand and Seal in presence of ROBT. ROSE,   WM. MOSELEY
          THOS. HAWKINS, ELIAS NEWMAN
  At a Court held for Essex County on the XVIth day of November MDCCXXXI
This Deed indented from WILLIAM MOSELEY to ROBERT BROOKE Gent was proved by the Oaths of all the Witnesses thereto & on his motion is admitted to record

pp.   KNOW ALL MEN by these presents that wee JOHN EVANS JUNR. & JOHN EVANS are
255-   held and firmly bound unto our Soveraign Lord GEORGE in the sum of One hun-
256   dred pounds Sterl. this XVIth day of November MDCCXXXI
          THE CONDITION of this Obligation is such that Whereas the above bound JOHN
EVANS JUNR. is by the Court of Essex County licensed to keep the FERRY usually called
PISCATAWAY FERRY Now if the sd JOHN EVANS JUNR. shall constantly keep two Sufficient boats (to wit) a foot boat & a horse boat with two able hands to attend the same
and also give passage without delay to the Inhabitants of this County & to such Publick
messages and expresses as may be mentioned in & by an Act of Assembly intituled an
Act for the better regulation & Settlement of Ferrys & for dispatch of Publick Expresses
to be Ferry Free & do perform all & whatsoever the Law enjoyne & truly & faithfully
comply with the duty & business of a FERRY KEEPER that then the above obligation to
be void otherwise to be in full force
in presence of HENRY ROBINSON   JNO. EVANS JUNR.
                                                       JNO. EVANS

At a Court held for Essex County on the XVIth day of November MDCCXXXI
JOHN EVANS JUNR. & JOHN EVANS acknowledged this bond to be their act & deed which
is admitted to record

pp.   KNOW ALL MEN by these presents that We JAMES GRIFFING, THOMAS BURNETT &
256-   WILLIAM ALLEN are held and firmly bound unto our Sovrn. Lord GEORGE the iid
257   in the just sum of Ten thousand pounds of tobacco this XVIth day of November
         MDCCXXXI
THE CONDITION of the above obligation is such that Whereas JAMES GRIFFIN hath obtained a licence to keep an ORDINARY at his House in TAPPA: TOWN if therefore sd
JAMES GRIFFIN doth constantly find & provided in his ORDINARY good wholesome and
cleanly lodgeing & diet for Travellers & Stableage fodder & provender or pasturage as
the Season of the year shall required for their Horses during the term of one whole
year from the date hereof & shall not suffer any unlawfull gaming in his House nor on
the Sabbath day suffer any to Tipple more than is necessary that then the above obligation to be void else to remain in force
in presence of HENRY ROBINSON   JAMES GRIFFING
                                       THOS. ₿ BURNETT WM   ALLEN
    At a Court held for Essex County on the XVIth day of November MDCCXXXI
JAMES GRIFFING, THOMAS BURNETT & WILLIAM ALLEN acknowledged this bond to be
their acts and deeds which is admitted to record

pp.   THIS INDENTURE made the 15th and 16th day of November in the year of our
257-   Loard one thousand seven hundred and thirty one Between THOMAS FITS JEFF-
262   RESS of the County of Essex in the Parish of Southfarnham of one part and
         ROBERT LEVERIT JUNER of the aforesd County and Parish of the other part Witt-
nesseth that the sd THOMAS FITS JEFFRESS by Indenture bearing date the day before the
date hereof did sell unto the sd ROBERT LEVERIT JUNR. all that parcell of land in the
aforesd County and Parish and bounded by the land of WILLIAM CHEANEY deced & the
land of ANNE COX and the land now in the possession of Mr. ROBERT BAYLOR and
binding upon one of the Branches of the DRAGON SWAMP oposite to the land of WIL-
LIAM COLE and comonly known by the land of RODGER BURGINE containing one hundred acres which sd land or woodland with all ways trees and all things being and appertaining To Have and To Hold unto the sd ROBERT LEVERETT his heirs and assigns
dureing the term of one year to the end that by virtue thereof and of the Statute for
transferring uses into possession that the sd ROBERT LEVERIT JUNR. may be in actual
possession of the sd premises Now This Indenture Witnesseth that the sd THOMAS FITS
JEFFRESS for the sum of Eleven pounds of good and lawfull Mony Curt. of Virginia and
the Sum of Thirteen hundred pounds of good and lawfull Tobacco in Caske paid by the sd
ROBERT LEVERIT unto the said THOMAS FITS JEFFRESS whereof he the sd THOMAS FITS
JEFFRESS hath sold unto the sd ROBERT LEVERIT JUNR all the aforesd parcell of land and
all the houses Orchards and other things appertaining To Have and To Hold unto the sd
ROBERT LEVERIT JUNR his heirs and assigns forever. In Witness whereof the sd parties
have set their hands and Seals
in presence of WM. COVINGTON,   THOMAS ₷ FITZ JEFFRESS
        SAMLL. FARGESON, THO: EDMONDSON
    At a Court held for Essex County on the XVIth day of November MDCCXXXI
THOMAS FITS JEFFRESS acknowledged this his Lease of Land to ROBERT LEVERETT JUNR.
which on his mocon is admitted to record
    Also the same day ELIZABETH the Wife of the sd THOMAS FITS JEFFRESS came into Court

and freely relinquished her right of dower in the land conveyed by this Release to the sd ROBERT LEVERETT JUNR. & admitted to record

KNOW ALL MEN by these presents that I THOS. FITS JEFFRESS of the County of Essex am held and firmly bound unto ROBERT LEVERIT JUNR. in the just sum of Forty pounds of good & lawfull mony of Virginia this 16th day of November 1731

THE CONDITION of this obligation is such that if THOS. FITS JEFFRESS shall at all times hereafter execute & keep every condition mentioned in the Indenture and THOS. FITS JEFFRESS & his Wife to ackowledge the sd Deeds in open Court when required that then the above obligation to be void or otherwise to stand in force

in presence of WM. COVINGTON　　　　　　　　　　　THOMAS ᨃFITS JEFFRESS
　　SAMLL. FARGESON, THO: EDMONDSON

At a Court held for Essex County on the XVIth day of November MDCCXXXI THOMAS FITS JEFFRESS acknowledged this bond to be his act & deed which is admitted to record

pp. 262-263　KNOW ALL MEN by these presents that I JOHN CORRIE of the Kingdom of Great Britain Mercht. do hereby appoint WILLIAM BEVERLEY of the County of Essex in the Colony of Virginia Gent my true and lawfull Attorney to receive from all and any person all goods debts belonging to me the sd JOHN CORRIE by Bill note or otherwise giving unto my sd Attorney my full power to sue prosecute any pesons whatsoever as also for any wrong or injury done to me by any person & upon recovery to give acquitances which shall be as sufficient as given by me confirming whatsoever my said Attorney shall lawfully do about the premises. In Witness whereof I have set my hand and seal this ninth day of August Anno Dom MDCCXXXI

in presence of HENRY ROBINSON　　　　　　　　JOHN CORRIE
　　MARK WEEKES

At a Court continued & held for Essex County at TAPPA. on the XXIId day of September MDCCXXXI This Power of Attorney from JOHN CORRIE to WILLIAM BEVERLEY gent was proved by the oath of MARK WEEKES one of the witnesses thereto

At a Court held for Essex County on the XVIth day of November MDCCXXXI This Power of Attorney from JOHN CORRIE Merchant to WILLIAM BEVERLEY Gent was further proved by the Oath of HENRY ROBINSON an other of the witnesses thereto & admitted to record

pp. 263-264　KNOW ALL MEN by these presents that we NICHOLAS SMITH & HENRY REEVES are held and firmly bound unto our Sovrn. Lord the King in the sum of Thirty thousand two hundred & ninety four and an half pounds of Lawfull merchantable tobacco. In Witness our hands this XVIIth day of November Anno Dom MDCCXXXI

THE CONDITION of the above obligation is such that Whereas NICHOLAS SMITH is admitted COLLECTOR of the County of Essex Now if the sd NICHOLAS SMITH shall faithfully collect the sum of Fifteen thousand one hundred & forty seven & an half pounds of Tobacco this day levyed by the Court of the aforesd County of Essex to the respective Creditors therein mentioned that then the above obligation to be void else remain in full force

in presence of W. BEVERLEY,　　　　　　　　NICHO. SMITH
　　HENRY ROBINSON　　　　　　　　　　　H. REEVES

At a Court continued & held for Essex County on the XVIIth day of November MDCCXXXI NICHOLAS SMITH & HENRY REEVES ackowledged this bond to be their act & deed which is admitted to record

pp. THIS INDENTURE made the fifteenth and sixteenth day of December in the fourth
264- year of the Reign of our Sovrn. Lord KING GEORGE the Second Anno Domini One
271 thousand seven hundred & thirty one Between WILLIAM MACKDONEL of the
Parish of St. Anns in the County of Essex Planter of one part and JOHN CARAGILL
Shoemaker of the Pish & County aforesd of the other part Witnesseth that for the sum of
three thousand five hundred pounds of Tobacco unto the sd WILLIAM MACKDONAL paid
he the sd WILLIAM MACKDONAL hath sold unto sd JOHN CARAGIL (in his actual possession now being by Virtue of Indenture of Bargain & Sale for one whole year and by
force of the Statute for the transferring of uses into possession) and to him and his
heirs forever all that tract of land containing fifty acres being part of a greater tract
of land being in the Parish and County aforesd being bounded beginning at a marked
red Oak by the MAIN ROAD and runing thence to a white Oak upon FOGGs line thence
runing along a Swamp called DOLLS MIRE to a marked white Oak, from thence to the
beginning tree, and all dwelling houses, kitchings, buildings, tobacco houses, Orchards & appurtenances whatsoever belonging To Have and To Hold the sd dividend of
land to the sole use & behoof of him the sd JOHN CARAGILL his heirs and Assigns forever. In Witness whereof the parties have set their hands and Seals
in the presence of RICHD. PARRY,   WILLIAM MACKDANNEL
        JNO. NANCE, the mark of ⊕ JAMES MACKDONEL
At a Court held for Essex County on the XXIst day of December MDCCXXXI
WILLIAM MACKDANNELL acknowledged this his Release of land Indented to JOHN
CARAGAN which on his motion is admitted to record
        KNOW ALL MEN by these presents that WILM. MACKDONEL of the Parish of St.
Anns in the County of Essex am bound unto JOHN CARRAGIL Shoemaker in the full sum
of Seven thousd. pounds of tobacco
THE CONDITION of the above obligation is that if WILLIAM MACKDONEL his heirs and
assigns shall at all times fullfill all articles mentioned in certain Indentures that then
this obligation to be void otherwise to stand in full force. Signed Sealed & delivered the
Sixteenth day of December 1731
in presence of RICHD. PARRY,   WILLIAM MACKDANNEL
        JNO. NANCE, the mark of ⊕ JAMES MACKDONEL
At a Court held for Essex County on the XXIst day of December MDCCXXXI
WILLIAM MACKDANNEL acknowledged this bond to be his act & deed which is admitted
to record

p. KNOW ALL MEN by these presents that we FRANCES LATON, JOHN EDMONDSON &
272 WILLIAM WORTHAM are held and firmly bound unto our Sovrn. Lord GEORGE
the 2d. in the full sum of Ten thousand pounds of Tobacco this XVIIIth day of
January Ano. Dom MDCCXXXI
THE CONDITION of the above obligation is such that Whereas said FRANCES LATON hath
obtained a License to keep an ORDINARY at her House in St. Anns Pish if therefore the
sd FRANCES LATON doth constantly find & provide in her ORDINARY good wholesome
and cleanly lodgeing & diet for Travellers & Stableage fodder & provender or pasturage
as the Season shall require for their Horses during the term of one whole year from the
date hereof & shall not suffer any unlawfull gaming in her House nor on the Sabbath
day suffer any to Tipple more than is necessary that then the above obligation to be
void else to remain in force
in presence of MARK WEEKES   FRANCES ⨍ LATON
                            JOHN EDMONDSON   WM. WORTHAM
At a Court held for Essex County on the XVIIIth day of January MDCCXXXI

FRANCES LATON, JOHN EDMONDSON & WILLIAM WORTHAM acknowledged this bond to be their act & deed which is admitted to record

p. 273   TO ALL TO WHOM these presents shall come Know Ye that Whereas JAMES & GEORGE NEWBELL hath formerly purchased a tract of land of BENJA. WATTKINS now deced containing two hundred acres more or less Joyntly togeather and never hath made any devision of the same untill now, Know ye that we the sd GEORGE and JAMES NEWBELL make a devision of the same as followeth vizt. that is to say begining at a corner red Oake standing at the end of a point by the head of a Marsh upon PEANKETANK SWAMP runing thence along a line of marked trees Southwardly to a tobacco house thence keeping near the same Course along a line of marked trees to the extend bounds to the line of the land whereon JAMES NEWBELL lives by a Pond, and the westermost part of the sd land is the choice or lot belonging to JAMES NEWBELL and the Eastermost part is the lot or part belonging to GEORGE NEWBELL. Given under our hands and Seals this 19th day of Janry. 1731
in presence of WM. COVINGTON   JAMES **M** NEWBELL
WM. COLE, HENRY **A** GRIMSTEAD   GEORGE **F** NEWBELL
At a Court held for Essex County on the XVth day of February MDCCXXXI
JAMES NEWBELL & GEORGE NEWBELL acknowledged this their Deed Poll for the partition of their land which on their motion is admitted to record

pp. 273-277   THIS INDENTURE made the Sixteenth and Seventeenth day of August in the year of our Lord one thousand Seven hundred & thirty one Between RICHARD COVINGTON of the Parish of St. Anns & County of Essex of one part & THOMAS WARING of the Parish & County aforesd of the other part Witnesseth that the sd RICHARD COVINGTON for the sum of fifteen pounds Eight shillings to JOHN SMITH of the Parish and County aforesd in hand paid whereof he the said RICHARD and JOHN doth hereby acknowledge and therewth fully discharge the sd THOMAS and by these presents doth grant unto the said THOMAS WARING his heirs and assignes thirty nine acres one hundred and twenty eight perches of land being in the Parish and County aforesd and bounded beginning at a Stooping dogwood Corner tree of the land of ROBERT PARKER late deced thence No. W. to a Corner Gum of his the sd RICHARD COVINGTONs & BENJAMIN WINSLOWs land in the Main Run of a Creek thence down the sd Creek to the beginning all which premises are now in the actual possession of him the sd THOMAS WARING by Virtue of one Indenture made for one year and all the Estate Right & demand whatsoever of him the sd RICHARD COVINGTON in the same Together with all woods timber & appurtenances belonging To Have and To Hold unto him the sd THOMAS WARING his heirs and assignes. In Witness whereof the parties have set their hands and Seals in presence of SIMON MILLER,
RICHD. WINSLOW, WM. SLOSS   RICHD. COVINGTON
At a Court held for Essex County on the XVth day of February MDCCXXXI
RICHARD COVINGTON acknowledged this his Release of land Indented to THOMAS WARING Gent which on his motion is admitted to record

pp. 277-278   TO ALL TO WHOM these presents shall come Know yee that I THOMAS COLEMAN of the County of KING & QUEEN doth hearby for divers good causes but more especially for the love and affection that I have and beare unto my loving Son ROBERT COLEMAN do freely give unto him all that parcell of land containing five hundred and forty acres in the County of Essex in the Parish of Southfarnham & bounded begining at a Corner Maple standing by the Run side at the mouth of the REEDY BRANCH runing thence up the several courses of the sd Branch to a Corner

white Oak of HENRY BAKERs thence South West along BAKERs line to a Pine where
lately stood a corner red Oake of HALLIARDs thence with HALLIARDs line a South by
East Course to a white Oake Corner to the sd HILLARD standing by the BEST LAND SWAMP
thence down the sd Swamp its several courses to the begining it being a tract of land
that was lately found to Escheat from one STEPHEN BEMBRIDGE and all the land within
the before recited bounds with all the appurtenances thereunto belonging I freely
give unto my before mentioned loving Son ROBERT COLEMAN & to his heirs forever
only reserving to my self the priviledge of makeing use of or occupying any part or
parcel thereof during my natural life. In Witness whereof I have set my hand & seal
this 15th day of February in the year of our Lord God one thousand seven hundred and
thirty one
in presence of WM.COVINGTON,   THOS.COLEMAN
        MARY CRANE, WM.COVINGTON JUNR.
    At a Court held for Essex County on the XVth day of February MDCCXXXI
THOMAS COLEMAN acknowledged his Deed Poll to his Son ROBERT COLEMAN which on his
motion is admitted to record

pp.   TO ALL TO WHOM these presents shall come I HENRY NEWTON of the County of
278-   Essex for the love and good will and affection I have and doe bear to my Son
279   HENRY NUTON JUNR. of the County aforesd have given and granted to my Son
         HENRY NUTON JUNR. his heirs & assigns a certain peice of land lying in the
County aforesd & adjoyning to the land that my sd Son HENRY bought of THOMAS NUTON
being about the quantity of forty acres bounded begining at a red Oak standing on the
side of the CHURCH ROAD and runing a strate corse to a tall Popler standing at the head
of a branch or bottom nigh the old tobo. house & from the sd Popler another strait corse
along a line of marked trees to a white Oak standing on the North side of the MAIN
COUNTY ROAD and runing up the sd Road to the line of Capt. SALVATOR MUSCOEs land &
along the sd MUSCOEs line to the foot of the hills by the WHITE OAK SWAMP & along the
foot of the sd Hills to the CHURCH ROAD & thence along the CHURCH ROAD to the first
mentioned red Oak it being part of my track of land I now live on To Have and To Hold
the sd parcell of land unto him the sd HENRY NEWTON JUNR. his heirs etc forever with
all the profits & appurtenances thereunto belonging absolutely without any manner of
Condition as I the sd HENRY NUTON absolutely & of my own accord let & put in farther
Testamoney in Witness whereof I have hereunto set my hand & Seale this 14th day of
Febry. 1731/2.
in presence of us JOHN ╪ KERGAN,   HENRY O NUTON
        JAMES DAVIS
    At a Court held for Essex County on the XXIst day of March MDCCXXXI
HENRY NEWTON acknoweldged this his Deed indented and livery and seizen thereon en-
doresed to HENRY NEWTON JUNR. which on his motion is admitted to record

pp.   KNOW ALL MEN by these presents that I OBADIAH COOKSON of BOSTON in the
279-   County of SUFFOLK and Province of MASSACHUSETS BAY in NEW ENGLAND Mer-
280   chant have named and do appoint my trusty & well beloved friend WILLIAM
         DAINGERFIELD Esqr. of Essex County in Virginia my true and lawfull Attorney
for me to demand sue for and receive of JOHN BATES of Essex County aforesd his heirs
etc. all debts to me due and owing giving my sd Attorney my full power to use all such
things as shall be necessary for the recovering of the sd Debt and generally to do in the
premises as fully as I myself might do if personally present, ratifying all and whatsoever my sd Attorney shall lawfully do therein. In Witness whereof I have hereunto set
my hand and Seale in Essex County aforesd this fifteenth day of March in the year of

our Lord one thousand seven hundred and thirty one and in the fourth year of the
Reign of our Soveraign Lord GEORGE the Second of Great Britain, france & Ireland etc.
in presence of PITT. SCANDRETT,   OBADH. COOKSON
    WM. DAINGERFIELD JUNR., ALEXANDER PARKER
  At a Court held for Essex County on the XXIst day of March MDCCXXXI
OBADIAH COOKSON acknowledged his Power of Attorney to WILLIAM DAINGERFIELD
Esqr. which on his motion is admitted to record

pp.   KNOW ALL MEN by these presents that I SARAH SMITH of the County of Essex and
280- Parish of St. Anns do constitute and appoint my friend BENJA. WINSLOW to be my
287   lawfull Attorney to acknowledge my right of Dower of a tract of land unto
       RICHARD COVINGTON or to his assigns. Witness my hand & Seal this 21st day of
March 1731/2
in presence of THOS. HAWKINS,   SARAH SMITH
    FRANCIS COVINGTON
  At a Court held for Essex County on the XXIst day of March MDCCXXXI
This Power of Attorney from SARAH SMITH to BENJA. WINSLOW was proved by the Oaths
of all the Witnesses thereto and admitted to record

      THIS INDENTURE made the twenty first and twentyeth day of March in the year
of our Lord God one thousand seven hundred and thirty one Between JOHN SMITH and
SARAH his Wife of the Pish of St. Anns in the County of Essex of one part and RICHARD
COVINGTON of the Parish & County aforesd of the other part Witnesseth that sd JOHN
SMITH and SARAH his Wife for the sum of Forty two pounds Sixteen shillings Current
money of Virga. hath sold unto sd RICHARD COVINGTON in his actual possession now
being one parcel of land or woodland with the appurtenances by virute of one Indenture for one whole year and the Statute for transferring uses into possession and to his
heirs forever all that parcel of land or wood land ground containing One hundred and
thirty two acres begining at a Corner white Oak to the sd COVINGTON & SMITH standing
in a large Branch and runing along a line of marked trees which did divide this land
from the land of the sd COVINGTON South East to two mark't pessimmon trees standing
by a large Marsh thence up the Marsh side to the mouth of the HORSEPEN CREEK thence
up the sd Creek to a large branch that divides this land from the land of PAGETTs thence
up the sd Branch to two marked white Oakes thence along a line of marked trees South
West to a Corner Ring Oak standing in the line of BENJA. WINSLOWs at or near the head
of another small Branch then down the sd Branch the severall courses and windings to
the beginning And all houses, outhouses, tobacco houses and appurtenances whatsoever thereunto belonging To Have and To Hold unto the said RICHARD COVINGTON his
heirs & assigns forever. In Witness whereof the parties have set their hands and Seals
in presence of THOS. HAWKINS,   JOHN SMITH
    FRANCIS COVINGTON, THOS. COVINGTON   SARAH SMITH
 At a Court held for Essex County at Tappa. on the XXIst day of March MDCCXXXI
JOHN SMITH & SARAH SMITH by BENJAMIN WINSLOW her Attorney acknowledged this
their release of land indented to RICHARD COVINGTON & the same being also proved by
the Oaths of all the Witnesses thereto on said RICHARDs motion is admitted to record

pp.   THIS INDENTURE made the twenty first day of March in the year of our Lord one
287- thousand seven hundred thirty one Between JOHN COOKE of St. Anns Parish in
289   County of Essex Planter of one part and EDWARD MASTERSON of the Parish and
      County aforesd Carpenter of other part Witnesseth that for the sum of two thou-
sand seven hundred and forty pounds of lawfull tobacco unto the sd JOHN COOKE in hand

paid by the sd EDWARD MASTERSON hath granted unto the sd EDWARD MASTERSON his
heirs and assigns forever all the half part or moiety of a GRIST MILL comonly called by
the name of TANDYS MILL with the land and appurtenances to the sd moiety belonging
and all the Estate rights and demands whatsoever of him the sd JOHN COOK To Have and
To Hold the said GRIST MILL with the land and appurtenances whatsoever hereby
granted unto the sd EDWARD MASTERSON his heirs and assigns forever. In Witness
whereof the parties have set their hands & Seals
in presence of RO: PARKER,   JOHN COOK
         SIMON MILLER
  At a Court held for Essex County at Tappa. on the XXIst day of March MDCCXXXI
JOHN COOK acknowledged this his Deed Poll to EDWARD MASTERSON which on his motion
is admitted to record

pp.   KNOW ALL MEN by these presents that we WILLIAM DUNN JUNR., EDWARD HAR-
289-   PER & WILLIAM GRAY are held and firmly bound unto our Sovrn. Lord GEORGE
290   the 2d. in the Just sum of ten thousand pounds of tobacco this XXIst day of
       March MDCCXXXI
THE CONDITION of the above obligation is such that Whereas the above bound WILLIAM
DUNN JUNR. & EDWARD HARPER have obtained a Licence to keep an ORDINARY at PER-
KINS ORDNY. if therefore the sd WILLIAM DUNN JR. & EDWARD HARPER do constantly
find & provide in their ORDINARY good wholesome Cleanly lodgeing and diet for Travellers and Stableage fodder and provender or pasturage as the Season shall require for
their Horses during the term of one year from the date hereof and not suffer any
unlawfull gameing in their House nor on the Sabbath suffer any to drink more then is
necessary that then this obligation to be null & of none effect else to stand in force
                                         WILLIAM DUNN JR.
                            EDWARD HARPER   WM. GRAY
  At a Court held for Essex County on the XXIst day of March MDCCXXXI
WILLIAM DUNN JR., EDWARD HARPER & WILLIAM GRAY acknowledged this bond to be
their act and deed which is admitted to record

pp.   KNOW ALL MEN by these presents that we THOMAS HARDY & JOHN FARGUSON are
290-   held and firmly bound unto our Soveraign Lord GEORGE the Second in the sum of
291   ten thousand pounds of Tobacco this XXIst day of March MDCCXXXI
       THE CONDITION of the above obligation is such that Whereas THOMAS HARDY hath
obtained a Licence to keep an ORDINARY at his House if therefore the said THOMAS doe
truly find and provide in his ORDINARY good wholesome Cleanly lodgeing and diet for
travellers and Stableage fodder and provender or pasturage as the Season of the year
shall require during the term of one year from the day of the date hereof and not suffer any unlawfull gameing in his House nor on the Sabbath suffer any to Drink more
then is necessary that then this obligation to be void else to stand in force
                                         THOS. HARDY
                                         JOHN FARGESON
  At a Court held for Essex County on the XXIst day of March MDCCXXXI
THOMAS HARDY acknowledged this bond to be his act & deed which is admitted to record

pp.   KNOW ALL MEN by these presents that we JOHN EDMONDSON of Essex County
291-   ORDINARY KEEPER & THOMAS EDMONDSON JUNR. of the same are held and firmly
292   bound unto JOHN FARGUSON in the sum of Two thousand pounds Sterl. the 15th
       day of Aprill Anno. Dom 1730
Whereas the above named JOHN FARGUSON at the instance and request of JOHN BATES

now Under Sheriff of Essex County became joyntly and severally with him & SAMUEL CLAYTON & the aforesd JOHN EDMONDSON bound to JAMES GARNETT now SHERIFF of Essex County in one obligation bearing date the Seventeenth day of June in the year of our Lord one thousand seven hundred and twenty nine of the penalty of one thousand pounds Current mony the Condition of which obligation is for the sd JOHN BATES pformance of the Office of Undersheriff and for other things incident to his Office

Now the Condition of the above obligation is such that if the above bound JOHN EDMONDSON & THOMAS EDMONDSON their heirs shall and will secure and save harmless the sd JOHN FARGUSON his heirs from the abovementioned obligation and conditon thereof soe pfected to sd JAMES GARNETT & from all manner of actions & costs whatsoever which may happen concerning the same to be sued commenced, brot against the sd JOHN FARGUSON at the suit of the sd JAMES GARNETT and also that they the sd JOHN EDMONDSON & THOMAS EDMONDSON shall at their own proper costs & pay the charges & expences of any suits brot. by sd JAMES GARNETT agst the sd JOHN FARGUSON on account of the sd JOHN FARGUSON pfecting the sd recited obligation that then the above obligation to be void otherwise to remain in force

in presence of RICHD. TYLER JUNR.,   JOHN EDMONDSON
    JOHN CASTON   THOS. EDMONDSON

At a Court held for Essex County on the XXIst day of March MDCCXXXI
This bond from JOHN EDMONDSON and THOMAS EDMONDSON JUNR. to JOHN FARGUSON was proved by the Oath of RICHARD TYLER JUNR. Gent a witness thereto & admitted to record

pp.   THIS INDENTURE made the two and Twentyeth day of February in the Fifth year
292- of the Reign of our Sovereign Lord GEORGE the Second and in the year of our
294   Lord one thousand seven hundred and thirty one Between MARK THOMAS of the
      County of WESTMORELAND Planter of one part and PITMAN SCANDRETT of the
County of Essex Merchant of other part Witnesseth that for the sum of Eleven pounds Currant mony of Virga. to the sd MARK THOMAS in hand paid by the sd PITMAN SCANDRETT he the sd MARK THOMAS hath sold unto the sd PITMAN SCANDRETT his heirs and assigns one full undivided fourth part of all that piece of land containing Two hundred acres being in the Parish of Southfarnham in the County of Essex which said Fourth part of the sd Two hundred acres of land descended unto ANN the late Wife of the sd MARK THOMAS now deceased as one of the Daughters and Coheirs of WILLIAM AYRES late of the sd County of Essex deceased and all the houses Orchards woods and appurtenances whatsoever thereunto belonging To Have and To Hold the sd fourth part of the sd Two hundred acres of land unto said PITMAN SCANDRETT during the time of the natural life of him the said MARK THOMAS paying unto the sd MARK THOMAS the yearly rent of one ear of Indian Corn upon the twenty fifth day of December in every year during the sd term if the same be lawfully demanded. In Witness whereof the sd Parties have set their hands and seals

in presence of T. WARING,   MARK THOMAS
    ROBT. ROSE, EDW: BARRADALL

At a Court held for Essex County at Tappa. on the XXIst day of March MDCCXXXI
This Deed indented from MARK THOMAS to PITMAN SCANDRETT was proved by the Oaths of the Witnesses thereto & on sd PITMANs motion was admitted to record

pp.   THIS INDENTURE made the 13th day of April in the year of our Lord God one
294- thousand seven hundred and Thirty Two between MARGARET SWINEY of the
296   County of Essex and Parish of Southfarnham of one part and RICHARD TYLER of
      the County and Parish aforesd of other part Witnesseth that sd MARGARET
SWINEY for the sum of Five pounds Currt. money of Virginia doth sell unto the sd

RICHARD TYLER his heirs and assigns forever all the right and Estate whatsoever which is or shall become due to the sd MARGARET SWINEY her heirs to a certain dividend of land being in the aforesd County of Essex and Parrish of South farnham containing fifty acres being part of a tract of One hundred acres of land formerly belonging to WILLIAM PRICE and bounded beginning upon the Creek in the Cove at a Corner white Oak being the Corner tree between the said land and RICHARD TYLER from thence up along the sd dividing line half a Mile & from thence to the line of Mr. JOHN HUNT thence down along the line of Mr. JOHN HUNT to his Corner upon the Creek from thence to the place where it first began and all the houses ways profitts and appurtenances and all the Estate right of her the sd MARGARET SWINEY To Have and To Hold unto the sd RICHARD TYLER his heirs and assigns forever. In Witness whereof the said MARGARET SWINEY have set her hand and Seale
in presence of JA: BOUGHAN,   MARGARET 🙰 SWINEY
        THOMAS BARKER

At a Court held for Essex County at Tappa. on the XVIIIth day of April MDCCXXXII MARGARET SWINEY acknowledged this her deed indented and livery and Seizin thereon endorsed to RICHARD TYLER which on his motion are admitted to record

pp.   KNOW ALL MEN by these presents that we JOHN VAWTER and WILLIAM GRAY
296-   are held and firmly bound unto our Sovrn. Lord GEORGE the Second in the full
297   sum of ten thousand pounds of Tobacco this XVIth day of May MDCCXXXII
        THE CONDITION of the above obligation is such that Whereas JOHN VAWTER hath
obtained a Licence to keep an ORDINARY at his House if Therefore if the said JOHN doth provide in his ORDINARY good wholesome cleanly lodgeing and diet for Travellers and Stableage fodder and Provender or pasturage as the Season of the year shall require for their Horses for one year from the date hereof, and not suffer any unlawfull gameing in his House, nor on the Sabbath to suffer any to Tipple more than is necessary that then this obligation to be void else to stand in force
                                              JNO. VAWTER
                                              WM. GRAY

At a Court held for Essex County at Tappa. on the XVIth day of May MDCCXXXII JOHN VAWTER & WILLIAM GRAY acknowledged this bond to be their act and deed which is admitted to record

pp.   THIS INDENTURE made the third day and fourth day of December in the year of
297-   of our Lord one thousand seven hundred and Thirty One Between ROBERT
302   GRESHAM of the Pish of St. Anns in the County of Essex of one part and JOHN
        MERRITT of the Pish and County aforesd of other part Witnesseth that the sd
ROBERT GRESHAM for the sum of Ten pounds Curt. mony hath sold unto the sd JOHN MERRITT (in his actual possession by virtue of one Indenture for one year and of the Statute for transferring uses into possession) and to his heirs and assigns forever one plantation or parcel of land containing seventy six acres being in the Pish of St. Anns of County aforesd and is the Plantation whereon WM. CARNAL now Dwelleth and bounded to the land of Mr. EDMUND BAGGE and unto the land of JOSEPH MUNDAY together with all Houses, out houses, woods and appurtenances thereunto belonging To Have and To Hold unto the said JOHN MERRITT his heirs and assigns forever against the lawfull claims of ROBERT GRESHAM forever. In Witness whereof the parties have set their hands and Seales
in presence of JAMES MERRITT,   ROBERT 🄱 GRESHAM
        CHARLES MUNDAY, JOHN MERRITT

At a Court held for Essex County on the XVIth day of May MDCCXXXII
ROBERT GRESHAM acknowledged this his Release of land indented to JOHN MERRITT
which on his motion if admitted to record

KNOW ALL MEN by these presents that I ROBT. GRESHAM am held and firmly
bound unto JOHN MERRITT in the sum of one hundred pounds Currt. this fifth day of
December in the year of our Lord Christ one thousand seven hundred and thirty one
THE CONDITION of the above obligation is such that if ROBERT GRESHAM do observe all
the Covenants mentioned in Indenture which ought to be fullfilled that then this
obligation to be voyd or otherwise to remain in force
in presence of JAMES MERRITT,   ROBERT ℞ GRESHAM
        CHARLES MUNDAY, JOHN MERRITT
At a Court held for Essex County on the XVIth day of May MDCCXXXII
ROBERT GRESHAM acknowledged this bond to be his act and deed which is admitted to
record

pp.   KNOW ALL MEN by these presents that I PITMAN SCANDRETT of Southfarnham
302-   Parish in the County of Essex do appoint my Brother ISAAC SCANDRETT of the
303   Parrish and County aforesaid to be my lawfull Attorney for me to ask demand
        and sue for and receive all debts as are or shall become due to me and to pay
money for me and to Contract for me and Let to farm any of my lands whatsoever
granting unto my said Attorney my full and lawfull Authority confirming all and
singular whatsoever my sd Attorney shall do about the premises. In Witness whereof I
have set my hand and Seale the Twenty seventh day of May in the Fifth year of the
Reign of our Sovereign Lord GEORGE the Second and in the year of our Lord God Seventeen hundred thirty and two
in presence of JOHN WILCOX,   PITTM. SCANDRETT
        JOHN DENHAM, ELIAS WAFFE
At a Court held for Essex County at Tappa. on the XXth day of June MDCCXXXII
This Power of Attorney from PITMAN SCANDRETT to ISAAC SCANDRETT was proved by
the oaths of ELIAS WAFFE & JOHN DENHAM two of the witnesses thereto and is admitted
to record.

pp.   KNOW ALL MEN by these presents that I JOHN WAMSLEY of LONDON TOWN in the
303-   County of ANN ARUNDELL in the Province of MARYLAND Inn Holder have made
304   and appoint Colo: WILLIAM BEVERLEY of Essex County in the Colony of Virginia
        my true and lawfull Attorney for me & in my name to ask, demand and receive
of & from JAMES STEWART alias JAMES BOOTH of Essex County aforesd Planter the sum of
Twenty eight pounds three shillings & 10 pence 1/2d Currt. money of the Province of
MARYLAND or any other Sum or Sums of money due & owing to me by the sd JAMES
STEWART alias BOOTH aforesd and upon (non) payment thereof for me and in my name
to sue & prosecute and proceed to Judgment the sd JAMES STEWART alias BOOTH and also
to perform all lawfull & reasonable acts for obtaining & discharging of the same giving
my sd Attorney my full power in the premises ratifying all and whatsoever my sd Attorney shall lawfully doe or cause to be done. In Witness whereof I have hereunto set
my hand and seal the thirteenth day of June MDCCXXXII
in presence of EDWARD ROYCROFT,   JOHN WAMSLEY
        JONAS RESTALL, THO: WATKINS
At a Court held for Essex County at Tappa. on the XXth day of June MDCCXXXII
This Power of Attorney from JOHN WAMSLEY to Colo. WILLIAM BEVERLEY was proved by
the Oaths of EDWARD ROYCROFT & Doctor THOMAS WATKINS two of the witnesses thereto
& is admitted to record

pp. MARYLD. SS. KNOW ALL MEN by these presents that I RICHARD HILL of
304- ANNARUNDL. COUNTY Practr. of Physick do by these presents constitute the
305 within named Collo. WM.BEVERLEY my Atty Impowering him hereby to sue for
   & recover of the wthin mentioned JAMES STEWARD alias BOOTH the sum of Eleven pounds three shillings & seven pence which he owes me as may appear by my acct.
signed by me of equal date with these presents & give my sd Attry. all the power of
constituting other Attorneys revokeing and discharging as fully as he could be autho-
rized to do by any more full letter of Atty. promiseing to ratifye whatever he may lawfully do in the premises. In Witness whereof I hereunto set my hand and seal this 14th
day of June 1732
in presence of THO: WATKINS,   RICHD. HILL
   EDWARD ROYCROFT
 At a Court held for Essex County at Tappa. on the XXth day of June MDCCXXXII
This Power of Attorney from RICHARD HILL to Colo. WILLIAM BEVERLEY was proved by
the Oaths of the Witnesses thereto and is admitted to record

pp. THIS INDENTURE made the 14th and 15th day of July in the year of our Lord God
305- one thousand seven hundred and thirty two Between WILLIAM COOPER of the
309 County of Essex in the Parish of Southfarnham of one part and JAMES TURNER of
   the aforesd County and Parish of the other part Witnesseth that the sd WILLIAM
COOPER by Indenture bearing date the day next before the date of these presents for the
consideration therein mentioned (five shillings) did bargain and sell unto the said
JAMES TURNER all that tract of land being within the aforesd County and Parish it
being all that tract of land lately purchased of RICHARD COOPER by the aforesd WILLM.
COOPER binding on the West side of the ROADE and binding on the land of FRANCES
YOUNG & the land of RICHARD BROWN according to the bounds exprest in the Deeds of
Sale from sd RICHARD COOPER unto the said WILLIAM COOPER containing fifty acers
which will more plaine appear on record which sd land with houses Orchards and all
other things thereon being and every part To Have and To Hold unto the aforesd JAMES
TURNER his heirs and assigns for the term of one whole year from thence next till the
term be compleated to the end that by Virtue thereof and of the Statute for transferring
uses into possession that the sd JAMES TURNER may be in actual possession of the premises and may be enabled to take and accept of a grant Release of the same
 Now This Indenture Witnesseth that the sd WILLIAM COOPER for the sum of Ten pounds
good and lawfull mony of Virginia doth hereby confirm unto the sd JAMES TURNER his
heirs and assigns the aforemenconed tract of land & premises and all the right to hold
to him the sd JAMES TURNER his heirs and assigns forever. In Witness whereof the sd
partise have set their hands and seals
in presence of us WM. COVINGTON,   WM. ⊃ COOPER
   RICHD. COVINGTON, RICHD. ✖ BRIZENDEN
 At a Court held for Essex County on ye XIXth day of June MDCCXXXII
ELIZABETH COOPER the Wife of the within named WILLIAM COOPER came into Court and
freely relinquished her right of dower of and in the land conveyed by this Deed from
the sd WILLIAM COOPER to the within named JAMES TURNER, which on his motion is
recorded (on margin)
 At a Court held for Essex County on the XVIIIth day of July MDCCXXXII
WILLIAM COOPER acknowledged this his Release of land indented to JAMES TURNER
which on his motion is admitted to record
   KNOW ALL MEN by these presents that I WILLIAM COOPER am held and firmly
bound unto JAMES TURNER in the full sum of Twenty five pounds good and lawfull
money of Virginia this 15th day of July 1732

THE CONDITION of this obligation is such that if the above bounden WILLIAM COOPER do truly keep all the Covenants mentioned in Indenture and that the Wife of the sd WIL-LIAM COOPER do acknowledge her right of dower of the sd land in open Court when thereunto required by the sd JAMES TURNER that then this obligation to be void otherwise to stand in force

in presence of WM. COVINGTON,   WM. ⟩ COOPER
            RICHD. COVINGTON, RICHD. ✗ BRIZENDEN
  At a Court held for Essex County on the XVIIIth day of July MDCCXXXII
WILLIAM COOPER acknowledged this bond to be his act & deed which is admitted to record

pp.   THIS INDENTURE made the Seventh day of July in the Sixth year of the Reign of
310-   our Soveraign Lord GEORGE the Second and in the year of our Lord one thousand
314   seven hundred & Thirty two Between TOBIAS INGRAM of the County of Essex &
         JANE his Wife of one part and ROBERT BROOKE of the same County Gent and
PHEBE his Wife of the other part WHEREAS the sd TOBIAS INGRAM is and stands possessed of a certain parcell of land containing three hundred and thirty three acres scituate lying and being in the Parish of St. Anns in the sd County of Essex hereinafter particularly described And Whereas the sd ROBERT BROOKE stands seized of a certain parcell of land containing Two hundred ninety nine acres and a half scituate lying and being in the aforesd Parish of St. Anns in the County of Essex and also in a certain peice of land contaiing one hundred and seventy five acres of land scituate lying and being in the sd Parish and County both herein after particularly described And Whereas the sd TOBIAS INGRAM and ROBERT BROOKE are minded and willing to exchange the sd lands and Tenements one for the other that is to say the sd ROBERT BROOKE shall have the sd lands & tenements whereof the sd TOBIAS INGRAM is possessed as aforesd and that the sd TOBIAS INGRAM shall have the sd lands and tenements whereof the sd ROBERT BROOKE is and stands seized as aforesd.
  Now This Indenture Witnesseth that in consideration and in pursuance of the sd Exchange and also for the sum of five shillings of lawfull money to the sd TOBIAS INGRAM paid by the sd ROBERT BROOKE at or before the Sealing of these presents they the sd TOBIAS INGRAM and JANE his Wife have exchanged sold transferred and confirmed unto the sd ROBERT BROOKE all that the aforesd moiety or half part of the sd Three hundred and thirty three acres of land herein before mentioned the same being part of a certain parcell of land containing four hundred acres formerly sold and conveyed by one WILLIAM MOSELEY deceased unto TOBIAS INGRAM Deced Grandfather to the sd TOBIAS INGRAM party to these presents by Deed bearing date the Seventeenth day of August one thousand Six hundred and fifty seven and afterwards confirmed to THOMAS INGRAM Father of the sd TOBIAS INGRAM party to these presents by EDWARD MOSELEY Son and Heir of the said WILLIAM MOSELEY by Deed bearing date the twelfth day of February one thousand seven hundred and Twelve which said Moiety or half part of the sd three hundred and thirty three acres of land is bounded as followeth that is to say begining at a white Oak stump in the fork of LITTLE OCCUPATION CREEK and running thence Southwest along the line of the sd ROBERT BROOKE to the southern Branch of the sd Creek commonly called CHEESEHIXON and up the same to the mouth of a Branch called the CABBIN BRANCH and thence along the line of the sd ROBERT BROOKE North West to a ROAD that leads to ROWZEE's NECK and up that ROAD to the line of DUNCAN ROBINSON and thence along the sd ROBINSONs line South East to a Hiccory Corner tree of sd ROBINSON thence along the sd ROBINSONs line South East to a white Oak Corner tree by the upper side of a Creek thence along the sd ROBINSONs line till the sd Creek divides into two parts and thence down the sd Creek to the beginning and all the houses, buildings trees

and appurtenances whatsoever to the said Premises belonging To Have and To Hold the sd Moiety or half part of the said Three hundred and thirty three acres of land and premises unto the sd ROBERT BROOKE his heirs and assigns forever:

And This Indenture Further Witnesseth that said ROBERT BROOKE & PHEBE his Wife in consideration and in pursuance of the sd Exchange for the sum of Five shillings paid by the said TOBIAS INGRAM have confirmed and by these presents sold unto the sd TOBIAS INGRAM all that tract of land herein before mentioned containing two hundred ninety nine acres and an half the same being formerly granted unto FRANCIS MERIWETHER deceased by PATENT bearing date the twentieth day of Aprill one thousand Six hundred and ninety four and by severall meanes & conveyances in the Law vested in ROBERT BROOKE deceased Father of the sd ROBERT BROOKE party to these presents and from the sd ROBERT BROOKE descended and came unto the sd ROBERT BROOKE party to these presents as his Eldest Son and heir at Law: And allso all that parcell of land herein before mentioned containing one hundred and seventy five acres the same being next and adjoyning unto the So. West of the land last mentioned and was formerly sold and conveyed by Indentures of Lease and Release bearing date the twenty fourth and twenty fifth day of August one thousand seven hundred twenty nine and all the houses, gardens. Orchards whatsoever to the sd severall prcells of land last mentioned also all the Estate right of them the said ROBERT BROOKE & PHEBE his Wife To Have and To Hold unto the sd TOBIAS INGRAM his heirs and Assigns. In Witness whereof they have set their hands and Seals

in presence of JAMES RULE,   TOBIAS INGRAM
               ROBERT GIBSON,   JANE + INGRAM
               JOHN FOREST   RO: BROOKE
                                                      PHEBE BROOKE

At a Court held for Essex County at Tappa. on the XVIIIth day of July MDCCXXXII TOBIAS INGRAM and JANE his Wife, ROBERT BROOKE Gent and PHEBE his Wife (the sd JANE & PHEBE being first privily examined by ALEXANDER PARKER Gent) Joyntly acknowledged this their Deed indented to each other which on their motion is admitted to record

pp.   KNOW ALL MEN by these presents that I HENRY BOUGHAN of the County of Essex
315-   and Parish of Southfarnham am held and firmly bound unto JAMES FARGESSON
317   of the County and Parish aforesaid in the penal sum of one hundred pounds
         Sterling money of great Britain
THE CONDITION of this obligation is such that if HENRY BOUGHAN in all things do fullfill and keep all and every the Award and Arbitrament final end & Judgment of Mr. ROBERT FARISH and MR. JAMES WOOD Arbitrators indifferently chosen as well on ye part of the above bound HENRY BOUGHAN as on ye part & behalf of JAMES FARGESSON to award determine & judge upon or concerning all manner of judgment, Suits, Trespasses or Controversies whatsoever had depending between the sd Parties at any time before the day of the date of these presents more especially concerning a certain divident of land now in dispute between the sd parties so as the sd Award and Judgment of the sd Arbitrators be made & put into writing under their hands & Seals and ready to be delivered to the sd parties and if the Arbitrators as aforesaid cannot agree upon the premises if then the sd HENRY BOUGHAN his heirs do for their part in all things well and truly keep all and every of the award and final end and judgment of such other person to be chosen at the discretion and by the sd Arbitrators for an umpire as well in the part & behalf of either of the sd parties conerning the sd Premises and put into writing indented under his hand & Seal and ready to be delivered to the sd partries or such of them as shall require the same That then this Obligation to be void otherwise to stand in

full force. In Witness whereof the sd HENRY BOUGHAN hath hereunto set his hand &
Seal this 20th day of May in the year of our Lord 1732
in presence of us JAMES JONES,   HENRY *HB* BOUGHAN
          THOMAS BARKER
    Memorandum That the sd Arbitrators to give their determination at or before the 29th
day of June next
    At a Court held for Essex County on the XVIIIth day of July MDCCXXXII
This bond from HENRY BOUGHAN to JAMES FERGUSON was proved by the Oath of JAMES
JONES a witness thereto and admitted to record
    In a Case of Diferance between HENRY BOUGHAN on the one part and JAMES FERGISON
on the other part both in South farnham Pish in Essex County have made choys of
JAMES WOOD & ROBERT FARIS to Arbitrate & make a final determination of the sd case
in diference & the said parties haveing bound themselves in a bond to stand to the
award & determination of the sd Arbitrs. & we finding the Case very dificult to determine and according to their obligation have liberty to call to their assistance whome
the sd Arbitrators should think a fiting & Capeable person did request Mr. JAMES ED-
MONDSON to assist on this affair & accordingly have examined the lines of the old
PATTEN belonging to Mr. HENRY BOUGHAN & also a sale of JAMES FARGISSONs out of a
PATTEN of JOHN HARPERs and doe find the outline of the old PATTEN runing West down
to the TOUN MARSH leaveing out the land in dispute between the sd BOUGHAN & FERGIS-
SON Therefore we find the land in dispute belongs to the sd JAMES FERGISSON. Given
under our hands & Seals this 29th day of June 1732
                                    J. WOOD
               ROBERT FARISH   JAMES EDMONDSON
    At a Court held for Essex County on the XVIIIth day of July MDCCXXXII
JAMES FERGUSON presented this Arbitrament & on his motion the same is admitted to
record

pp.   KNOW ALL MEN by these presents that we WILLIAM TAYLOR, NATHANIEL FOGG
317-   & PEARCE GRIFFIN are held and firmly bound unto our Sovereign Lord GEORGE
318   the Second in the sum of Tenn thousand pounds of tobo. this 18th day of July
        Ano. Dm. 1732
    THE CONDITION of the above obligation is such that whereas WILLIAM TAYLOR hath
obtained a Licence to keep an ORDINARY at his House if Therefore the sd WILLIAM TAY-
LOR constantly find & provide in his ORDINARY good wholesome cleanly lodgeing and
diet for Travellers and Stableage fodder and provender or pasturage as the Season requires for their Horses, during the term of one year from the date hereof and not
suffer any unlawfull gameing in his House nor on the Sabbath day suffer any to Tipple
more then is necessary that then this obligation to be null & of none effect, else to
stand in force   WM. + TAYLER
               NATHL. FOGG   PIERCE + GRIFFIN
    At a Court held for Essex County on the XVIIIth day of July MDCCXXXII
WILLIAM TAYLOR, NATHANIEL FOGG & PIERCE GRIFFIN acknowledged this bond to be
their act and deed which is admitted to record

pp.   THIS INDENTURE made this eighteenth day of July in the year of our Lord one
318-   thousand seven hundred & thirty two Between JAMES BOOTH of the County of
322   Essex Planter of one part and WILLIAM BEVERLEY of the same of the other part
    Witnesseth that Whereas by an Indented Deed of Release bearing date the twen-
ty third day of September in the year of our Lord one thousand seven hundred & twenty
seven for the sums of money therein expressed which the sd JAMES BOOTH did then owe

to the sd WILLIAM BEVERLEY the sd JAMES BOOTH did thereby give sell & assign unto
the sd WILLIAM BEVERLEY his heirs & assigns being the plantation whereon the said
JAMES BOOTH then lived and all his other lands, Islands & marshes adjoyning thereto
and all the estate right claim & demands whatsoever to the same belonging To Have and
To Hold the said premises & every part thereof unto the sd WILLIAM BEVERLEY his
heirs & assigns forever but with this express limitation & reservation that in case the
sd JAMES BOOTH should within the space of four years ensuing pay unto the sd WIL-
LIAM BEVERLEY the sum of one hundred & fifty eight pounds Eighteen shillings & two
pence Sterl. money of England & two hundred Seventy & six pounds thirteen Shillings
& one penny Current money together with the interest of Six p cent p Ann on the sd
severall sums that then in such case it should be lawfull for the said WILLAM BEVERLEY
to grant & reconvey the said granted premises unto the sd JAMES BOOTH his heirs or
assigns for his & their proper use. And Whereas the said JAMES BOOTH by his other
Indented Deed of Release bearing date the Tenth day of October in the year of our Lord
one thousand seven hundred and twenty eight for consideration of three hundred
seventy one pounds eighteen shillings & three pence Sterl. paid by the sd WILLIAM for
divers others causes did thereby Release & quit claim to all equity of redemption in the
premises and did confirm the sd land (except the marshes adjoyning to the land of
RICHARD COVINGTON & lyeing right before the same & on the same side of BRICES CREEK
and also an half acre of land being the place where his Ancestors lye BURIED reserved
by the sd JAMES BOOTH to him & his heirs forever for a BURYING PLACE)
  Now the said JAMES BOOTH for the consideration received and for the further sum of
five shillings of good and lawfull money of great Britain paid by WILLIAM BEVERLEY
doth clearly grant unto the sd WILLIAM BEVERLEY all the Six hundred acres & all his
other lands Island & marshes adjoyning thereto and also the sd marshes adjoyning to
the land of RICHARD COVINGTON together with all appurtenances whatsoever
belonging To Have and To Hold unto the said WILLIAM BEVERLEY his heirs and assigns
forever. In Witness whereof the parties have set their hands & Seals
in presence of JAS. CRAIK,   JAMES BOOTH
        ALEXR. THOARS, MARK WEEKES
  At a Court held for Essex County at Tappa. on the XVIIIth day of July Anno Dom
MDCCXXXII JAMES BOOTH acknowledged his Deed indented & livery and Seizin thereon
endorsed to WILLIAM BEVERLEY Gent which on his motion is admitted to record

pp.   THIS INDENTURE made the Seventh and Eighteenth day of July in the Sixth year
322-   of the Reign of our Sovereign Lord GEORGE the Second and in the year of our
329   Lord one thousand seven hundred and thirty two Between ELIAS DEJARNAT of
         the Pish of St. John in the County of KING WILLIAM Planter and ELIZABETH his
Wife of one part and the honourable JOHN ROBINSON of the Parish of Southfarnham in
the County of Essex Esqr. of the other part Witnesseth that the sd ELIAS DEJARNAT and
ELIZABETH his Wife for the sum of Forty pounds Sterling doth sell unto the said JOHN
ROBINSON (in his actual possession by virtue of a bargain and sale for one year and by
the Statute for transferring uses into possession) and to his heirs & assigns, all those
two severall peices or parcells of land adjoyning and Contiguous to each other containing one hundred and fifty acres being in the aforesd Parish of South farnham in
the sd County of Essex where THOMAS HINDS late of the sd County deced dwelt and now
in the tenure or occupation of one WALTER LEONARD, one hundred acres part thereof
being bounded beginning at a marked white oak Corner tree to the land of one JOHN
MITCHELL and runing thence by MITCHELLs land South East to a marked white Oak
standing by a Branch called the GREEN SWAMP thence West South West to a marked
white Oak thence North West down a Swamp called BEAVERDAM SWAMP to a marked

white Oak, thence East North East to the beginning, and fifty one acres of land the resi-due thereof beginning at a marked Dogwood a Corner tree of one THOMAS GREEN deced and runing thence North East to a Sasafrass and Hickory standing in a valley in the line of Capt. ANTHONY SMITH deced and on the East side of the MAIN ROAD that leads to PISCATAWAY FERRY and runing thence along the sd SMITHs line South East to a scrubby Hicory Corner tree of the sd SMITHs and one JOHN MITCHELL and thence along the sd MITCHELLs line North to a red Oak on a level and thence North East to the begin-ning And all houses, Outhouses, Woods and appurtenances whatsoever belonging To Have and To Hold the sd severall parcells of land unto the sd JOHN ROBINSON his heirs and assigns forever. In Witness whereof the partys have set their hands and Seals in presence of MARK WEEKES,   ELIAS DEJARNAT
     W. BEVERLEY   ELIZABETH DEJARNAT

At a Court held for Essex County at Tappa. on the XVIIIth day of July Ano Dm MDCCXXXII ELIAS DEJARNAT and ELIZABETH his Wife (the sd ELIZABETH being first privily exa-mined) acknowledged this their Release of land indented & receipt thereon endorsed to the Honble. JOHN ROBINSON Esqr. which on his motion are admitted to record

     KNOW ALL MEN by these presents that I ELIAS DEJARNAT am held and firmly bound unto the honourable JOHN ROBINSON in the sum of Eighty pounds Sterl. the eighteenth day of July in the Sixth year of the Reign of our Sovereign Lord GEORGE the Second Anno Domini one thousand seven hundred and thirty two

THE CONDITION of this obligation is such that if ELIAS DEJARNAT and ELIZABETH his Wife shall at all times observe the Covenants mentioned in Agreement which ought to be observed according to the true intent of the Indenture that then this obligation to be void otherwise to remain in full force
in presence of MARK WEEKES,   ELIAS DEJARNAT
     W. BEVERLEY

At a Court held for Essex County at Tappa. on the XVIIIth day of July Ano Dm MDCCXXXII ELIAS DEJARNAT acknowledged this bond to be his act and deed which is admitted to record

pp.   KNOW ALL MEN by these presents that we SAMUEL CLAYTON of the County of
329-   Essex and RICHARD TYLER JUNR. of the same County Gent are held and firmly
330   bound unto ALEXANDER BAILLIE, RICHARD OSWOULD & COMPANY Merchants in
     GLASGOW their Exrs. or assignes in the sum of Twenty six pounds this XIXth day
of July MDCCXXXII

THE CONDITION of this obligation is such that Whereas Judgment being this day given in Essex County Court unto the sd ALEXANDER BAILLIE, RICHARD OSWOULD & COMPANY Merchants against the above bound SAMUEL CLAYTON in an action of debt depending & the sd SAMUEL CLAYTON had an Appeal granted him to the Eighth day of the next General Court giveing Security according to Law if Therefore sd SAMUEL CLAYTON Appellant shall accordingly appear and prosecute the sd Appeal at the sd next General Court and perform the Judgment of the sd Court & pay the damage of fifteen p cent which the Law gives upon the principal debt, damages & costs of the County Court this day recovered as aforesd if cast in the sd Appeal that then the above obligation to be Void otherwise to stand in full force
                               SAMLL. CLAYTON
                               RICHD. TYLER JUNR.

At a Court held for Essex County at Tappa. on the XIXth day of July MDCCXXXII SAMUEL CLAYTON & RICHARD TYLER JUNR. Gent acknowledged this bond to be their act and deed which is admitted to record

pp.   ESSEX SS. WHEREAS Several Laws have appointed and confirmed to this County
330-   of Essex fifty acres of land for a TOWN and Whereas WILLIAM DAINGERFIELD
331   Esqr., SALVATOR MUSCOE, BENJAMIN ROBINSON & WILLIAM BEVERLEY Gent are
       by Order of the Court of the sd County of Essex appointed Feoffees in Trust to
dispose of the sd land Now This Indenture Witnesseth that the sd WILLIAM DAINGER-
FIELD & WILLIAM BEVERLEY Feoffees aforesd in consideration of six hundred and forty
pounds of Tobacco & Cask to them paid by JAMES GRIFFIN have granted to the sd JAMES
GRIFFIN and his heirs four half acres or lotts of land in the BURGH of TAPPAHANNOCK
being part of the sd Fifty acres & numbered forty five, fifty six, fifty seven & fifty
eight To Have and To hold the said lotts to sd JAMES GRIFFIN in full manner as is
directed by Act made at a General Assembly begun at WILLIAMSBURGH the Thirteenth
day of October in the year of our Lord one thousand Seven hundred and Five entituled
an Act for Establishing ports & Towns he or they paying one ounce of flax seed and two
ounces of hemp seed on the tenth day of October annually to the Director & Benchers of
the BURGH of TAPPAHANNOCK when they shall be elected and to their Successors provided that the sd JAMES GRIFFIN without delay proceed to build and finish on each of
the sd lotts within twelve months after the date hereof one good house to contain
twenty foot square at the least otherwise this grant to be Void & liable to be purchased
by any other person. In Witness whereof the parties have set their hands and Seals the
Nineteenth day of July Anno Dm. One thousand seven hundred and thirty two
in presence of us JOHN MEGGS,   WM. DAINGERFIELD
               MARK WEEKES   W. BEVERLEY
    At a Court continued & held for Essex County at Tappa. on the XIXth day of July
MDCCXXXII WILLIAM DAINGERFIELD Esqr. & WILLIAM BEVERLEY Gent Feoffees of the
TOWN of TAPPA. acknowledged their deed indented & livery & Seizin thereon endorsed
to JAMES GRIFFIN which are admitted to record

pp.   KNOW ALL MEN by these presents that I JOHN MILLS late of the County of Essex
332-   and Parish of St. Anns do appoint and in my place put JAMES JONES of the County
337   aforesaid and Parish of Southfarnham to be my lawfull Attorney for me to ack-
       nowledge a set of Deeds of Lease and Release to TIMOTHY DISCOLL bearing date
the Eleventh & Twelveth dayes of August one thousand seven hundred and thirty two in
Essex County Court when he shall be thereunto requested confirming all and every
thing whatsoever my said Attorney shall lawfully doe in my name as if I was there my
self. In Witness whereof I have set my hand this 12th day of August in the year of our
Lord God one thousand seven hundred and thirty two
in presence of JOHN CROXTON,   JOHN Ɨ MILLS
              SAMLL. S THOMPSON
    At a Court held for Essex County at Tappa. on the XVth day of August MDCCXXXII
This Power of Attorney from JOHN MILLS to JAMES JONES was proved by the Oaths of
JOHN CROXTON and SAMUEL THOMPSON witnesses thereto & is admitted to record

       THIS INDENTURE made the eleventh and twelveth day of August in the year of
our Lord Christ one thousand seven hundred and thirty and two Between JOHN MILLS of
the County of Essex & Parish of St. Anns Son of JOHN MILLS of the aforesaid County &
Parish deced of one part and TIMOTHY DISCOLL of the aforesd County of Essex & Parish
of Southfarnham of the other part Witnesseth that the sd JOHN MILLS for the sum of
thirty pounds Current money of Virginia doth sell unto sd TIMOTHY DISCOLL in his
actual possession now being by virtue of a bargain and sale for one year and by force
of the Statute for transferring uses into possession and to his heirs & assigns forever
all the claim or demand whatsoever to all his lands and plantations in the County of
Essex and more especially to a certain devidend of land in the County before mentioned
formerly belonging to his sd Father JOHN MILLS of the sd County deced containing two

hundred acres of land being on the head of LITLE OCEPATIA CREEK on the South side thereof bounded on the land of Mr. ROBERT JONES deced and land of Capt. SALVATOR MUSCOE and the land of Major ROBERT BROOKE with the rights and appertinances thereof all houses, buildings, paths, advantages appertaining or which formerly have been accepted with the same being in the County of Essex and Parish of St. Anns To Have and To Hold the said lands above mentioned unto the sd TIMOTHY DISCOLL his heirs & assigns In Witness whereof JOHN MILLS hereunto set his hand and Seal

in presence of JOHN CROXTON,   JOHN **I** MILLS
      SAMLL. **5** THOMPSON, THOMAS YOUNGER

At a Court held for Essex County on the XIXth day of September MDCCXXXII JOHN MILLS by JAMES JONES his Attorney acknowledged this his release of land indented to TIMOTHY DISCOLL which on his motion is admitted to record

pp.   KNOW ALL MEN by these presents that I ROBERT HOCKLEY of Esix County have
337-   for sundry good causes & weighty considerations appointed in my stead & place
338   my trusty and well beloved Wife DIANAH HOCKLEY of the aforesd County my true
      & lawfull Atturney my being now rendered uncapable of any Service do appoint my said Wife my Atturney to ask demand and levy and receive for me and in my name of any person of any County giving and granting my sole & full power in the premises to sue arrest imprison and condemn for me and in my name in any Court before any Judge or Justice & discharge in my name to make & deliver any bill or bond for me or in my stead & again at her pleasure to revoke and further to perform & finish for me all things which shall be necessary touching the premises as fully and entirely as I could do about the same ratifying whatsoever my sd Atturney shall do. In Witness whereof I the sd ROBERT HOCKLEY have set my hand and seal this 15th day of Augt. in the Sixt year of the Reign of our Soveraign Lord GEORGE the Second King of great Brittain etc and in the year of our Lord One thousand seven hundred and thirty & two

in presence of JOHN BRYANT   ROBT. **R** HOCKLEY
      JET VERNON

At a Court held for Essex County on the XIXth day of September MDCCXXXII This Power of Attorney from ROBERT HOCKLEY to DIANAH his Wife was proved by the oaths of the Witnesses thereto & is admitted to record

pp.   THIS INDENTURE made this second day of September in the year of our Lord one
339-   thousand seven hundred thirty and two Between TOBIAS INGHRAM of St. Anns
341   Parish in Essex County of one part and JAMES SAMUEL & JOHN MARTIN both of
      the Parish & County abovesaid of the other part Witnesseth that the sd TOBIAS INGRAM for sum of Five pounds Current money of Virginia doth grant unto the sd JAMES SAMUEL & JOHN MARTIN their heirs & assigns for the full space of term of twenty and one years one certain parcel of land containing ninty nine and one half acres being part of a tract of land granted to the sd TOBIAS INGHRAM by Majr. ROBERT BROOKE lying & being in the Parish & County abovesd and bounded on one side by WILLIAM GOULDINGs line and to be layd off between two other tracts of land granted by sd TOBIAS INGHRAM one to JOHN BATES JUNR. and the other to JOSEPH SORRILL so as to contain the abovesd quantity of ninty nine and one half acres and all the appurtenances whatsoever belonging To Have and To Hold the sd land unto them the sd JAMES SAMUEL & JOHN MARTIN their heirs and assigns forever, paying yearly the quit rents of the abovesd land and also one ear of Indian Corn to TOBIAS INGHRAM or his assigns the same being lawfully demanded and that his Wife JANE will relinquish her right of dower in the premises when thereunto required. In Witness whereof the above party have set their

hands and seals
in presence of WILLIAM DOBSON,   TOBIAS INGRAM
         FOSTER SAMUEL, ROBERT FARMAR
   At a Court held for Essex County on the XIXth day of September MDCCXXXII
TOBIAS INGRAM acknowledged this his Lease of Land indented and livery and Seizin
thereon endorsed to JAMES SAMUEL & JOHN MARTIN which on their motion are admitted to record

p.   KNOW ALL MEN by these presents that we THOMAS RAY JUNR., THOMAS RAY
341   SENR. & JOSEPH REEVES are held and firmly bound unto our Sovereign Lord
        GEORGE the Second in the full sum of ten thousand pounds of tobacco this XIXth
day of September MDCCXXXII
THE CONDITION of the above obligation is such that whereas the above bound THOMAS
RAY JUNR. hath obtained a Licence to keep an ORDINARY at SANDERS ORDINARY in the
sd County if Therefore the sd THOMAS RAY JUNR. doth constantly provide in his ORDI-
NARY good wholesome & cleanly Lodging & diet for Travellers & Stableage fodder &
provender or pasturages & provender as the Season shall require for their Horses for &
during the term of one year from the date hereof & shall not permitt any unlawfull
gameing in his House nor on the Sabbath day suffer any to Tipple more than is necessary that then the above obligation to be void else to be in full power
                                      THOS. RAY JNR.
                           THOS. RAY   JOS. REEVES
   At a Court held for Essex County on the XIXth day of September MDCCXXXII
THOMAS RAY JUNR., THOMAS RAY SENR. & JOSEPH REEVES acknowledged this bond to be
their act & deed which is admitted to record

p.   Virga. SS. KNOW ALL MEN by these presents that I EDWARD ROYCROFT of ANN
342   ARUNDL. COTY. in the Province of MARYLAND do constitute Colo. WILLIAM
        BEVERLEY of Essex County in the Colony of Virginia my Attorney impowering
him hereby to sue for and recover of JAMES STUART alias BOOTH the sume of Seven
pounds seventeen shillings & five pence half penny Current money wch he owes to me
as will appear by Account and I give my sd Attorney full power revoking and discharging in as ample manner as I my self could do if I were personally present. In Witness
whereof I set my hand and Seal this 21st day of June MDCCXXXII
in presence of THO: WATKINS,   EDWARD ROYCROFT
         BENJA.   VAWTER, MARK WEEKES
   At a Court held for Essex County on the XIXth day of September MDCCXXXII
This Power of Attorney from EDWARD ROYCROFT to Colonel WILLIAM BEVERLEY was
proved by the Oaths of MARK WEEKES & BENJAMIN VAWTER two of the witnesses thereto & admitted to record

pp.   THIS INDENTURE made the ninth and tenth day of May in the year of our Lord
342-   Christ one thousand seven hundred and thirty two Between THOMAS COVINGTON
348   in the County of Essex Planter of one part and WILLIAM WEBB of the Parish and
        County aforesd Planter of other part Witnesseth that the sd THOMAS COVINGTON
for the sum of fourty pounds Sterl. doth grant unto the sd WILLIAM WEBB his heirs &
assigns forever (in his actual possession by virtue of Indenture for one year and of the
Statute for transferring uses into possession) one plantation or percel of land woodland
ground and premises containing one hundred & twenty five acres of land & being in
the Parish of Southfarnham in the County of Essex and bounded begining at a COOLE
SPRING on the GLEAB BRANCH so called at two great IRON MINE STONES lying at the sd

Spring thence down the said Branch its several courses to the GLEAB SWAMP thence down its several courses to the land of THOS. COOPERs thence along the sd COOPERs line to land of JAMES TURNER thence along the sd TURNERs line and the line of WILLIAM BRISLEY there lands the several courses thereof to a marked Corner red Oake standing in the line of this sd PATENT nigh the head of a bottom on the ROAD leading to PISCATA-WAY SMITHS ROALING HOUSE thence a strait course to the beginning place COOLE SPRING which said land and premises was given the sd THOMAS COVINGTON by his reputed Father WILLIAM COVINGTON of Essex County deced as may appear by the sd WILLM. COVINGTONs last Will and Testament in writing recorded in this said County purchased by the sd WILLIAM COVINGTON of LARKIN CHEW & by PATENT granted to ARTHUR HODGES dated October the Tenth Anno d. one thousand Six hundred & eighty nine together with all houses improvements and appurtenances belonging To Have and To Hold to the sd WILLIAM WEBB his heirs and assigns forever. In Witness whereof the parties have set their hands and seals
in presence of us ROBT. X DUAWAY,   THOS. COVINGTON
    WILLM. ☩ BOREING, MICAJAH EVANES,
    SAMUEL CLAYTON, RICHARD ☩ JOHNSON,
    JOS: ANDERSON
   At a Court held for Essex County on the XIXth day of September MDCCXXXII
This Release of Land indented from THOMAS COVINGTON to WILLIAM WEBB was proved by the Oath of JOSEPH ANDERSON one of the witnesses thereto
   At a Court continued & held for Essex County on the XXth day of September MDCCXXXII
This Release of Land indented from THOMAS COVINGTON to WILLIAM WEBB was further proved by the Oaths of MICAJAH EVANES & RICHARD JOHNSON two other of the witnesses thereto & admitted to record

pp.   THIS INDENTURE made the fourteenth and fifteenth day of July in the year of
349-   our Lord God one thousand Seven hundred and thirty two in the Reign of our
354   Soveraign Lord KING GEORGE over England Between RICHARD JONES Planter the
         Subscriber hereof of Southfarnham Parish in Essex County in Virginia of one
part and PETER MITCHELL of the sd Parish and County of the other part Witness that the sd RICHARD JONES by Indenture bearing date the day next before the date hereof hath bargained and sold unto the sd PETER MITCHELL for the consideration therein expressed (five shillings) a tract of land being in the abovesd Parish & County on the South side of the RAPPA. RIVER being part of the land and plantation whereon said RICHARD JONES now lives on containing forty acres being part of a PATTENT of land granted to JOHN LACY deceased bearing date Anno 1662, the sd Tract of land being bounded be-gining at a Corner Hiccory near a PATH in LACYs line, thence North East to a white Oake by the abovesd RICHARD JONES Old Feild thence South East to an old Tree blown down, thence North East to a Corner white Oake under a Hill thence North West to a red Oake pressing tree under the sd Hill & thence South to a Pine on a hill side thence South West to a Doggwood tree by the sd JONES old feild thence South West to a Corner red Oake saplin thence South West to two red Oake saplins in the old line near the MAIN ROAD thence South East to the begining Corner Hickory Together with all woods, houseings fencing and appurtenances belonging unto the sd forty acres of land with warranty and the statute for transferring uses into possession from time to time
   Now This Indenture Witnesseth that the sd RICHARD JONES for the just sum of Two thousand six hundred & sixty six pounds of tobacco he doth sell unto sd PETER MITCHELL his heirs & assigns the sd forty acres of land together with all rights belonging. In Witness whereof the sd RICHARD JONES set his hand and seal

in presents of JNO. EVANS JUNR.,   RICHD. JONES Plantr.
             CATHERINE EVANS, JOS. ANDERSON
  At a Court held for Essex County at Tappa. on Tuesday the XVIIth day of October Ano. Dm
MDCCXXXII RICHARD JONES Planter acknowledged his Release of land Indented to PETER
MITCHELL which on his motion is admitted to record

pp.   THIS INDENTURE made the XVIIth day of August in the year of our Lord Christ
354-   one thousand seven hundred and thirty two between WILLIAM CARNALL &
356   MARY his Wife both of the Parish of St. Anns in the County of Essex of one part
        and JOHN MERRITT of the County & Parish aforesd of the other part Witnesseth
that said WILLIAM CARNALL & MARY his Wife for sum of fifteen pounds Current money
of Virginia hath sold unto the said JOHN MERRITT all that parcell of land and premises
whereon the sd WM. CARNALL now dwells containing Seventy Six acres being in the
Parish and County aforesd and bounded with the lands of JOSEPH MUNDAY & Mr. ED-
MUND BAGGE (which sd plantation is called by the name of GRESHAM's PLANTATION)
Together with all houses, improvements, trees whatsoever thereunto belonging To
Have and To Hold the aforesd plantation or land unto the sd JOHN MERRIT his heirs and
assigns forever paying yearly one pepper Corn at the feast of St. Michael the Archangel only if the same be lawfully demanded by sd WM. CARNALL & MARY his Wife (the
rents and Services which from henceforth shall grow due and ought to be performed to
our Sovereign Lord the King). In Witness whereof the parties have set their hands and
seals in presence of ROBERT ⟨R⟩ GRESHAM,   WILLIAM X CARNALL
             CHARLES MUNDAY, JOHN MERRITT   MARY ⟨M⟩ CARNALL
  At a Court held for Essex County at Tappa. on Tuesday the XVIIth day of October Ano.
Dm. MDCCXXXII WILLIAM CARNALL & MARY his Wife (the said MARY being first privily examined by ALEXANDER PARKER Gent) acknowledged this their deed indented and
livery and Seizin thereon endorsed to JOHN MERRITT which on his motion is admitted to
record

p.   KNOW ALL MEN by these presents that we NICHOLAS SMITH Gent. SHERIFF of
357   Essex County & JOHN VAWTER are held and firmly bound unto WILLIAM
        DAINGERFIELD, THOMAS WARING & SALVATOR MUSCOE & THOMAS STHRESHLY
JUNR. Gent. Justices of the County of Essex in the sum of ninety Seven thousand six
hundred & nine pounds of Tobacco this XXIst day of November Ano dm MDCCXXXII
  Whereas the above bound NICHOLAS SMITH is by the Court of Essex County aforesd appointed COLLECTOR of the County and Country Levey for the County of Essex for the year
MDCCXXXII Now the Condition of the above obligation is that if the said NICHOLAS SMITH
shall well and truly collect the sd County and Country levey and truly pay to the several
respective Creditors the sums to them due amounting in the whole to forty eight thou-
snd eight hundred and fifty four and an half pounds of tobacco and also save harmless
and keep indemnifyed the sd Justices from all Suits & trouble whatsoever that may happen to them on account of the non payment of the sd levey or any part thereof that
then the above obligation to be void otherwise to be of force
                                                    NICHO. SMITH
                                                    JOHN VAWTER
  At a Court held for Essex County at Tappa. on the XXIth day of November MDCCXXXII
NICHOLAS SMITH & JOHN VAWTER acknowledged this bond to be their act and deed
which is admitted to record

p.   KNOW ALL MEN by these presents that we ROBERT WILLIS and THOMAS HARDY
358   are held and firmly bound unto our Sovereign Lord GEORGE the 2d. in the sum of
        Twenty pounds Sterling we bind ouselves this XXIst day of November MDCCXXXII
The Condition of the above obligation is such that Whereas ROBERT WILLIS is by the
Court of Essex County Licensed to keep the FERRY from TAPPAHANNOCK to WEBLEY
PAVEYs and to NAYLORs HOLE now if the sd ROBERT WILLIS shall constantly keep two
sufficient boats (to wit) a foot boat and a Horse boat with two able hands to attend the
same and also give passage without delay to such publick Messages and expresses as
may be mentioned in and by Act of Assembly Intituled an Act for the regulation and
Settlement of FERRYS and for dispatch of Publick Expresses to be FERRY free & do and
perform all and whatsoever the Laws require and truly perform the duty and business
of a FERRY KEEPER that then the above obligation to be void otherwise to be in full
force   ROBERT WILLIS
                                                         THOS. HARDY
     At a Court held for Essex County at Tappa. on Tuesday the XXIst day of November
MDCCXXXII   ROBERT WILLIS & THOMAS HARDY ackowledged this bond to be their act
and deed which is admitted to record

pp.   KNOW ALL MEN by these presents that we ROBERT WILLIS and THOMAS HARDY
358-   are held and firmly bound unto our Sovereign Lord GEORGE the 2d in the sum of
359   ten thousand pounds of tobacco this XXIst day of November MDCCXXXII·
        THE CONDITION of the above obligation is such that Whereas the above bound
ROBERT WILLIS hath obtained a Licence to keep an ORDINARY at his Hosue in TAPPA.
now if thereof the sd ROBERT WILLIS find and provide in his ORDINARY good wholesome and cleanly lodgeing and diet for travellers and Stableage fodder and provender
or pasturage and provender as the Season of the year shall require for their Horses
during the term of one whole year from the day hereof and shall not permit any
unlawfull gameing in his House nor on the Sabbath day suffer any to Tipple more than
is necessary that then this above obligation to be void else to be in force
                                                         ROBERT WILLIS
                                                         THOS. HARDY
     At a Court held for Essex County at Tappa. on Tuesday the XXIst day of November
MDCCXXXII ROBERT WILLIS & THOMAS HARDY acknowledged this bond to be their act
and deed which is admitted to record

pp.   TO ALL CHRISTIAN PEOPLE to whom these presents shall come I JOHN LACEY of
359-   the Parish of South farnham in the County of Essex Planter send Greeting.
360   Know ye that I the sd JOHN LACEY for divers causes but especially for the
        natural love and affection which I have unto my perticular friend and neigh-
bour RICHARD JONES Planter of the aforesd County have given unto the sd RICHARD
JONES Planter all that plantation and tract of land given to me by my Brother JONATHAN
LACEY deceased scituate lying and being in the abovesd County of Essex being the land
and plantation whereon I now live containing Eighty acres To Have and To Hold the said
Plantation and land and all houses Orchards and appurtenances whatsoever belonging
and also all the rents and profits unto the said RICHARD JONES Planter his heirs and
assigns forever Reserveing Nevertheless unto me the sd JOHN LACY the free use and
Occupation of any part of the sd land and plantation dureing my naturall life if I shall
desire or require or demand the same any thing herein before contained to the contrary. In Witness whereof I have set my hand and Seale this ninth day of October in
the Sixth year of the Reign of our Sovereign Lord GEORGE the Second Anno Dm.
MDCCXXXII

in presence of THOS. ☞ BALIST,   JOHN LACEY 4
       WM. CALECOTE, JAMES JOHNSTON
   At a Court held for Essex County at Tappa. on the XXIst day of November MDCCXXXII
This Deed Poll for land from JOHN LACEY to RICHARD JONES Planter was proved by the
Oaths of all the witnesses thereto & is admitted to record

p.   THIS INDENTURE made the XXIst day of November MDCCXXXII Between GEORGE
361   STUBBLEFIELD Carpinter of the Parish of St. Ann & County of Essex of one part
         and EDWARD GOODE Son of RICHARD GOODE desd. of about eighteen years of age
Planter of Parish and County aforesaid of other part Witnesseth that the sd EDWARD
GOODE for divers good causes but more especially for to learn the art trade and mistery
of a Carpenter doth put and bind himself as an Apprintice and Servant to the sd GEORGE
STUBBLEFIELD and by these presents doth of his own free will bind himself for and
during the space and time of five years from the first day of October last and from
thence to be fully compleated all which time said EDWARD GOODE his said Master shall
faithfully serve & his lawfull commands obay In Consideration of the above Service the
sd GEORGE STUBBLEFIELD doth oblige himself to learn and instruct the sd EDWARD GOOD
in the art and mistery abovesaid and to find him suffitient diat Cloathing washing and
lodging dureing the abovesd time of five years and to give to the sd EDWARD at the expiration of the sd time one full Sute of good new apparel. In Witness whereof the
parties have set their hands and Seals
in presence of SALVATOR MUSCOE,   GEORGE STUBBLEFIELD
       JNO. VAWTER, THOS. JONES   EDWARD GOODE
   At a Court held for Essex County at Tappa. on Tuesday the XXIst day of November
MDCCXXXII GEORGE STUBBLEFIELD acknowledged this Indenture to be his act and deed
which on his motion is admitted to record

pp.   THIS INDENTURE made the fifteenth day of December in the Sixth year of the
362-   reign of our Sovereign Lord GEORGE the second Anno Dm. one thousand seven
364   hundred and thirty two Between SILVESTER AMIS of the Parrish of Ware in the
         County of GLOUCESTER Gent of one part and PETER KEMP of the Parrish of Petso
in the sd County Gent of other part Witnesseth that the sd SILVESTER AMIS for the sum
of fifty one pounds thirteen Shillings Current money of Virginia do sell unto the said
PETER KEMP and to his heirs all that tract of land being in Essex County and bounded
Begining at a great Corner marked Pine divideing this land from a tract of land belonging to Major GEORGE MORRISS and JAMES VAUGHAN and runing thence South to a
Corner Stooping red Oak by a Branch side thence South East to a Corner Pine on a point
by the same Branch thence down the same Branch again South to two Corner white
Oakes in the sd Branch belonging to THOMAS GAINES thence along the sd GAINES's line
East to a Corner Stooping red Oake at the head of a Branch thence North East to a great
leaning white Oake on the head of a deep valley issueing out of a Branch of HOSKINS
CREEK thence West to the begining containing three hundred seventy five acres of
land To Have and To Hold the said land unto the said PETER KEMP and to his heirs and
assignes forever. In Witness whereof the said SILVESTER AMIS hath set his hand & Seal
in presence of us ALEXR. ROANE,   SILVESTER AMIS
       JAMES REDFERN
   At a Court held for Essex County at Tappa. on the XIXth day of December MDCCXXXII
SILVESTER AMIS Gent ackowledged this Deed indented to PETER KEMP to be his act and
Deed which is ordered to be recorded

p.   KNOW ALL MEN by these presents that we JAMES GRIFFIN, WM. ROANE & JAMES
364   RENNOLDS are held and firmly bound unto our Sovereign Lord GEORGE the 2d.
        in the full sum of ten thousand pounds of Tobacco this 19th day of December
1732. THE CONDITION of the above obligation is such that whereas JAMES GRIFFIN hath
this day obtained a Licence to keep an ORDINARY at TAPPA. TOWN if therefore the sd
JAMES GRIFFIN doth constantly provide in his ORDINARY good wholesome & cleanly
lodgeing & diet for travellers & Stableage fodder & provender or pasturage & provender
as the Season shall require for their horses for and during the term of one whole year
from the date hereof & shall not suffer or permitt any unlawfull gameing in his House
nor on the Sabbath day suffer any to Tipple or drink more then is necessary that then
the above obligation to be void else to remain in force
                                            JAMES GRIFFING
                            WM. ROANE   JAMES RENNOLDS
  At a Court held for Essex County at Tappa. on the XIXth day of December MDCCXXXII
JAMES GRIFFIN, WILLIAM ROANE & JAMES RENNOLDS acknowledged this bond to be
their act and deed which is ordered to be recorded

pp.   THIS INDENTURE made the twentyeth and the one and twentyeth day of Novem-
365-   ber in the year of our Lord God according to the Computation now used in the
369   Church of great Britain Seaventeen hundred thirty and two Between JOSEPH
        DIMILLO of Southfarnham Pish in the County of Essex Planter of one part and
JOHN MEGGS of the Pish & County aforesd of other part Witnesseth that the sd JOSEPH
DIMILLO for the sum of Seaventeen pounds Current money of Virga. hath sold unto the
said JOHN MEGGS in his actual possession now being by virtue of one Indenture for one
whole year and of the statute for transferring uses into possession and to his heirs and
assigns forever all that plantation or parcell of land containing three hundred acres
which sd land is now adjoyning part of the plantation whereon ARGOLL BLACKSTONE
deced formerly dwelt being in the Pish and County aforesaid and all the houses, barnes,
Stables, timber and appurtenances wtsoever appertaining To Have and To Hold unto the
said JOHN MEGGS his heirs and assigns forever. In Witness whereof the parties have set
their hands and Seals
in presence of JAMES WEBB,   JOSEPH DIMILLO
        JAMES FARGESON
  At a Court held for Essex County at Tappa. on the XIXth day of December MDCCXXXII
JOSEPH DIMILLO acknowledged this his Release indented which on the motion of the sd
JOHN was ordered to be recorded

pp.   KNOW ALL MEN by these presents that I KATHERINE SHORT Wife of THOMAS
369-   SHORT of the Parish of St. Ann in Essex County do hereby nominate and appoint
370   my loveing and trusty friend WILLIAM BEVERLEY Gentleman as my lawfull
        Atturney in my name to acknowledge all the right of dower I have to one par-
cel of land which my sd Husband did sell unto JOHN NANCE deced by Deeds bearing date
May 15th 1731. Witness my hand & Seale this 16th Janry. 1732
in presence of JNO. VAWTER,   KATHERINE C SHORT
        D. GAINES, EDWARD F MURRAH
  At a Court held for Essex County at Tappa. on the XVIth day of January MDCCXXXII
This Power of Attorney from KATHERINE SHORT the Wife of THOMAS SHORT to WILLIAM
BEVERLEY Gentleman was proved by the Oaths of DANIEL GAINES & JOHN VAWTER two of
the witnesses thereto and admitted to record, and the sd WILLIAM by virtue thereof relinquished the sd KATHERINE's Dower in the land within which is admitted to record

pp.
370-
376

THIS INDENTURE made the eighteenth and nineteenth day of September in the year of our Lord God according to the Computation now used by the Church of Great Brittain Seventeen hundred thirty and two Between RICHARD BRIZANDINE of Southfarnham Pish in County of Essex Planter of one part and JAMES WEBB of the sd Pish & County Gent. of other part Witnesseth that the sd RICHARD BRIZANDINE for the Summe of four thousand pounds of good sound and merchantable tobacco to him paid he hath sold unto the said JAMES WEBB his heirs and assignes forever the lands in his actual possession now being by virtue of one Indenture for one year and by Statute for transferring uses into possession all that parcel of land conteyning ninety acres being part of a tract of land formerly sold by one SAMUEL GREEN to one JOHN GUNN and by the sd RICHARD BRIZANDINE purchased of JOHN HALL Son and Heir of SARAH GREEN and is adjoyning to a pcl of land the sd JAMES WEBB lately purchased of one SAMUEL GREEN lying on the DRAGON SWAMP with all its right and appurtenances together with all houses gardens lands waters profits belonging wch sd premises are in the Parish of Southfarnham aforesd and all To Have and To Hold to him the sd JAMES WEBB his heirs and assignes for ever. In Witness whereof the parties have set their hands & Seals in presence of JAMES COLLICOAT,   RICHARD ✝ BRIZANDINE
WILLIAM COLLICOAT, SAMLL. GREEN
At a Court held for Essex County at Tappa. on the XVIth day of January MDCCXXXII RICHARD BRIZANDINE ackowledged this Release indented to JAMES WEBB to be his act and deed which on the motion of the sd JAMES is admitted to record

pp.
376-
380

THIS INDENTURE made the Seventeenth day of October in the year of our Lord Christ one thousand seven hundred thirty and two Between BENJAMIN GRAVES of the Pish of Southfarnham in County of Essex Plantr. of one part and JAMES MUNDAY and THOMAS MERRITT of the Pish of St. Ann in the County aforesd Plantrs. of the other part Witnesseth that the sd BENJAMIN GRAVES for the sum of Two thousand pounds of tobacco hath gratned unto the sd JAMES MUNDAY & THOMAS MERRITT their heirs & assignes all that plantation tract of land and woodland whereon his Father JOHN GRAVES of the Pish of St. Ann in County aforesd deced lived at the time of his death containing two hundred acres (more of less) One hundred and fifty acres of which was taken away by a Survey made by Capt. XTOPHER BEVERLEY etc. being in the Pish of St. Ann in the County aforesd & bounded as followeth Vizt. on the land of Capt. XTOPHER BEVERLEY, CHARLES MUNDAYs, SAMLL. LOYDs, Colo. JOSEPH SMITHs deced and the sd JAMES MUNDAYs land with all & Singular it's rights houses edifices woods and appurtenances belonging which said Two hundred acres of land is part of a greater tract taken up by NICHOLAS CATLETT and WILLIAM MOSELEY of the County aforesd deced and the aforesd Two hundred acres conveyed by the sd NICHOLAS CATLETT to PETER JOHNSON and by PETER JOHNSON conveyed to one WILLIAM GANNOCK and by WILLIAM GANNOCK conveyed to JOHN GRAVES Father to the sd BENJAMIN GRAVES ptie to these presents by Conveyance bearing date the twenty ninth day of September one thousand Six hundred Eighty five as p the records of Essex County Court may appear To Have and To Hold the said land and all & singular the premises unto the said JAMES MUNDAY and THOS. MERRIT their heirs & assigns forever. In Witness whereof the parties have set their hands and Seals
in presence of JAMES MERRITT,   BENGIMIN ✝ GRAVES
THOMAS ⊤ MUNDAY, ROBERT I HAMBELTUN
At a Court held for Essex County at Tappa. on the XVIth day of January MDCCXXXII BENJAMIN GRAVES ackowledged this Deed of Feoffment indented with the Livery & Seizein thereon endorsed to JAMES MUNDAY & THOMAS MERRITT to be his act and deed which on the motion of the sd JAMES & THOMAS is admitted to record

pp.   THIS INDENTURE made the twelfth and thirteenth day of January in the year of
380-   our Lord God one thousand seven hundred and thirty two Between JOSEPH AN-
387   DERSON of the Parish of Southfarnham in County of Essex Planter of one part
       and JOHN ROBINSON of the Parrish of Southfarnham in County of Essex Esqr. of
the other part Witnesseth that the sd JOSEPH ANDERSON for the sum of Thirty eight
pounds Ten shillings of lawfull money of Virginia hath sold unto the sd JOHN ROBINSON
in his actual possession now being of the plantation hereafter mentioned by virtue of
Indenture for one year and of the statute for transferring uses into possession and to
his heirs forever all that plantation or persell of land containing One hundred & thirty
acres being in the Parrish of Southfarnham and County of Essex aforesd which was
granted to sd JOSEPH ANDERSON by PATTENT bearing date the twenty fourth day of
February One thousand Seven hundred and thirty in the Fourth year of the reign of
our Sovereign Lord GEORGE the Second and is bounded beginning at a Corner Hickory
of this land and the land of Mr. CLAYTON & Capt. REUBEN WELCH and running thence
along the sd WELCH's line South East to a Corner red Oak thence South West to a Corner
white Oak of this land & the land of THOMAS CROW thence along the sd CROWs line North
West to a red Oak on the upper side of a valley joining on the lands of FRANCIS MOORE
thence along an irregular line of mark't trees which divides this and the land of OWEN
OWINGS which if brought in a strait line will be North East to the beginning And all
houses buildings timber & appurtenances whatsoever belonging and all the Estate
right To Have and To Hold unto the sd JOHN ROBINSON his heirs and assigns forever. In
Witness whereof the parties have set their hands and seals
in presence of us FRANCIS SMITH,   JOS: ANDERSON
       RICHARD JONES, CATHARINE ROBINSON
At a Court held for Essex County at Tappa. on the XVIth day of January MDCCXXXII
JOSEPH ANDERSON acknowledged this his Release indented with the Receipt thereon endorsed to the Honble. JOHN ROBINSON Esqr. to be his act and deed which is admitted to
record

pp.   THIS INDENTURE made the Nineteenth day of March in the year of our Lord
387-   Christ according to the Computation now used in the Church of Great Brittain
388   one thousand seven hundred thirty and two Between GARRET BURN of the Pish
       of St. Anns in County of Essex of one part and FRANCIS GOULDMAN of the afore-
sd Pish and County of other part Witnesseth that ye sd GARRET for the sum of Twenty
shilling to him in hand paid doth sell and confirm unto the sd FRANCIS GOULDMAN and
to his heirs and assignes forever all his Estate Right and demand of and in one Plantation and pcell of land containing fifty acres being in the Pish & County aforesd and
bounded Vizt. binding on the land of Mr. EDMD. BAGGE, the land of CHARLES MUNDAY
and the land of JOHN LAWSON it be the land whereon the sd GARRET BURN formerly
lived and wch he purchased from DANLL. DISKEN and whereon JAMES MERRET now
lives To Have and To Hold the aforesd Plantation and every of their appurtenances unto
the sd FRANCIS GOULDMAN his heirs and assigns forever against him the sd GARRET
BURN his heirs or any other psons claiming under him. In Witness whereof the pties
have set their hands and Seals
in presence of JOHN SMITH   GARRIT BURN
At a Court held for Essex County at Tappa. on the XXth day of March MDCCXXXII
GARRET BURN acknwledged this his Deed indented with the livery & seizen thereon to
FRANCIS GOULDMAN which on his motion is admitted to record

pp.   THIS INDENTURE made the Sixteenth day of March in the Sixth yeare of the
388-   reigne of our Sovereigne Lord GEORGE the Second in the yeare of our Lord one

390   thousand seaven hundred thirty and two Betweene WILLIAM BROOKES of ye
        Parish of St. Anns in the County of Essex of one part and THOMAS SHORT of the
Parish and County aforesd of other part Witnesseth that ye sd WILLIAM BROOKS for ye
sum of Twenty pounds Curt. mony of Virginia to him paid hath granted unto the sd
THOMAS SHORT his heirs and assignes forever One hundred and fifty acres of land
being in ye Parish and County aforesaid bounded begining at a white Oake about foure
poles above ye MAIN ROADE Corner tree to HAWKINS PATTENT thence with HAWKINS
line North East to the first above mentioned beginning togeather with all and singular
the profits and appurtenances whatsoever belonging and all ye Estate rights of him the
sd WILLIAM BROOKES To Have and To Hold unto ye sd THOMAS SHORT his heirs and assignes forever and allso yt ye sd WILLIAM BROOKES his heirs etc will acknowledge this
Deede in Essex County Court, and that his Wife FRANCES will then and there relinquishe
her right of Dower in ye premises when required. In Witness whereof the sd partys
have set their hands and seals
in presence of JNO. VAWTER,   WM. BROOKS
     WM. SHORT, THOMAS TILLER
  At a Court held for Essex County at Tappa. on ye XXth day of March MDCCXXXII
WM. BROOKS acknowledged this his Deed of Feofment indented & livery & seizin to THO-
MAS SHORT which on his motion is admitted to record
  Also the same day Came into Court FRANCES ye Wife of the sd WM. BROOKS & freely relinquished her right of Dower in ye land conveyed by this Deed to THOMAS SHORT wch
was admitted to record

pp.   THIS INDENTURE made the nineteenth day of March one thousand seven hun-
391-   dred and thirty Three Between JOHN LAWSON of the Parrish of St. Anns and
393   County of Essex Planter of one part and JOHN STOKES of the aforesd Parrish and
        County Carpenter of other part Witnesseth that for the sume of Six pounds Five
shillings Currt. money of Virginia unto the said JOHN LAWSON in hand paid he doth sell
& confirm unto the sd JOHN STOKES his heirs and assigns all that his part of a tract of
land being in the above Parrish and County containing One hundred acres, the which
said part being the halfe of the sd hundred acres together with all Houses Orchards and
trees to the same belonging and all the Estate right whatsoever of him the said JOHN
LAWSON To Have and To Hold unto the said JOHN STOKES his heirs and assigns forever.
In Witness whereof the parties have set their hands and seals
in presents of us .W. RENNOLDS,   JOHN ( ) LAWSON
     JAMES MARRITT
  At a Court held for Essex County at Tappa. on the XXth day of March MDCCXXXII
JOHN LAWSON acknowledged this Deed indented with the Livery and Seizen thereon endorsed to JOHN STOKES which on his motion is admitted to record
     KNOW ALL MEN by these presents that I JOHN LAWSON am held and firmly bound
unto JOHN STOKES in the sum of Twelve pounds Ten shillings Curt. money of Virginia
this nineteenth day of March 1732/3.
  THE CONDITION of this obligation is such that if JOHN LAWSON shall truely keep all the
agreements mentioned in Indenture that then this obligation to be void else to stand in
full force
in presence of W. RENNOLDS,   JOHN ⊙ LAWSON
     JAMES MARRITT
  At a Court held for Essex County at Tappa. on the XXth day of March MDCCXXXII
JOHN LAWSON acknowledged this bond to JOHN STOKES to be his act and deed which is
admitted to record

pp.   THIS INDENTURE made the Thirteenth day of March in the Sixth year of the
393-   Reign of our Sovereign Lord GEORGE the Second & Anno Domini one thousand
396   seven hundred thirty two Between SILVESTER AMIS of the County of GLOU-
         CESTER of one part & PETER KEMP of the said County of the other part Witnesseth
that the said SILVESTER AMIS for the sum of Fifty one pounds Thirteen shillings Current money of Virginia hath sold unto the said PETER KEMP his heirs and assigns forever all that tract of land being in Essex County containing three hundred and seventy
five acres bounded Beginning at a great corner marked Pine devideing this land from a
Tract of land belonging to Major GEORGE MORRIS and JAMES VAUGHAN and runing
thence South to a corner Stooping red Oak by a Branch side thence South East to a Corner Pine on a point by the same Branch thence down the same Branch again South to
two Corner white Oaks in the said Branch belonging to THOMAS GAINES thence along
the said GAINES's line East to a Corner stooping red Oak at the head of a Branch thence
North East to a great leaning white Oak on the head of a deep valley or Bottom issueing
out of a branch of HOSKINS CREEK thence West North West to the beginning place
where it begun together with all houses, buildings, waters & all other advantages to the
said three hundred and seventy five acres of land all which sd granted premises are
now in the actual possession of him the said PETER KEMP by vertue of Indenture of
Lease for the term of one year bearing date the day before the date hereof & by force of
the Statute for transferring uses into possession To Have and To Hold the said land &
premises unto him the said PETER KEMP his heirs and assigns forever. In Witness
whereof the sd SILVESTER AMIS to this present Indenture hath set his hand & Seal
in presence of us SAMLL. SMITH,   SILVESTER AMIS
         CHARLES WORTHAM
   At a Court held for Essex County at Tappa. on the XXth day of March Ano Dom MDCCXXXII
SILVESTER AMIS acknowledged this his Release indented to PETER KEMP which is admitted to record

pp.   THIS INDENTURE made the Second day of January in the year of our Lord God one
396-   thousand seven hundred thirty two three by and Between TOBIAS INGRAM of St.
398   Anns Parish in Essex County of one part and JAMES SAMUEL and JOHN MARTIN
         both of the sd Parrish & County of the other part Witnesseth that the sd TOBIAS
INGRAM in consideration of three thousand three hundred pounds of good sound Merchantable Tobo. by the sd JAMES SAMUEL and JOHN MARTIN to the sd TOBIAS INGRAM
paid whereof he hath granted & confirmed unto them the said JAMES SAMUEL & JOHN
MARTIN their heirs and assigns for and during the space and term of twenty one years
one certain tract of land containing One hundred acres being part of a tract of land
granted to the sd TOBIAS INGRAM by Majr. ROBERT BROOKS lying and being in the
Parish & County aforesd and bounded upon the RANGE & COPLINs lines and so as to contain One hundred acres as aforesd together with all and singular the profitts and appurtenances whatsoever to the said land belonging To Have and To Hold unto them the
said JAMES SAMUEL and JOHN MARTIN during the abovesd Term of Twenty and one
years from the date hereof and from thence to be fully ended they paying yearly the
Quitrents of the abovesaid Land and also one ear of Indian Corn to the said TOBIAS
INGRAM or his assigns if demanded and also that he the said TOBIAS INGRAM will acknowledge the said Lease unto them in Essex County Court and that his Wife JANE will
then and there Relinquish her right of Dower in the premises when thereunto required. In Witness whereof the above party hath sett their hands and Seals
in presence of JOS. SORRILL,   TOBIAS INGRAM
         JOHN BATES JUR., ROBERT FARMAR

At a Court held for Essex County at Tappa. on ye XIXth day of March Ano Dom MDCCXXXII
TOBIAS INGRAM acknowledged this Lease of land indented to JAMES SAMUEL & JOHN
MARTIN together with the Livery & Seizen thereon endorsed which is admitted to
record

pp.   TO ALL CHRISTIAN PEOPLE to whome these presents shall come I EMANUEL WIL-
398-   LIAMS of the Parrish of Southfarnham in County of Essex send Greeting. Know
399   ye that I the said EMANUEL WILLIAMS in consideration of the natural affection
       and fatherly love which I have to my well beloved Son HUGH WILLIAMS, as also
for diverse other good causes, have given & confirm'd and by these presents do give
unto my Son HUGH WILLIAMS One hundred & fifty acres of land being part of the land I
now live on & joining to the land of WILLIAM BROOCKE with all and singular its rights
together with all houses, buildings, profits and appurtenances whatsoever belonging
To Have and To Hold the said One hundred and fifty acres of land and all the premises
unto my said Son HUGH WILLIAMS to the only proper use & behoof of the said HUGH
WILLIAMS his heirs and assigns forever, and I will forever defend by these presents.
In Witness whereof I have set my hand & seal this 17th day of February in the year of
our Lord one thousand seven hundred Thirty and two three
in presence of HUGH WILLIAMS,   EMMANUEL WILLIAMS
     WILLIAM CALLICOAT, RICHARD R REASON
 At a Court held for Essex County at Tappa. on the XXth day of March MDCCXXXII
EMANUEL WILLIAMS acknowledged his Deed indented with the Livery & seizen thereon
endorsed to HUGH WILLIAMS which is admitted to record

pp;   KNOW ALL MEN by these presents yt I JOHANNAH COLEMAN Wife of RICHARD
399-   COLEMAN of ye County of HANNOVER in Saint Martins Parrish doe Constitute &
400   apoint Mr. EDMUN BOOKER of ye County of Essex in Saint Anns Parrish my true
       and lawfull Atorney to acknowledge my right of Dower to Mr. NATHANIELL FOG
which I have in a parsell of land which my husband RICHRD. COLEMAN sold sum time
agoe to Mr. NATHANIELL FOG ye said land lieing in Essex County & my husband RICHRD.
COLEMAN acknowledged ye same to ye said For & whereas I did not then acknowledge
my right of Dower which I have in ye said land therefore I doe by this Instrument of
righting impower my frend Mr. EDMUN BOOKER to acknowledge ye said land to Mr.
NATHANIELL FOG notifieing & confirmeing wt. my said Attorney shall doe. In Witnis
whereof I have hereunto set my hand & Seale this 19th day of March 1732/3
Testes DANIELL CLAYTON,   JOHANNAH COLEMAN
     JOHN CLARKE
 At a Court held for Essex County at Tappa. on the XXth day of March MDCCXXXII
This Power of Attorney from JOHANNA COLEMAN to EDMOND BOOKER was proved by ye
Oaths of all the witnesses thereto & was admitted to record

pp.   THIS INDENTURE witnesseth that EDMUND PAGETT natural & lawfull Sone of
400-   EPHRAIM PAGETT late of the Parish of St. Anns in the County of Essex deced an
401   Orphan of ye age of Seventeen years by and wth the approbation & consent of
       ye Court of Essex County doth by these presents put himself Apprentice to WIL-
LIAM BEVERLEY of ye sd County Gent. with him to dwell & serve for and during the full
term of three whole years to begin from ye day of ye date hereof during which time ye
sd apprentice his sd Master shall serve, his secrets keep & Comands obey, hurt to his
Master he shall not doe nor cause or procure to be done by others, the goods of his sd
Master he shall not imbezel purloin or waste the same but in all things as a good and
faithfull apprentice bear and behave himself toward his sd Master, fornication the sd

Apprentice shall not committ, Matrimony he shall not contract, at Cards or Dice he shall not play, he shall not absent himself day or night without consent of his sd Master, and the sd Master shall find and provide Sufficient meat, drink, washing lodging and Clothing during his Apprenticeship wth due Correction and at the expiration of ye sd apprentice his sd Master is to give one new suit of wearing Cloaths. In Witness whereof ye sd parties have set their hands and Seals this XXth day of March Anno Dom MDCCXXXII in presence of us　　　　　　　　　　　　　EDMD. PAGETT
　　　　BENJA. WINSLOW, FRAS. SMITH　　　　　　W. BEVERLEY

At a Court held for Essex County at Tappa. on ye XXth day of March MDCCXXXII EDMOND PAGETT by & with the Consent of ye Court bound himself an apprentice to WILLIAM BEVERLEY gent. & with ye sd WILLIAM signed this Indenture in Court which is admitted to record

p.　KNOW ALL MEN by these presents that we ROBERT PARKER & JOHN EDMONDSON
401　are held and firmly bound unto our Sovereign Lord GEORGE ye 2d. in ye full sum
　　of ten thousand pounds of Tobo this XXth day of March MDCCXXXII

THE CONDITION of ye above obligation is such that Whereas FRANCES LAYTON hath obtained a Licence to keep an ORDINARY at her House if therefore ye sd FRANCES doth constantly find and provide in her ORDINARY good wholesome & cleanly lodging & diet for travellers and Stableage fodder and provender or pasturage & provender as ye Season of ye year shall require for their Horses for and during ye term of one whole year from ye day of ye date hereof and shall not suffer any unlawfull gameing in her house nor on ye Sabbath day suffer any to Tipple more then is necessary that then ye above obligation to be void else to remain in force

　　　　　　　　　　　　　　　　　　RO. PARKER
　　　　　　　　　　　　　　　　　　JON. EDMONDSON

At a Court held for Essex County at Tappa. on ye 20th day of March 1732 ROBERT PARKER & JOHN EDMONDSON acknowledged this bond to be their act & deed which was ordered to be recorded

pp.　KNOW ALL MEN by these presents that we SUSANNA FOWLER, EDWARD ROWZEE
401-　& BENJA. ROWZEE are held and firmly bound unto WM. DAINGERFIELD, SALR.
403　MUSCOE, ROBT. BROOKE, ALEXR. PARKER, WM. BROOKE & THOS. STHRESHLY JUNR.
　　Gent Justices of the County of Essex & their heirs in ye sum of one thousand pounds Currt. mony we bind ourselves this 17th day of Aprill Anno Dom MDCCXXXIII

THE CONDITION of the above obligation is such that if the above bound SUSANNA FOWLER Administratrx. of all ye goods chattles and credits of WM. FOWLER deceased do make or cause to be made a true and perfect inventory of all and singular the goods chattles and credits of the sd deced which shall come to her hands and ye same so made do exhibit or cause to be exhibited in ye Court of Essex at such times as she shall be thereunto required by ye said Court and further do make a true and just account of all her actings and doings therein when required and all the rest of ye sd goods chattles & credits wch shall be found upon account being first examined & allowed by ye Justices of ye Court shall deliver & pay unto such persons as the Justices shall order and provided & if it shall hereafter appear that any last Will and Testament was made by ye sd deced & the Exr. or Exrs. therein named do exhibit ye same in ye sd Court making request to have it allowed and approved accordingly if ye sd SUSANNA being thereunto required do render and deliver up her Letters of Admon. approbation of such Testament being first had and made in the sd Court that then ye above obligation to be void and of none effect

　　　　　　　　　　　SUSANNA 〇 FOWLER
　　　　　EDWARD ROWZEE　　　BENJA. ROWZEE

At a Court held for Essex County at Tappa. on ye XVIIth day of April MDCCXXXIII
SUSANNA FOWLER, EDWARD ROWZEE & BENJA. ROWZEE acknowledged this their bond to
be their act and deed wch is ordered to be recorded

pp. THIS INDENTURE made the fifteenth and Sixteenth day of April in the Sixth year
403- of the reign of our Sovereign Lord GEORGE the second and in the year of our
409 Lord one thousand seven hundred and thirty three Between RICHARD CORTHORN
of the Parish of Southfarnham in County of Essex Planter of one part and the
Honorable JOHN ROBINSON of the same Parish and County Esqr. of other part Witnesseth
that for the sum of fifteen pounds Sterling to the said RICHARD CORTHORN in hand paid
he doth hereby grant unto the said JOHN ROBINSON (in his actual possession now being
by virtue of a Bargain and Sale for one year and by force of the Statute for transferring uses into possession) and to his heirs and assigns forever all that parcell of land
containing Seventeen acres being upon the mouth of PISCATTAWAY CREEK in the
Parish and County aforesaid Begining at a small white Oak at the head of BUSHES OLD
SPRING BRANCH and runing then North East to a small hickory in the old field thence
North East to a small red Oak by the head of the MYRTLE SWAMP and thence down the
said Swamp according to the several meanders thereof to the begining the same being
formerly purchased by him the said RICHARD CORTHORN of one RICHARD BUSH and
granted to him by said RICHARD BUSH by Deed bearing date the Twenty ninth day of
May in the year of our Lord one thousand seven hundred and Six and all houses,
buildings, waters and appurtenances whatsoever belonging and all the Estate right
whatsoever To Have and To Hold unto the said JOHN ROBINSON his heirs and assigns
forever. In Witness whereof the partys have set their hands and Seals
in presence of EDW: BARRADALL,   RICHARD *RC* CORTHORN
          W. BEVERLEY
At a Court held for Essex County at Tappa. on the XVIIth day of April MDCCXXXIII
RICHARD CORTHORN acknowledged this Release of land indented with the Receipt thereon endorsed to the Honble. JOHN ROBINSON Esqr. which is admitted to record
          KNOW ALL MEN by these presents that I RICHARD CORTHORN am held and firmly
bound unto the Honorable JOHN ROBINSON in the sum of Thirty pounds Sterling dated
the Sixteenth day of April in the Sixth year of the reign of our Sovereign Lord GEORGE
the second & Anno Domini 1733
THE CONDITION of this obligation is such that if the above bound RICHARD CORTHORN
shall at all time truely observe all Covenants which on his part ought to be observed as
expressed in Indenture that then this Obliglation to be void or otherwise to remain in
force in presence of EDW. BARRADALL   RICHARD *RC* CORTHORN
          W. BEVERLEY
At a Court held for Essex County at Tappa. on the XVIIth day of Aprill MDCCXXXIII
RICHARD CORTHORN acknowledged this bond to be his act and deed which is admitted to
record

pp. THIS INDENTURE made the twenty fourth day of March in the year of our Lord
410- Christ according to the Computation now used in the Church of Great Brittain
412 one thousand seven hundred thirty and two Between FRANCIS GOULDMAN of the
County of Essex of one part and JOHN WILCOX of the aforesd County Gent. of the
other part Witnesseth that sd FRANCIS GOULDMAN for the sum of Ten pounds Curt. mony
of Virga. hath granted unto JOHN WILCOX and to his heirs and assignes forever a plantation and tract of land containing Fifty acres being in the Pish of St. Anns and County
aforesd and bounded on the land of JOSEPH & CHARLES MUNDAY, JOHN LAWSON & EDMD.
BAGGE & it being the land formerly purchased by one GARRET BURN from DANLL. DIS-

KIN and by the sd GARRET BURN sold & conveyed to FRANCIS GOULDMAN ptie to these presents, relation being had to the records of the aforesd County may more fully appear with the appurtenances together wth all houses buildings Orchards trees profits wtsoever To Have and To Hold unto ye sd JOHN WILCOX his heirs and assigns to their own proper use. In Witness whereof the pties have set their hands and seals
in presence of SALVATOR MUSCOE,   FRANCIS GOULDMAN
        RICHARD COVINGTON, JOHN SMITH,
        EDWD. E RILEY
    At a Court held for Essex County at Tappa. on Tuesday the XVIIth day of April MDCCXXXIII This Deed indented with the livery and Seizin thereon endorsed from FRANCIS GOULDMAN to JOHN WILCOX gent was proved by the oaths of all the Witnesses thereto and on his motion the same is admitted to record

pp.   THIS INDENTURE made the fourteenth day of May in the year of our Lord Christ
412-   one thousand seven hundred and thirty three Between JOHN NEWTON of the Pish
415   of St. Anns in the County of Essex Plantr. of the one part and JOHN CIRGAN of the
            aforesd Pish and County Plantr. of the other part Witnesseth that the sd JOHN
NEWTON for and in consideration of one Negro man named Dick of the value of Twenty & seven pounds Currt. money of Virginia to him paid by sd JOHN CIRGAN he the sd JOHN NEWTON hath sold unto the sd JOHN CIRGAN his heirs and assigns one parcell of land or woodland ground containing Forty acres being in the Pish & County aforesd and bounded begining at a red Oak standing on the MAIN ROAD side it being a Corner tree of the land purchased by Capt. SALVATOR MUSCOE from WM. STOAKS and a line tree of the said NEWTON ptie to these presents from thence along the sd NEWTONs line to two corner red Oaks being corner trees of the land of the abovesd JOHN CIRGAN standing in a vallie at ye head of DOLLS MIRE from thence along sd JOHN NEWTONs line to a corner red Oake thence along sd NEWTONs line to a large white Oake Corner tree to sd JOHN NEWTON, Colo. WILLIAM BEVERLEY & THOMAS DAVIS from thence to the MAIN ROAD thence up ye MAINE ROAD to the red Oak where it first began Including all the land claimed by the sd JOHN NEWTON on the West side of the aforesd MAINE ROAD with all & Singular the appurtenances thereunto belonging togethr. with all houses, gardens profits whatsoever appertaining which sd Forty acres of land is part of One hundred and Ninety acres of land purchased by HENRY NEWTON of the aforesaid Pish & county deced Grand Father of the sd JOHN NEWTON ptie to these presents from Mr. HUMPHREY BOOTH late of the Pish & County aforesd deced as by the records of the County Court of Essex may more fully appear To Have and To Hold the sd parcel of land to the only use and behoof of the said JOHN CIRGAN his heirs & assignes. In Witness whereof the pties first above named have set their hands and Seals
in presence of SALVATOR MUSCOE,   JOHN NEWTON
        THO: EDWARDS
    AT a Court held for Essex County at Tappa. on ye XVth day of May Anno Dom MDCCXXXIII JOHN NEWTON ackowledged this his Deed indented with the livery & Seizen thereon endorsed to be his act and deed wch is admitted to record

p.   KNOW ALL MEN by these presents that we ALEXANDER PARKER, THOMAS
416   WARING and ROBERT BROOKE of Essex County gent are held and firmly bound
            unto our Sovern. Lord GEORGE the Second of Great Britain in the Just Sum of one thousand pounds Sterling Witness our hands this fifteenth day of May in the year of our Lord one thousand seven hundred & thirty three
    THE CONDITION of the above obligation is such that whereas the above bound ALEXANDER PARKER gent is by Comission from the Honble the Governor appoint SHERIFF of

this County of Essex Now if the aforesd ALEXANDER PARKER shall render to the Auditor
& Receiver General of his Matys Revenues a particular perfect account of all his Matys
rents and dues arising in the said County & also due payment make of all other Publick
dues & fees put into his hands to collect in the said County unto the several persons to
whom the same shall be payable, and true performance make of all matters relating to
his Office dureing his continuance therein: Then the above obligation to be void & of
none effect otherwise to remain in force

ALEXANDER PARKER

T. WARING   RO: BROOKE

At a Court held for Essex County at Tappa. on ye XVth day of May MDCCXXXIII
This Bond was acknowledged by ALEXANDER PARKER, THOMAS WARING & ROBERT
BROOKE Gent to be their act & deed which is ordered to be recorded

pp.   KNOW ALL MEN by these presents that we THOMAS HARDY & JOHN EDMONDSON
416-   are held and firmly bound unto our Sovereign Lord GEORGE the 2d in the just
417   sum of ten thousand pounds of Tobacco we bind ourselves this XVth day of May
        Ano Dom MDCCXXXIII
THE CONDITION of ye above obligation is that Whereas THOMAS HARDY hath obtained a
Licence to keep an ORDINARY at his House if therefore sd THOMAS HARDY doth constantly provide in his ORDINARY good wholsom & cleanly Lodging and diet for Travellers & Stableage fodder and provender or pasturage and provender as the Season of the
year shall require for their Horses for and during ye term of one whole year from the
day of the date hereof and shall not suffer any unlawfull gameing in his House nor on
the Sabbath day suffer any to Tipple more then is necessary that then the above obligation to be void else to remain in full force

THOS. HARDY

JNO. EDMONDSON

At a Court held for Essex County at Tappa. on ye XVth day of May MDCCXXXIII
THOMAS HARDY & JOHN EDMONDSON acknowledged this bond to be their act and deed
which is odered to be recorded

pp.   THIS INDENTURE made the ninth and tenth day of April in ye year of our Lord
417-   God one thousand seven hundred & thirty three Between RICHARD BEALE of the
421   Parish of Southfarnham Essex County in Virginia of one part and THOMAS
        CAUTHORN of the Parish County and Colony aforesd of the other part Witnesseth
that the sd RICHARD BEALE for Seventeen acres of land lying near PISCATAWAY CREEK
on the South side thereof joyning to the land of the heires of Mr. THOMAS MERRI-
WETHER which sd land was bought by RICHARD CAUTHORN of RICHD. BUSH as may by
Deed more at large appeare & Eight hundred pounds of Tobacco to him the sd RICHARD
BEALE in hand paid or well secured to be paid by the said THOMAS CAUTHORN at or before the Ensealing of these presents whereof he the sd RICHD. BEALE doth grant unto
the sd THOMAS CAUTHORN and to his heirs a certain tract of land containing sixty acres
which sd land & plantation the sd RICHD. BEALE purchased of RICHD. JOHNSON by Deeds
bearing date the 29th March 1728 & by the sd RICHARD JOHNSON purchased of RICHD.
JONES and MARY his Wife by Deeds dated ye 5th day of January 1721 as will more at
large appeare Begining at a Corner in JOHN EVANS line formerly Capt. JOSIAH PICKES
his land thence along the line of the sd PICKES and this Sixty acres South East along
THOMAS JOHNSONs line to a drove Stake thence adjoyning the said THOMAS JOHNSON his
land Northwest to a white Oak thence North East to a white Oak thence to the Begining
togather with all and singular the waies waters profitts & appurtenances whatsoever to
the sd Land & plantation belonging all which said Sixty acres of land and likewise all

the houses and premises are now in the actual possession of him the sd THOMAS CAU-
THORN by virtue of an Indenture of Bargain and Sale for one year and by Virtue of the
statute for transferring uses into possession and all the Estate right and demand whatsoever To Have and To Hold unto the sd THOMAS CAUTHORN his heirs and assignes forever. In Wittness whereof the sd RICHD. hath set his hand and seal
in presence of SAMLL. CLAYTON,   RICHD. BEALE
       JOHN ✠ HOSKINGS; MARTHA ⋀ HOSKINGS
    At a Court held for Essex County at Tappa. on the XVth day of May MDCCXXXIII
RICHARD BEALE acknowledged this his Release of land Indented to THOMAS CAUTHORN
to be his act and deed & ELIZABETH ye Wife of the sd RICHD. freely relinquished her
Dower of & in ye lands & premises conveyed by this Deed to the said THOMAS CAUTHORN
which is admitted to record

pp.   THIS INDENTURE made the fourteenth and fifteenth day of May in the year of
421-   our Lord Christ one thousand seven hundred and thirty three Between ROBT.
426   FOSTER of the Parish of St. Drisdall in County of KING & QUEEN Planter of one
          part and WILLIAM TAYLOR of the Parish of St. Anns in the County of Essex of the
other part Witnesseth that the sd ROBT. FOSTER for the sum of Thirty & six pounds Curt.
money doth sell unto the sd WILLIAM TAYLOR in his actual possession by virtue of one
Indenture for one year & of the Statute for transferring uses into possession one parcel
of land woodland containing One hundred acres & being in the Parish of St. Anns in the
County of Essex and bounded beginning at a sweet Gum standing in the Main Swamp of
GILSONS RUN and runing up the West side of a large Branch that Issueth out of the sd
main GILSONS SWAMP to the first fork of the sd Branch and from thence along the West
Fork to a Maple standing in the sd Branch standing nigh the line of JOHN GARNETT and
from thence through the woods to a Poplar standing on a Stoney Hill in the Plantation
of the sd WM. TAYLOR & from thence down a Row of Chery Trees a strait Corse to the
Main Run of GILLSONS SWAMP & so down ye Main Run to include all that percell of land
wch JOHN FOSTER conveyed to the sd ROBT. FOSTER as p the sd Conveyance & all ways
waters trees & appurtenances belonging To Have and To Hold to the proper use and
behoof of him the said WILLIAM TAYLOR his heirs & assigns forever. In Witness
whereof the parties have set their hands and Seals
in presence of us THOMAS WARREN,   ROBT. FOSTER
       THOS. SAMUEL, JAMES   NOEL
    At a Court held for Essex County at Tappa. on the XVth day of May MDCCXXXIII
ROBERT FOSTER acknowledged this his Release of land indented to WILLIAM TAYLOR to
be his act and deed & MARY the Wife of the sd ROBERT freely relinquished her dower in
the lands conveyed to the sd WILLIAM TAYLOR which on his motion is admitted to
record

pp.   TO ALL CHRISTIAN PEOPLE to whome these presents shall come I NICHOLAS
426-   SMITH of the Parrish of Southfarnham in the County of Essex send Greeting.
427   Know ye that I the sd NICHOLAS SMITH as well for the Natural affection and
          fatherly love which I have unto my Beloved Son NICHOLAS SMITH as also for
divers other causes have given and do fully and absolutely grant unto my said Son
NICHOLAS SMITH & to his heirs and assigns forever one certain percel of land being in
Southfarnham Parrish in the County of Essex & joining to the land I now live on containing Three hundred acres bounded begining at a Popler standing in my MILL
SWAMP & runing thence North West along a line of marked trees Parting this land and
the land of EDWARD BOMAR to a Corner red Oak parting this land & the land of WILLIAM
DOBYNS deceased, thence North East to a Quarter North along the line parting this land

& the land of DOBBYNS to another Corner red Oak parting this land & the land of JOHN
CHEYNEY to a white Oak standing on the South side of JOHN CHEYNEYS SPRING BRANCH
thence down the Branch until it comes into my MILL SWAMP thence up the MILL
SWAMP to the begining with all & singular its Rights Buildings, Orchards, Pastures or
any profits and heriditaments whatsoever belonging and all the Estate right of me the
sd NICHOLAS SMITH To Have and to Hold the said Tract of land with the appurtenances to
my sd Son NICHOLAS SMITH to the only proper use & behoof of him my said Son his
heirs & assigns forever. In Witness whereof I have sett my hand and Seal this 15th day
of May in the year of our Lord one thousand seven hundred & thirty three
in presence of SAMLL. SMITH,   NICHO. SMITH
        FRANS. SMITH
    At a Court held for Essex County at Tappa. on ye XVth day of May MDCCXXXIII
NICHOLAS SMITH acknowledged his Deed of Gift indented with ye livery & Seizen thereon endorsed to his Son NICHOLAS SMITH to be his act & deed which is admitted to record

p.   KNOW ALL MEN by these presents that I JAMES RULE of the City of LINLITHGOW
428   in the Kingdom of Great Brittain Mercht do constitute and appoint THOMAS
        JONES of ye County of Essex my true & lawfull Attorney with full power to de-
mand sue for and receive in my name and for my use all sums of mony or Tobo. which
remain due to me in the Colony of Virginia. As Witness my hand and seal this 2d. day of
September 1732
Test   WILLIAM JONES,   JAMES RULE
        JAMES AOTKINS
    At a Court held for Essex County at Tappa. on the XVth day of May MDCCXXXIII
This Power of Attorny from JAMES RULE to THOMAS JONES was proved by the oaths of ye
Witnesses thereto & admitted to record

pp.   KNOW ALL MEN by these presents that I THOMAS MASON and ANN my Wife of the
428-   Parrish of Southfarnham and County of Essex are holden and firmly bound unto
429   MARY FRANK of the Parrish and County aforesd and to her heirs etc. the full
        sum of One hundred pounds Currant money of Virginia this 5th day of Septemr.
1732. THE CONDITION of this obligation is such that whereas the above bound THOMAS
MASON and ANN his Wife and the above named MARY FRANK hath an equall right and
title to a certain parcell of land in the Parrish and County aforesd containing Two hundred & forty eighty acres and both parties haveing agreed to make a devition of the sd
land hath made choice of Capt. JAMES WOOD of KING & QUEEN COUNTY to Survey and divide the said land between the aforesd parties and if the sd THOS. MASON and ANN and
their heirs etc. doe forever hereafter abide by the Judgment Survey and Division that
the said JAMES WOOD doth make soe that sd MARY FRANK her heirs etc. or any of them
be never hereafter molested by sd THOMAS MASON and his heirs in the peaceable and
quiet possession of the bounds made that then this obligation to be void otherwise to
remain in full force
in presence of J. WOOD,   THO. MASON
        JOHN FARGESON. DENNIS D DUN   ANN A MASON
    At a Court held for Essex County at Tappa. on ye XVth day of May MDCCXXXIII
This Bond from THOMAS MASON & ANN MASON to MARY FRANK was proved by the oath
of JOHN FARGESON a witness thereto and admitted to record

p.   KNOW ALL MEN by these presents that we JON. VAWTER & WM. GRAY are held
429   and firmly bound unto our Sovereign Lord George ye 2d in ye full sum of Ten
        thousand pounds of Tobo this 15th day of May MDCCXXXIII.

THE CONDITION of ye above obligation is that Whereas JON. VAWTER hath obtained a
Licence to keep an ORDINARY at his House in this County if Therefore the sd JNO.
VAWTER doth constantly provide in his ORDINARY good wholsome and clenly lodging
and diet for travellers & Stableage fodder & provender or pasturage and provender as
the Season shall require for their Horses for and during the term of one whole year
from ye day of the date hereof and shall not permitt any unlawfull gameing in his
House nor on ye Sabbath day suffer any to Tipple more then is necessary that then this
obligation to be void else to stand in force

JNO. VAWTER
WM. GRAY

At a Court held for Essex County at Tappa. on ye XVth day of May MDCCXXXIII
This bond was acknowledged by JOHN VAWTER and WILLIAM GRAY to be their act &
deed & by the Court was ordered to be recorded

pp.   KNOW ALL MEN by these presents that we GEORGE BECKHAM, WILLIAM TAYLOR
429-   & THOMAS DANIELL are held & firmly bound unto THOMAS WARING, SALVATOR
430   MUSCOE, JAMES GARNETT & RICHARD TYLER JUNR. Gentlemen Justices of ye
        County of Essex & their heirs and Successors in the sum of Two hundred pounds
Sterling this XVth day of May MDCCXXXIII
THE CONDITION of ye above obligation is such that if the said GEORGE BECKHAM Guardian of ANN BERRY his heirs & Admrs. do truly pay unto the sd Orphan all such Estates
as now is or hereafter shall come to ye hands of sd GEORGE BECKHAM as soon as sd Orphan shall attain to lawfull age or when required by sd Justices of the peace of the
County of Essex as also to keep harmless the sd Justices from all Trouble that may arise
about ye sd Estate that then this obligation to be void elce to remain in full force

GEORGE X BECKHAM
WILLIAM +++TAYLOR   THO: DANIELL

At a Court held for Essex County at Tappa. on ye XVth day of May MDCCXXXIII
GEORGE BECKHAM, WILLIAM TAYLOR & THOMAS DANIELL acknowledged this bond to be
their act and deed which was ordered to be recorded

pp.   KNOW ALL MEN by these presents that we JOHN MEGGS & RICHARD BEALE are
430-   held & firmly bound unto JOHN BATES his heirs or assigns in the sum of twenty
431   four pounds dated this XVIth day of May MDCCXXXIII
        THE CONDITION of the above obligation is such that whereas Judgmt. being this
day given in Essex County Court unto sd JOHN BATES against JOHN MEGGS in an action of
Trespass on ye Case depending between (them) & the sd JOHN MEGGS had an appeal
granted him to the 8th day of the next Generall Court giveing Security according to Law
if therefore the sd JOHN MEGGS appellant as aforesd shall accordingly appear and
prosecute the sd appeal at the sd next General Court and pform the Judgment of the sd
Court and pay the damages of fifteen p cent which the Law gives upon the principal
debt damages & Costs of County Court this day recovered if cast in the sd appeal that
then the above obligation to be void otherwise to be in full power.

JOHN MEGGS
RICHD. BEALE

At a Court contd. & held for Essex County at Tappa. on ye XVIth day of May MDCCXXXIII
JOHN MEGGS & RICHARD BEALE acknowledged this bond to JOHN BATES to be their act &
deed wch on his motion is admitted to record

p.   KNOW ALL MEN by these presents that I JOHN WOOD of the County of Essex Tayler
431   do hereby appoint JOSEPH LEMAN of the aforesd County my true and lawfull
         Attorney for me to demand and receive all sums of mony or Tobo due to me in
the sd County or else where and to give discharges & acquitances for the same, and on
the refusal of payment to prosecute and act therein as tho I myself were personally
present. In Witness whereof I have set my hand and Seal the 10th of Apl. 1733
in presence of RALPH FARMAR,   JOHN WOOD
         ELIZA. JONES
   At a Court held for Essex County at Tappa. on the XIXth day of June MDCCXXXIII
This Power of Attorney from JOHN WOOD to JOSEPH LEEMAN was proved by the Oaths of
both ye Witnesses thereto and was admitted to record

pp.   KNOW ALL MEN by these presents that we ANDREW CROSBIE of DUMFRIES Mer-
431-   chant for my self and Company and JOHN CORRIE of DUMFRIES aforesd Mer-
432   chant have for sundry good causes appointed in our staed and place put our
         Trusty and well beloved friends JAMES CORBETT & EBENEZER YOUNG of DUMFRIES
aforesd Merchants and ROBT. SPENCE Commander of the Good Ship *SUCCESS OF
DUMFRIES* and each of them our true and lawfull Attorneys for us to demand sue for
recover and receive fourteen thousand three hundred and forty nine pounds of Tobacco contained in a bond granted by Captain BENJAMIN WINSLOW dated the first day of
September last past payable on the first day of May next and two thousand eight hundred & seventy pounds of Tobacco contained in another bond granted by RICHARD TUN-
STALL both which bonds were Lodged by me the said JOHN CORRIE with Mr. JAMES REID
of URBANA in Virginia as his Receipt dated the fifteenth of September aforesd makes
appear As also seven hundred and twenty pounds of Tobacco containd in a Bill or order
drawn by Collonell WILLIAM BEVERLIE of Essex County in Virginia aforesd the 24th day
of July last upon Mr. JAMES REID payable to me the sd JOHN CORRIE by these presents
granting to our sd Attorneys authority in the premises to take all lawfull ways and
means for the recovery of the aforesd Tobaccos and upon receipt deliver Receipts
which shall be as good as if granted by us and in our names to perform as we or any of
us in our own persons might do about the same confirming whatsoever our sd Attorneys shall do. In Witness whereof we hereunto set our hands and seals the second day
of March in the Sixth year of the Reign of our Sovereign Lord GEORGE the Second Anno
Domini 1732/3 in presence of and before these Witnesses WILLIAM McMURDO of DUM-
FRIES aforesd Merchant and JAMES EWART writer there
in presence of WILLIAM McMURDO,   ANDREW CROSBIE
         JA: EWART   JOHN   CORRIE
   At a Court held for Essex County at Tappa. on the XIXth day of June MDCCXXXIII
The above written Power of Attorney from ANDREW CROSBIE and JOHN CORRIE to JAMES
CORBETT & EBENEZER YOUNG was proved by the oath of WILLIAM McMURDO one of the
witnesses thereto and was admitted to record

p.   KNOW ALL MEN by these presents that we JOHN SMITH, RICHARD COVINGTON &
433   THOMAS COVINGTON are held and firmly bound unto our Sovereign Lord GEORGE
         the Second in the just sum of Ten thousand pounds of Tobo this XIXth day of June
MDCCXXXIII. THE CONDITION of the above obligation is such that whereas JOHN SMITH
hath obtained a Licence to keep an ORDINARY at his House If therefore the sd JOHN
SMITH doth constantly provide in his ORDINARY good wholesome & cleanly lodging and
diet for Travellers & Stableage fodder and provender or pasturage and provender as the
season shall require for their Horses for the term of one whole year from the day herof
and shall not pmit any unlawfull gameing in his House nor suffer any to Tipple more

than is necessary that then this obligation to be void else to remain in force
JOHN SMITH
RICHD. COVINGTON THOS. COVINGTON

At a Court continued and held for Essex County at Tappa. on the XXth day of June
MDCCXXXIII JOHN SMITH, RICHARD COVINGTON and THOMAS COVINGTON acknowledged
this bond to be their act and deed which was ordered to be recorded

pp.   KNOW ALL MEN by these presents that I MARY MANN of ye County of Essex and
433-   Parish of Saint Annes doe appoint my well beloved friend GEORGE GREEN of the
434   above sd County and Parish my Sole and lawfull Attorney to recover by Law or
      any proceedures thereto relating all maner of debts whatsoever as he shall
think fitting and judge to be justly recoverable to me the sd MARY MANN as if I myself
were there present. In Witness whereof I have hereunto set my hand and seal this
Twenty fourth day of January in the year of our Lord 1732/3
Testes   SIMON MILLER,   MARY 𝓜 MANN
        WILLIAM ✗ EAGLETONE

At a Court held for Essex County at Tappa. on the XIXth day of June MDCCXXXIII
This Power of Attorney from MARY MANN to GEORGE GREEN was proved by the Oaths of
the witnesses thereto & was admitted to record

p.   KNOW ALL MEN by these presents that we WM. DUNN, EDWARD HARPER & WIL-
434   LIAM GRAY are held and firmly bound unto our Sovereign Lord GEORGE ye
      Second in the sum of Ten thousand pounds of Tobo this XXth day of June
MDCCXXXIII. THE CONDITION of the above obligation is such that whereas WILLIAM
DUNN & EDWARD HARPER hath obtained a licence to keep an ORDINARY at their House
in Southfarnham Pish if Therefore the sd WILLIAM DUNN & EDWARD HARPER doth
constantly provide in their ORDINARY good wholesome & cleanly lodging and diet for
Travellers & Stablegage fodder and provender or pasturage and provender as the Season shall require for their Horses for the term of one whole year from the day hereof
and shall not permit any unlawfull gameing in their house nor on the Sabbath day to
suffer any to Tipple more then is necessary that then this obligation to be void else to
be in force

WM. DUNN
EDWD. HARPER WM. GRAY

At a Court continued and held for Essex County at Tappa. on the XXth day of June
MDCCXXXIII WILLIAM DUNN, EDWARD HARPER & WILLIAM GRAY acknowledged this
bond to be their act & deed which is ordered to be recorded

pp.   THIS INDENTUREmade the 10th day of July in the Six yeare of our Soveren Lord
435-   KING ye GEORGE ye 2d. Anno Domini 1733 Between MASSEY YARRINGTON of the
437   County of Essex & Parish of Southfarnham of one part and GEORGE WRIGHT of
      the Parish and County aforesaid of other part Witnesseth that the sd MASSEY
YARRINGTON for the consideration of Twelve pounds six Shillings currant money to
him paid by these presents doe grant unto the sd GEORGE WRIGHT in his actual possession now being by virtue of a bargain and sale to him made of the percell of land with
ye appurtenances herein after mentioned by Indenture baring date the day before the
date hereof for four months from the next before the day of date of that Indenture and
by force of the Statute for transferring uses into possession his heirs all that percell of
land being in the Parish and County aforesd containing Forty one acres begining att a
Corner Spanish Oak of MASSEY YARRINGTON and WILLIAM MASH runing down the
Branch to the mouth of the sd Branch thence down the next Branch to the MainWes-

tern Branch and downe the Swamp to an Ash by the Run side thence up another
Branch its several Corses to a Fork of the Branch thence South West to a corner Hiccory
of MASSEY YARREINGTON and WILLIAM MASH thence South West to a white Oak and
South West to the begining together with all houses commodities and appurtainances
thereunto belonging To Have and To Hold unto the sd GEORGE WRIGHT and his heirs forever. In Witness whereof he hath set his hand and seal
in presents of us HENRY COX,   MASSEY YARRINGTON
      MATHEW COX
  At a Court held for Essex County at Tappa. on the XVIIth day of July MDCCXXXIII
MASSEY YARRINGTON acknowledged this Indenture to GEORGE WRIGHT to be his act &
deed which on his motion is admitted to record

pp.   THIS INDENTURE made the Twenty six and Twenty seven day of June in the year
437-   of our Lord Christ one thousand seven hundred and thirty three Between JAMES
441   BOOTH of the County of Essex Husbandman on the one part and FRANCIS COVING-
       TON of the same County Planter of the other part Witnesseth that sd JAMES BOOTH
for the sum of Sixty pounds of Current money of Virginia hath sold unto the sd FRAN-
CIS COVINGTON in his actual possession now being by virtue of a bargaine & sale by
Indenture for one year and by force & virtue of the Statute for transferring uses into
possession & to his heirs & assigns all that percell of land in the sd County of Essex
whereon the sd FRANCIS COVINGTON formerly Dwelt and adjoyning unto the land of
CHRISTOPHER BEVERLEY & unto the land of HENRY TANDY and also unto the land of
THOMAS MERIWEATHER containing Two hundred acres with all & singular the out
houses, buildings, advantages and appurtenances whatsoever to the sd plantation belonging and all Estate right of JAMES BOOTH To Have and To Hold unto the sd FRANCIS
COVINGTON his heirs and assigns forever. In Witness whereof the parties have set their
hands and Seals
in presence of BENJA. VAWTER,   JAMES BOOTH
      WM. GRAY, JNO. BATES
      J. BILLOPS
  At a Court held for Essex County at Tappa. on the XVIIth day of July MDCCXXXIII
JAMES BOOTH acknowledged this Release indented to FRANCIS COVINGTON to be his act &
deed which is admitted to record.

The following appears after the end of Deed Book 19.

REGISTER OF CERTIFICATES GRANTED
SINCE APRIL 1st ANO. 1730 for PASSES

To Whom Granted	Date of the Notes	When Published	Date of the Certificates
WILLIAM DICKERY	18th of May 1730	19th of May 1730	5th of June 1730
JOHN MCCULLOCK Mercht	No date	19th of May 1730	12th of Septr. 1730
WILLIAM LOTHERINGTON	21st of July 1730	22d of July 1730	2d of August 1730
ADAM REID	21. of July 1730	21st of July 1730	4th of Sept 1730
RICHARD PARRY	15th of August 1732	15th of August 1732	26 of August 1732
JAMES RULE	" of July 1732	18th of July 1732	6th of Septr 1732
LEONARD HILL	(no entries)		

ADCOCK. Elizabeth 41; Henry 2; Joseph 41.
ADKINSON. Nicholas 17.
ALDERSON. Ann 20, 21; James 20, 21, 27.
ALLEN. William 63.
AMIS. Silvester 85, 86, 90.
ANDERSON. Joseph 82, 83, 88.
ANDREWS. Ann 42; George 42;
 George Junr. 42; George Senr. 42.
AOTKINS. James 97.
ARMISTEAD. Colo. Henry 32; John 6, 7.
AUBERY. Henry 11; Richard 11.
AYRES. Ann 70; William 27.

BAGGE. Edmund 25, 26, 58, 71, 83, 88, 93.
BAILLIE. Alexander 78.
BAKER. Henry 67.
BALIST. Thos. 85.
BARBEE. John 31.
BARBER. Ann (Foster) 19; Samuel 19.
BARKER. Thomas 36, 51, 71, 76.
BARRADALL. Edw. 34, 70, 93.
BARTLETT. James 49; John 50.
BATES. John 59, 67, 69, 70, 98, 101;
 John Junr. 80, 90; John Senior 54;
 Ordinary 59.
BATTALEY. M. 11.
BAYLOR. Robert 55, 63.
BEALE. Elizabeth 96; Richard 95, 96, 98.
BEAZLEY. Burying Place 17; Henry 17;
 John 17; William 17; Winefred 17.
BECKHAM. George 98.
BELAND. Joseph 41.
BEMBRIDGE. Stephen 67.
BERRICK (BARWICK). Ann 27.
BERRY. Ann 98.
BEVERLEY. Christopher 24, 50, 53, 87, 101;
 Henry 18; W. 1, 9, 16, 20, 22, 23, 53, 78, 92,
 93, 101; William 34, 35, 64, 73, 76, 77, 79,
 86, 91, 92; Collo. William 54, 72, 81, 94, 99;
 Major William 50; Xpher 32.
BIBBY. John 47, 48.
BILLUPS. Dorothy (Aubery) 11; J. 101;
 John 11; Richard 17.
BIRD. Philemon 24.
BISWELL (BEIZWELL). Jeremiah 10; Robert 45;
 Samuel 17, 27, 28, 52.
BLACKSTONE. Argoll 86.
BLANTON. Ann 34; Patent 34; Thomas 34;
 Thomas (Elder) 34.
BOMER. Edward 55, 56, 96.
BOOKER. Edmun 91.

BOOTH. Burying Place 77; Humphrey 94;
 James 50, 51, 72, 73, 76, 77, 81, 101.
BOREING. Willm. 82.
BOUGHAN. Henry 75, 76; Henry Junior 51, 52;
 James 25, 71; John 36, 51, 60; Line of 24;
 Susanna 60.
BOULLER. John 46, 47.
BOULWARE. James 16.
BRADBURY. Ann 2.
BRANCHES: Assages 24; Bushes Old Spring 93;
 Cabbin 74; Cheyneys Spring 97; Church
 Spring 13; Gleab 81; Graves Spring 23;
 Middle 36. 51; Mirey 5; Muddy 33;
 Reedy 66.
BREDGAR. Line of 40.
BRIDGE. Henry Browns 51; White Marsh 13;
 Wm. Jones 7.
BRIDGER. Land of 13.
BRISLEY. William 82.
BRIZENDINE. Richard 55, 56, 73, 87.
BRONAUGH. Ann 15.
BROOCKE. Samuel 3; Thomas 3; William 91.
BROOKE. Frances 89; Humphry 21. 24;
 John 5, 6; Phebe 22, 74, 75; Robert 1, 6, 7,
 8, 20, 22, 23, 24, 58, 61, 62, 74, 75, 92, 94, 95;
 Robert (Elder) 62, 75; Major Robert 80, 90;
 Susanna 22; William 2, 20, 21, 22, 45, 52,
 89, 92.
BROWN. Charles Junr. 11; Charles Senr. 11;
 Francis 36, 51; Henry 51; James 3; Line of 17;
 Mary 11; Richard 73; Samuell 33, 52.
BRUSHWOOD. John 18.
BRYANT. Frances 60; John 24, 38, 60, 80;
 Thomas 10.
BURGYNE. Roger 55, 63.
BURN. Garritt 88, 93, 94.
BURNETT. Thomas 63.
BUSH. John 5, 6; Richard 55, 56, 93, 95;
 Sarah 5, 6.
BUTLER. John 45.
BUTTIN. Thomas 19.
BYROM. James 50.

CALECOTE. William 85, 91.
CARAGILL. John 65.
CARELL. Edmond 46, 47.
CAREY. Hugh 16, 17, 27, 28.
CARNALL. Mary 83; William 71, 83.
CARTAGENA: King of Spain 38.
CARTER. John 23; Katherine 35; Richard 35.
CASTON. John 70.

CATLETT. Nicholas 49, 87.

CAWTHORNE (CAUTHORNE). Richard 17, 18, 96; Thomas 95, 96.

CHAIR. Charles 40.

CHALKLY. Benjamin 2, 3.

CHANEY (CHEYNEY). John 97; William 38, 40, 48, 55, 63.

CHEAP. Patrick 54.

CHEW. Larkin 82.

CHURCHES. 11, 13, 58; Churchwarden 20; Glebe 20; of Great Britain 17, 40, 47, 86, 87, 88; Path 13; Spring Branch 13.

CIRGAN. John 94.

CLARK(E). Benjamin 2; Edward 31, 33; John 91.

CLAYTON. Daniell 91; Mr. 88; Samuel 2, 20, 26, 27, 40, 47, 48, 54, 59, 70, 78, 82, 96; Susan 40.

CLEMENT. John 52.

CLERK OF COURT. Beverley 1, 23; Tunstall 23.

CLOTWORTHY. Roger 49.

COGHILL. James 56, 57; Patent 56, 57.

COLE. William 55, 63, 66.

COLEMAN. James 22, 45, 46; Joannah 91; Ordinary 22, 45, 46; Patent of 45; Richard 33, 34, 45, 91; Robert 66, 67; Thomas 50, 66, 67.

COLLECTOR: County of Essex 19, 20, 42, 83.

COLLICOAT. James 87; William 87.

CONNER. Timothy 24.

COOK(E). John 2, 8, 68, 69; Susanna (Pell) 2; Thomas 46, 47; William 2.

COOKSON. Obadiah 67, 68.

COOPER. Elizabeth 73; Richard 44, 73; Thomas 35, 60, 82; William 73, 74.

COPLIN. Line of 90.

CORBETT. James 40, 99.

CORNE. James & Company 34.

CORRIE. John 64, 99.

COTHORN. Richard 93.

COUNTIES; Caroline 17, 30, 38, 49; Gloucester 33, 54, 85, 90; Goochland 61; Hanover 91; Henrico 2; King & Queen 5, 24, 33, 43, 44, 50, 53, 66, 96, 97; King George 22, 42; King William 77; Middlesex 11, 38, 48; New Kent 56; Northampton 16; Prince William 61; Richmond 3, 19, 50; Spotsilvania 34, 57; Westmoreland 47, 70.

COVINGTON. Francis 21, 50, 51, 68, 101; Land of 33; Richard 21, 24, 25, 66, 68, 73, 74, 77, 94, 99, 100; Thomas 21, 31, 51, 81, 82, 99, 100; William 31, 48, 49, 51, 52, 53, (contd)

COVINGTON (contd). William (contd). 63, 64, 66, 67, 73, 74, 82; William Junr. 67.

COX. Anne 55, 63; Francis 5; Henry 101; Line of 5; Mathew 101; William 3, 5.

CRAIK. James 77.

CRANE. Ferry 27; Francis 26, 27; Mary 67; Ordinary 26.

CREATON. Henry 40.

CREEKS: Blackburns 52; Brices 77; Cheesehixon 74; Cheesetuxsen 1; Cockellshell 33, 57; Gelson 19, 43; Horsepen 68; Hoskinses 18, 30, 85, 90; Little Occupation 15, 74, 80; Main Occupation 15; Mattapony 24; Mill 43; Occupacy 31; Piscataway 18, 44, 47, 54, 93, 95; Wassanousen 1, 22.

CROSBY. Andrew 99; George 28; James 10, 11; Mary 10, 11.

CROW. Thomas 38, 40, 88.

CROXTON. Ann 36, 37, 38; John 36, 37, 38, 51, 79, 80.

CRUST. Sarah 56.

CUFFE. Sarah 40.

CUMTON. Richard 41.

CURTIS. R. Junr. 6.

DAILY. Daniel 12; Timothy 43.

DAINGERFIELD. William 9, 19, 24, 25, 67, 68, 79, 83, 92; William Junr. 68.

DANIELLL. James Junr. 52; Thomas 98.

DAVIS. Evan 30, 44; James 67; Line of 7; Thomas 43, 94.

DEJARNAT. Elias 77, 78; Elizabeth 77, 78.

DENHAM. John 72.

DICKERY. William 1, 102.

DICKS. James 13.

DIKE. John 7; Judith 7.

DILLON. Thomas 35.

DIMILLO. Joseph 61, 86.

DISCOLL. Timothy 79, 80.

DISKIN. Daniell 45, 88, 93, 94.

DOBSON. William 81.

DOBYNS. Daniel 2, 38, 48, 49; William 96.

DOWNS. Sarah 8; Thomas 8.

DRISCOLL. Timothy 15.

DUAWAY. Robt. 82.

DUDLEY. Ordinary 6; Peter 6, 50; Richard 50.

DUNN. Dennis 97; Ordinary 51, 69, 100; William 100; William Junr. 51, 69.

EAGLETONE. William 100.

EDMONDSON. Constant 10; James 4, 76; John 4, 7, 14, 26, 44, 45, 65, 66, 69, 70, 92, 95; Ordinary 4, 69; Thomas 10, 35, 63, 64; Thomas Junr. 17, 69, 70.

EDWARDS. Tho: 44, 94.

ELLET. Major 5.

ENGLAND. Bristell 22, 52; County of Cumberland 28, 59; London 4, 8, 9.

EVANS. Benjamin 3, 4; Catherine 83; Jane 3, 4; John 3, 14, 15, 62, 63, 95; John Junr. 62, 63, 83; Micajah 82; Thomas 3, 4.

EWART. James 99.

FARGUSON. James 75, 76, 86; John 26, 27, 36, 37, 38, 69, 97; Samll. 59, 63, 64.

FARISH. Robert 75, 76.

FARMER. Ralph 99; Robert 81, 90.

FERRY: Piscataway 62, 78; Tappahannock 27, 84; To Naylors Hole 84; Willis 84.

FISHER. Benjamin 35; Line of 24.

FITZJEFFRIS. Elizabeth 63; Thomas 48, 54, 55, 63, 64.

FLOWERS. Isaac 45; Martha 45.

FOGG. Elizabeth 27; Line of 65; Nathaniel 1, 33, 58, 60, 76, 91.

FOREST. John 75.

FORWARD. Jonathan 9.

FOSTER. Ann 19; Burying Place 19; John 19, 45, 96; John Junr. 19; Mary 96; Robert 96.

FOWLER. Susanna 92, 93; William 92.

FRANK. Mary 97.

FRAZER. John 23; William 48.

FRIE. John 9.

GAINES. Daniel 56, 57, 58, 86; Mr. 42; Thomas 85, 90.

GAMES. Elizabeth 27.

GARNETT. James 11, 15, 16, 19, 20, 21, 24. 25, 35, 50, 70, 98; John 96.

GATEWOOD. James 48, 49, 54; John 30, 48; Katherine (Carter) 35; Line of 10; Thomas 41; William 35.

GEORGE. John 13, 20, 48, 55, 56; Robert Senior 20.

GETAR (GEATER). John 49, 50.

GIBSON. Elizabeth 49, 50; Robert 23, 75; William 49, 50.

GODFREY. Pt. 27, 40, 41.

GODSON. Doctor 14.

GOLDEN. William 16, 28.

GOOCH. William 39.

GOODE. Edward 86; Richard 86.

GOULDING. William 80.

GOULDMAN. Colo. 31; Ed. 25; Francis 12, 24, 25, 28, 29, 30, 31, 32, 43, 44, 88, 93, 94; Colo. Francis 12, 29; Plantation 30; Winifrid 24, 25.

GRAVES. Alexander 38, 48, 49; Benjamin 87; Francis 33; John 87; Land of 23; Mary 48; Robert 40, 45, 46; Spring Branch 23; Thomas 34.

GRAY. Abner 58; William 4, 8, 26, 51, 69, 71, 97, 98, 100, 101.

GRAYSON. Land of 21.

GREEN. Daniel 40; George 100; Samuel 40, 41, 56, 87; Samuel (Elder) 40; Sarah 56, 87; Thomas 78.

GREENSMITH. John 15.

GREGORY. Richard 54.

GRESHAM (GRISANE). Charles 25; Frances (Parker) 25; Robert 25, 26, 51, 58, 71, 72, 83.

GRIFFIN. James 16, 41, 79, 86; Ordinary 16, 41, 86; Pearce 76.

GRIFFING. James 63; John 27, 48; Ordinary 63.

GRIGGS. John 30.

GRIMSTEAD. Henry 66.

GUNN. John 56, 87.

HAILL. John 41; Jonathan 43.

HALL. Charles 56; John 55, 56, 87; Sarah 56.

HALLEWRIN (HALLURING). Milleced 61; Samuel 61.

HAMBLETON. Robert 87.

HANKIN. William 20.

HARDY. Ordinary 14, 44, 69, 95; Thomas 14, 44, 45, 69, 84, 95.

HARPER. Edward 44, 51, 69, 100; John 76.

HART. John 24.

HARWAR. Orphans of 13; Thomas 13.

HAWKINS. Capt. John 52; Patent 89; Thomas 10, 53, 62, 68.

HAY. Timothy 24.

HAYES. John 15, 39.

HEALY. Thomas 3.

HENSHAW. Saml. 2.

HICKMAN. R. 39.

HILL. Leonard 13, 14, 102; Richard 73.

HILLARD. Line of 67.

HILTON. John 61.

HINES (HINDS). John 15; Thomas 40, 77.

HIPKINS. James 13.

HOCKLEY. Dianah 80; Robert 80.
HODGES. Arthur 44, 82.
HODGKINSON. Bartholomew 19; Patent of 19.
HODSON. John 10.
HOLDER. James 29, 31, 32.
HOSKINGS. John 96; Martha 96.
HOWARD. Thomas 1.
HOWELL. John 4.
HUDSON. Elizabeth 40; Elizabeth Junr. 40;
  Isaac 55, 56.
HUNT. George 31; John 29, 31, 32, 71;
  John (Younger) 31; William 31.

INGRAM. Jane 74, 75, 80, 90; Landing of 22;
  Thomas 74; Tobias 1, 22, 23, 74, 75, 80, 81,
  90, 91; Tobias (Elder) 74.
IRELAND. Dublin 32.

JACKSON. Mr. 58.
JEFFERIES. William 38.
JOHNSON. Peter 87; Richard 82, 95;
  Thomas 95; William 54.
JOHNSTON. James 85.
JONES. Ambe 36; Francis 36; James 14, 16,
  76, 79; Mary 95; Richard 7, 82, 83, 84, 85,
  88, 95; Robert 1, 34, 80; Samuel 2;
  Thomas 8, 15, 58, 85, 97; William 1, 7, 97.
JORDAN. John 3.
JOURNEY. William 17.

KARNALL. Mary 58, 59; William 58, 59.
KEMP. Peter 55, 85, 90; William 54, 55.
KENNY. Mr. 58.
KETON. Elizabeth 5; William 5.
KIDD. Elizabeth 10; Thomas 10, 35.
KIRGAN (KERGAN). John 7, 67.

LACEY. John 84, 85; Jonathan 84.
LAMBERT. Jonathan 52.
LANDRUM. Martha 27; William 27, 28.
LAREMORE. Mary 7, 8.
LATANE. Lewis 9.
LATON. Frances 65, 66, 92; Ordinary 65, 92.
LAWSON. John 88, 89, 93.
LEEMON. Joseph 6, 99.
LEONARD. Walter 77.
LEVERIT. Robert Junr. 63, 64.
LICORISH. Wil 2, 4.
LONG. Bloomfield 42; John 42; Richard 52.
LOTHERINGTON. William 102.
LOURY. W. 4.

LOYD. Samll. 87; Thomas 25, 26, 43;
  William 22.

McCULLOCH. John 34, 35, 102.
McDANIEL. Arthur 7.
McMURDO. William 99.

MACKDONELL. James 65; William 65.
MAGWIRE. Roger 6.
MAN(N). Joseph 36, 37; Mary 36, 37, 100.
MARRITT. Thomas 23, 34.
MARSH. William 17, 18.
MARTIN. John 80, 81, 90, 91.
MARYLAND: 9, 28; Annarundl 73, 81;
  London Town 72.
MASH. William 100, 101.
MASON. Ann 97; Thomas 97.
MASTERSON. Edward 68, 69.
MAYFIELD. Abraham 1, 58.
MECORMICK Stephen 57.
MEDLEY. Eleaner 13, 14.
MEGGS. John 17, 79, 86, 98.
MERIWETHER. Francis 75; Mr. 17;
  Thomas 19, 50, 95, 101.
MERRITT. James 71, 72, 87, 88, 89;
  John 58, 59, 71, 72, 83; Thomas 87.
METCALF. Gilbert 19; Susanna 19.
MILL: Road 35; Smiths 21, 96; Tandys 8, 69.
MILLER. John 42; Simon 52, 60, 61, 66, 69, 100.
MILLS. John 79, 80; John (Elder) 79.
MITCHELL. John 35, 77, 78; Peter 82, 83.
MONCASTER. Land of 25.
MOORE (MORE). Francis 88; George 32.
MORGAN. Dorothy 32; Edward 12, 25;
  Evan 32; Marck 11, 25.
MORRISS. George 85; Major 90.
MOSELEY. Benjamin 62; Edward 61, 62, 74;
  Elizabeth 62; William 61, 62, 74, 87.
MOSS. John 47; Richard 47; Robert 47;
  Robert (Younger) 47; Thomas 47; William 47.
MOTLEY. Henery 56, 57; John 46, 60.
MUNDAY. Charles 71, 72, 83, 87, 88, 93;
  James 23, 87; John 23; Joseph 58, 71, 83, 93;
  Thomas 23, 87; Thomas Elder 23.
MURROUGH. Edward 45, 57, 58, 86;
  Martha (Flowers) 45.
MUSCOE. Elizabeth 47; Mary 47; Salvator 1, 6,
  7, 8, 21, 23, 33, 35, 42, 47, 79, 83, 85, 92, 94,
  98; Capt. Salvator 11, 67, 80, 94.

NALL. Agness 25.

NANCE. John 46, 47, 56, 57, 65.
NEWBELL. George 66; James 66.
NEWBLE. Nathaniel 56.
NEW ENGLAND: Boston 67.
NEWMAN. Elias 62.
NEW SPAIN: Viceroyes 39.
NEWTON (NUTON). Henry 67, 94; Henry
  Junr. 67; John 94; Thomas 67.
NICHOLSON. Clement 28.
NISBET. Wm. 11.
NOELL. Cornelius 56; Daniel 28; James 1, 96.
NORTH. Anthony Senr. 19; William 19.
NORTH BRITAIN. Dumfries 34, 40, 99;
  Glasgow 78; Linlithgow 97.
NORTH CAROLINA. Albemar 3.

ONEAL. John 33; Mary 33.
ORDINARIES: Bates 59; Coleman 22, 45;
  Crane 26; Dunn & Harper 69; Edmond-
  son 4, 69; Griffin 16, 41, 86; Griffing 63;
  Hardy 14, 69, 95; Laton 65, 92; Perkins 51,
  69; Ray 81; Sanders 22, 45, 81; Smith 29,
  99; Taylor 76; Vawter 4, 26, 53, 71, 98.
OSBORN. Thomas 3.
OSWOULD. Richard 78.
OWINGS. Owen 48, 88.

PADDINSON. Thomas 40.
PAGETT. Edmund 91, 92; Ephraim 91, 92;
  Land of 68.
PAIN. Charles 39, 60.
PAMPLIN. Nicholas 43, 44; Nicholas Juner 43;
  Sarah 43; William 43.
PARKER. Alexander 9, 19, 21, 31, 35, 54, 68,
  75, 83, 92, 94, 95; Frances 25; Robert 16,
  25, 29, 33, 34, 35, 52, 66, 69, 92.
PARR. Phillip 35.
PARRY. Richard 65, 102.
PARSONS. Elizabeth 27.
PATENTS: Anderson 88; Bibby 48;
  Blanton 34; Boughan 76; Coghill 56;
  Coleman 45; Covington, Boughan & Williams
  25; Doctor 14; Flowers 43; Fogg 2;
  Harper 76; Hawkins 89; Hodges 82;
  Hodkinson 19; Jones 1; Lacy 82; Meri-
  wether 75; Muscoe 11; Paddinson 40;
  Payne 42; West 2; West & Clotworthy 49;
  Williamson 55.
PATH. 17, 31, 44; Coxes 3; Lacys 82;
  Smiths Mill 21.
PATTERSON. Jos. 13.

PAVEY. Webley 84.
PAYNE. Robert 15; Robert Junr. 42;
  Robert Senr. 42.
PEARSON. William 28.
PECK. John 28.
PELL. Susanna 2; Timothy 2.
PERRY. Aaron 7; Mary 53.
PERU. Viceroyes 39.
PHRAIZIER. Amey 25.
PICKES. Capt. Josiah 95.
PICKET. John 3, 5, 6; Road 5, 6.
PITTS. David 52.
PLUMMER. Thomas 45, 49, 52.
PLACES. Beverdam 45; Burying Place 17, 19,
  77; Burtons Range 24; Coole Spring 81, 82;
  Covetions Deed 21; Dolls Mire 94; Gouldmans
  Quarter 31; Greshams Plantation 83; Ingrams
  Landing 22; Iron Mine Stones 81; Island 43;
  Kennys Plantation 58; Mire Ponn 14; Naylors
  Hole 27, 84; Piscataway Roaling House 82;
  Range 90; Rowzees Neck 74; Thomas Quarter
  39, 60; Toun Marsh 76.
POWELL. Mary 49, 50; Thomas 49, 50.
PRICE. John 8; William 71.
PROCLAMATION: Cessation of Hostilities Between
  his Majesty & King of Spain 38, 39.

RAMSEY. Thomas 16, 28; William 27, 28.
RANSOME. Frances 39, 60; Robert 39, 60.
RAY. Thomas Junr. 81; Thomas Senr. 81.
REASON. Richard 91.
REDFERN. James 85.
REEVES. Henry 64; John 40, 41, 54; Joseph 81.
REID. Adam 102; James 99.
RENNOLDS. James 16, 34, 41, 86; Line of 33;
  W. 43, 44, 89.
RESTALL. Jonas 72.
REYNOLDS. Benja. 5; Corneles 42; Mary 52;
  Thomas 52.
RICE. Jacob 11, 12.
RICHESON. Peter 39, 60; William 39, 60.
RILEY. Edwd. 94.
RIVERS: Rappa. 14, 40, 42, 57, 82.
ROADS: 73; Church 67; County 25; Main 7, 21,
  31, 44, 54, 65, 67, 78, 82, 89, 94; Mill 30, 35;
  Pickets 5, 6; Piscataway Roaling House 82;
  Roleing 25; Rowzees Neck 74; White Marsh
  Bridge 13.
ROANE. Alexander 85; Sarah 30; W. 12, 18,
  19, 43, 44; William 30, 43, 86.
ROBARDS. Griffing 48.

TRADES/OCCUPATIONS (contd). Practr. of
  Physick 73; Shoemaker 65; Taylor 2, 45,
  47; Writer 99.
TRAINUM. Charles 30, 31; Lidia 30, 31.
TUNSTALL. R. 24; Richard 23, 24, 99;
  Thomas 8.
TURNER. James 73, 82.
TYLER. Catharine 14, 39; John 59;
  Richard 14, 59, 70, 71; Richard Junr. 2, 3, 7,
  15, 39, 60, 70, 78, 98.

UPSHAW. Hannah 18, 19; Jeremiah 18, 19, 34;
  William 18, 19; Capt. Willm. 18.

VAUGHAN. James 85, 90.
VAWTER. Benjamin 81, 101; David 16;
  John 4, 10, 26, 33, 53, 56, 57, 58, 71, 83, 85,
  86, 89, 97, 98; Margaret 16; Ordinary 4, 26,
  53, 71, 98; William 16, 17.
VERNON. Jet 80.
VIRGIL. Mary 50.

WAFFE. Elias 72.
WAGGENER. Benjamin 50.
WALKER. John 28, 59.
WALL. James 9; Mary 9.
WALSH. Robert 58.
WAMSLEY. John 72.
WAREING. Land of 21; Thomas 9, 22, 39, 42,
  43, 52, 53, 66, 70, 83, 94, 95, 98.
WARREN. Samuel 27; Thomas 31, 96.
WATTKINS. Alice 61; Benjamin 66;
  Thomas 73, 81; Doctr. Thomas 72;
  William 61.
WEBB. James 40, 41, 86, 87; John 47, 48;
  Mary 31; William 81, 82.
WEEKES. Mark 29, 43, 64, 65, 77, 78, 79.
WELCH. Capt. Reuben 17, 36, 88.
WEST. Richard 49.
WEST INDIES. Spanish Governments 39.
WHARTON. Michael 58.
WHEATON. Elizabeth 46.
WHITE. Edward 11.
WILCOX. John 21, 72, 93, 94.
WILLARD. Martin 53.
WILLIAMS. Emal. 13; Emanuel 91;
  Hugh 3, 91; William 25.
WILLIAMSON. Thomas 55; Thomas Juner 35.

WILLIS. Ferry 84; Ordinary 84; Robert 84.
WILSON. William 60.
WILTSHIRE. Richard 45, 46.
WINSLOW. Benjamin 19, 20, 21, 27, 50, 60, 61,
  66, 68, 92; Captain Benjamin 99; Line of 21;
  Richard 66.
WISE. Richard 8, 9.
WOOD. J. 97; James 75, 76; Capt. James 97;
  John 1, 99; Thomas 17, 51.
WORTHAM. Charles 90; William 65, 66.
WORTHY. John 4.
WRIGHT. George 3, 100, 101.

YARRINGTON. Massey 100, 101.
YOUNG. Catherine 39, 60; Ebenezer 99;
  Frances 73; Henry 14, 15, 59; Katrine 14;
  Line of 17; William 14, 39, 60; Williamson 14.
YOUNGER. John 32, 36, 37, 38; Thomas 80.

Heritage Books by Ruth and Sam Sparacio:

Abstracts of Account Books of Edward Dixon, Merchant of Port Royal, Virginia, Volume I: 1743–1747

Abstracts of Account Books of Edward Dixon, Merchant of Port Royal, Virginia, Volume II

Albemarle County, Virginia Deed and Will Book Abstracts, 1748–1752

Albemarle County, Virginia Deed Book Abstracts, 1758–1761

Albemarle County, Virginia Deed Book Abstracts, 1761–1764

Albemarle County, Virginia Deed Book Abstracts, 1764–1768

Albemarle County, Virginia Deed Book Abstracts, 1768–1770

Albemarle County, Virginia Deed Book Abstracts, 1776–1778

Albemarle County, Virginia Deed Book Abstracts, 1778–1780

Albemarle County, Virginia Deed Book Abstracts, 1780–1783

Albemarle County, Virginia Deed Book Abstracts, 1787–1790

Albemarle County, Virginia Deed Book Abstracts, 1790–1791

Albemarle County, Virginia Deed Book Abstracts, 1791–1793

Augusta County, Virginia Land Tax Books, 1782–1788

Augusta County, Virginia Land Tax Books, 1788–1790

Amherst County, Virginia Land Tax Books, 1789–1791

Caroline County, Virginia Order Book Abstracts, 1765

Caroline County, Virginia Order Book Abstracts, 1767–1768

Caroline County, Virginia Order Book Abstracts, 1768–1770

Caroline County, Virginia Order Book Abstracts, 1770–1771

Caroline County, Virginia Order Book, 1765–1767

Caroline County, Virginia Order Book, 1771–1772

Caroline County, Virginia Order Book, 1786–1787

Caroline County, Virginia Order Book, 1787, Part 1

Caroline County, Virginia Order Book, 1788

Culpeper County, Virginia Deed Book Abstracts, 1795–1796

Culpeper County, Virginia Land Tax Book, 1782–1786

Culpeper County, Virginia Land Tax Book, 1787–1789

Culpeper County, Virginia Minute Book, 1763–1764

Digest of Family Relationships, 1650–1692, from Virginia County Court Records

Digest of Family Relationships, 1720–1750, from Virginia County Court Records

Digest of Family Relationships, 1750–1763, from Virginia County Court Records

Digest of Family Relationships, 1764–1775, from Virginia County Court Records

Essex County, Virginia Deed and Will Abstracts, 1695–1697

Essex County, Virginia Deed and Will Abstracts, 1697–1699

Essex County, Virginia Deed and Will Abstracts, 1699–1701

Essex County, Virginia Deed and Will Abstracts, 1701–1703

Essex County, Virginia Deed and Will Abstracts, 1745–1749

Essex County, Virginia Deed and Will Book, 1692–1693

Essex County, Virginia Deed and Will Book, 1693–1694

Essex County, Virginia Deed and Will Book, 1694–1695

Essex County, Virginia Deed and Will Book, 1753–1754 and 1750

Essex County, Virginia Deed Book, 1724–1728

Essex County, Virginia Deed Book, 1728–1733

Essex County, Virginia Deed Book, 1733–1738

Essex County, Virginia Deed Book, 1738–1742

Essex County, Virginia Deed Book, 1742–1745

Essex County, Virginia Deed Book, 1749–1751

Essex County, Virginia Deed Book, 1751–1753

Essex County, Virginia Land Trials Abstracts, 1711–1716 and 1715–1741

Essex County, Virginia Order Book Abstracts, 1699–1702

Essex County, Virginia Order Book Abstracts, 1716–1723, Part 1

Essex County, Virginia Order Book Abstracts, 1716–1723, Part 2

Essex County, Virginia Order Book Abstracts, 1716–1723, Part 3

Essex County, Virginia Order Book Abstracts, 1716–1723, Part 4

Essex County, Virginia Order Book Abstracts, 1723–1725, Part 1

Essex County, Virginia Order Book Abstracts, 1723–1725, Part 2

Essex County, Virginia Order Book Abstracts, 1725–1729, Part 1

Essex County, Virginia Order Book Abstracts, 1727–1729

Essex County, Virginia Order Book, 1695–1699

Fairfax County, Virginia Deed Abstracts, 1799–1800 and 1803–1804

Fairfax County, Virginia Deed Abstracts, 1804–1805

Fairfax County, Virginia Deed Book Abstracts, 1799

Fairfax County, Virginia Deed Book, 1798–1799

Fairfax County, Virginia Land Causes, 1788–1824

Fauquier County, Virginia Minute Book, 1759–1761

Fauquier County, Virginia Minute Book, 1761–1762

Fauquier County, Virginia Minute Book, 1766–1767

Fauquier County, Virginia Minute Book, 1767–1769

Fauquier County, Virginia Minute Book, 1769–1771

Hanover County, Virginia Land Tax Book, 1782–1788

Hanover County, Virginia Land Tax Book, 1789–1793

Hanover County, Virginia Land Tax Book, 1793–1796

King George County, Virginia Order Book Abstracts, 1721–1723

King George County, Virginia Deed Book Abstracts, 1721–1735

King George County, Virginia Deed Book Abstracts, 1735–1752

King George County, Virginia Deed Book Abstracts, 1753–1773

King George County, Virginia Will Book Abstracts, 1752–1780

King William County, Virginia Record Book, 1702–1705

King William County, Virginia Record Book, 1705–1721

King William County, Virginia Record Book, 1722 and 1785–1786

Lancaster County, Virginia Deed and Will Book, 1652–1657

Lancaster County, Virginia Deed and Will Book, 1654–1661

Lancaster County, Virginia Deed and Will Book, 1661–1702 (1661–1666 and 1699–1702)

Lancaster County, Virginia Deed Book Abstracts, 1701–1706

Lancaster County, Virginia Deed Book, 1710–1714

Lancaster County, Virginia Order Book Abstracts, 1656–1661

Lancaster County, Virginia Order Book Abstracts, 1662–1666

Lancaster County, Virginia Order Book Abstracts, 1666–1669

Lancaster County, Virginia Order Book Abstracts, 1670–1674

Lancaster County, Virginia Order Book Abstracts, 1674–1678

Lancaster County, Virginia Order Book Abstracts, 1678–1681

Lancaster County, Virginia Order Book Abstracts, 1682–1687

Lancaster County, Virginia Order Book Abstracts, 1729–1732

Lancaster County, Virginia Order Book Abstracts, 1736–1739

Lancaster County, Virginia Order Book Abstracts, 1739–1742

Lancaster County, Virginia Order Book, 1687–1691

Lancaster County, Virginia Order Book, 1691–1695

Lancaster County, Virginia Order Book, 1695–1699

Lancaster County, Virginia Order Book, 1699–1701

Lancaster County, Virginia Order Book, 1701–1703

Lancaster County, Virginia Order Book, 1703–1706

Lancaster County, Virginia Order Book, 1732–1736

Lancaster County, Virginia Will Book, 1675–1689

Richmond County, Virginia Deed Book Abstracts, 1705–1708

Richmond County, Virginia Deed Book Abstracts, 1708–1711

Richmond County, Virginia Deed Book Abstracts, 1711–1714

Richmond County, Virginia Deed Book Abstracts, 1715–1718

Richmond County, Virginia Deed Book Abstracts, 1718–1719

Richmond County, Virginia Deed Book Abstracts, 1719–1721

Richmond County, Virginia Deed Book Abstracts, 1721–1725

Richmond County, Virginia Order Book Abstracts, 1694–1697

Richmond County, Virginia Order Book Abstracts, 1697–1699

Richmond County, Virginia Order Book abstracts, 1699–1701

Richmond County, Virginia Order Book Abstracts, 1714–1715

Richmond County, Virginia Order Book Abstracts, 1719–1721

Richmond County, Virginia Order Book, 1692–1694

Richmond County, Virginia Order Book, 1702–1704

Richmond County, Virginia Order Book, 1717–1718

Richmond County, Virginia Order Book, 1718–1719

Spotsylvania County, Virginia Deed Book, 1722–1725

Spotsylvania County, Virginia Deed Book, 1725–1728

Spotsylvania County, Virginia Deed Book: 1730–1731

Spotsylvania County, Virginia Order Book Abstracts, 1742–1744

Spotsylvania County, Virginia Order Book Abstracts, 1744–1746

Stafford County, Virginia Deed and Will Book, 1686–1689

Stafford County, Virginia Deed and Will Book, 1689–1693

Stafford County, Virginia Deed and Will Book, 1699–1709

Stafford County, Virginia Deed and Will Book, 1780–1786, and Scheme Book Orders, 1790–1793

Stafford County, Virginia Deed Book, 1722–1728 and 1755–1765

Stafford County, Virginia Order Book, 1664–1668 and 1689–1690

Stafford County, Virginia Order Book, 1691–1692

Stafford County, Virginia Order Book, 1692–1693

Stafford County, Virginia Will Book, 1729–1748

Stafford County, Virginia Will Book, 1748–1767

Westmoreland County, Virginia Deed and Will Abstracts, 1723–1726

Westmoreland County, Virginia Deed and Will Abstracts, 1726–1729

Westmoreland County, Virginia Deed and Will Abstracts, 1729–1732

Westmoreland County, Virginia Deed and Will Abstracts, 1732–1734

Westmoreland County, Virginia Deed and Will Abstracts, 1734–1736

Westmoreland County, Virginia Deed and Will Abstracts, 1736–1740

Westmoreland County, Virginia Deed and Will Abstracts, 1740–1742

Westmoreland County, Virginia Deed and Will Abstracts, 1742–1745

Westmoreland County, Virginia Deed and Will Abstracts, 1745–1747

Westmoreland County, Virginia Deed and Will Abstracts, 1747–1748

Westmoreland County, Virginia Deed and Will Abstracts, 1749–1751

Westmoreland County, Virginia Deed and Will Abstracts, 1751–1754

Westmoreland County, Virginia Deed and Will Abstracts, 1754–1756

Westmoreland County, Virginia Order Book, 1705–1707

Westmoreland County, Virginia Order Book, 1707–1709

Westmoreland County, Virginia Order Book, 1709–1712